SOUTH AFRICA'S FUTURE

South Africa's Future

From Crisis to Prosperity

Anthony Ginsberg

First published 1998 by Macmillan
an imprint of Macmillan Publishers Ltd
25 Eccleston Place, London SW1W 9NF
and Houndmills, Basingstoke, Hampshire, RG21 6XS

Associated companies throughout the world

ISBN 0 333 77536 8 PB
ISBN 0 333 72187 X HB

First published 1998 by St Martin's Press
Scholarly and Reference Division,
175 Fifth Avenue, New York, N.Y. 10010

ISBN 0 312 21503 7 HC

Library of Congress Cataloging-in-Publication Data
Ginsberg, Anthony Sanfield.
South Africa's future : from crisis to prosperity / Anthony Ginsberg.
p.   cm.
Includes bibliographical references and index.
ISBN 0–312–21503–7 (cloth : alk. paper)
1. South Africa—Politics and government—1994–   2. South Africa–
–Economic conditions—1991–   I. Title.
DT1974.G56   1998
338.968—dc21   98–12975
                                                      CIP

Any content, views of opinions presented in this book are solely those of the author and do
not in any way represent those of his previous or present employers.

Owing to the rapidly changing face of the international economy, certain statistics may
now be outdated.

To
my beautiful and loving wife Ruthy
Mom, Dad, Caryn and Dean
Granny Lily
&
to the warm, friendly people of South Africa

Contents

List of Figures and Tables

Figures

Tables

Introduction

"The budget should be balanced."
"The treasury should be refilled. Public debt should be reduced."
"The arrogance of the public officials should be controlled."

CICERO (106–43 BC)

EACH YEAR hundreds of new books are published relating to South Africa. While some entertain and others teach, few if any attempt to change the way South Africa operates. Although seemingly an impossible goal, the suggestions and recommendations in this book are designed to serve as a blueprint for a better South Africa which benefits all its citizens, many of whom cannot read this book because of widespread illiteracy throughout South Africa.

South Africa cannot continue on its present economic course. Although we benefit from living in a beautiful land, rich with minerals, we have squandered our assets over the years. It is time *om wakker te skrik* (to wake up) before South Africa slips further behind in the battle to become a country where the average citizen's standard of living can rise rather than fall, where jobs are readily available, and where our political leaders are held far more accountable and are put under pressure to perform — or otherwise risk losing their jobs.

This book details the dangers facing South Africa if we do not adopt new policies that will bolster international and local confidence in our country, our people and our currency.

South Africans deserve to feel financially secure — it is a legitimate part of the South African dream. But this will remain unattainable without a stable currency, a free market for labour, a healthy and viable opposition in parliament and an economy that can achieve sustained growth of at least 5% to 6% for the next decade. It is time for a new way of thinking in South Africa if we are to ever achieve prosperity for the majority of South Africans rather than just for a tiny elite.

1

Purpose of this book

It has been my intention to write this book for a non-academic
audience. In doing the research for the book, too often I came
across well-written and thought-provoking academic articles and
treatises that remain buried in university libraries and that for the
most part are ignored or never read by the electorate and those
policy-makers who can effect change in South Africa.

Before setting out to write this book on South Africa's future,
many people asked me what my purpose was, and what hidden,
sinister motives I might be harbouring.

Although it is not my intention for this book to serve as a
criticism of current South African economic and political policies,
and by implication the current ANC government, the undeniable
day-to-day realities which most South Africans have to live with
and the uncertain financial and economic future many of us are
facing may result in the subject matter proving to be a trifle
sensitive for even the most thick-skinned members of our society.

Many so-called experts on Africa have tried to caricature
Africans in general and South Africans in particular as a people
who do not accept criticism or dissent easily. It has been suggested
that by writing this book I would become *persona non grata*, or
even worse, a *volks veraaier* (a traitor), in my own country. It is my
hope and wish that the reception of this book might disprove
these notions and that my ideas will be seen for what they are:
those of a patriotic South African who cares for the future of his
country — a future that will see South Africa's economic potential
realised, where the last vestiges of unequal opportunity will be
discarded forever, freedom of expression will be treated with far
more respect than has been the case with our neighbours to the
north, and the voting public will be better informed on the issues
of the day.

Of course, there will always be critics who will attack such a
book, but this book will have succeeded in its purpose if it enlivens
the debate and irks certain special-interest groups.

The truth

If the truth hurts so be it. By raising the hard facts and figures
published by our own government and other sources, I hope to
show that we in South Africa have a tremendous challenge ahead
of us: an economic, social and political challenge that if
successfully met will have profound implications for the entire

African continent, and for other peoples of the world who have yet to overcome historical conflicts, jealousies and prejudice.

However, in order to meet this challenge head on and to be able to find solutions we have to know what we have inherited from over 40 years of corrupt apartheid rule and over 300 years of white dominance.

This book is intended to stir debate as to why certain ineffectual policies remain, by illustrating how such policies benefit a select group in South Africa. The book illustrates why the South African consumer has suffered most over the past two decades as inflation and protectionist trade policies have led to an ever spiralling cost of living. At the same time I attempt to show why South Africans continue to see the value of their currency diminish, while their taxes continue to rise.

Remedies to generate economic growth based on lessons learnt around the world are suggested, and these have the potential to make South Africa a prosperous country once more. Whether this book will make a meaningful contribution to this enterprise only the future will show.

This book also serves to address the reasons for South Africa's high unemployment and the related massive crime wave, draconian import tariffs, diminishing value of the rand, high tax rates and the lack of long-term foreign investment. It is intended to show that South Africa is still controlled by a monopoly of five to ten industrial companies which oppose changing much of the status quo and which enjoy total control of the domestic South African market. These companies, along with government and our largest labour unions, are largely responsible for the limited number of foreign investors coming to our shores. Many foreign companies now operating in South Africa generate few jobs as they operate only as marketing, sales and distribution arms for their foreign parents. Other newcomers have acquired local South African firms, without providing any new jobs.

South Africa's inability to attract long-term direct foreign investment can also be blamed on the Reserve Bank's restrictive monetary policy, which has stunted growth relative to other emerging market economies. The prime overdraft rate rose by 4% between May and July 1998, reaching a 13-year high, while our currency has lost a quarter of its value against both the dollar and the pound in the first half of 1998.

By comparison with other emerging markets South Africa is now simultaneously bottom of the growth league and top of the interest rate league (see Figures 1 and 2).

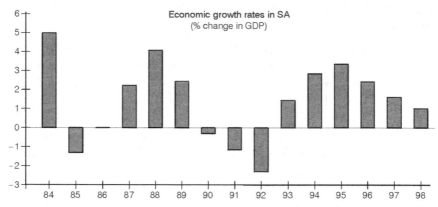

Figure 1 *Economic growth rates in South Africa (percentage change in GDP)*

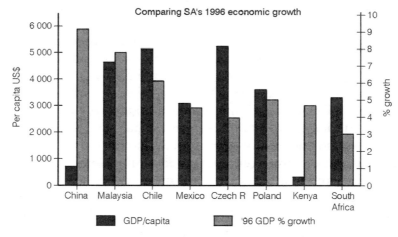

Figure 2 *Comparing South Africa's 1996 economic growth with that of other countries*

The Challenge

So what is the challenge? How are we to create a prosperous society where by the year 2005 our unemployment rate will have fallen below 10% — requiring the creation of well over 3 million jobs in the next decade? How do we rid ourselves of the high level of crime that plagues many of our cities and towns, making Johannesburg the murder capital of the world? In South Africa we currently enjoy other special benefits, such as living with the daily fear of our cars being hijacked, while about 50% of our black male population between the ages of 18 and 35 years remains unemployed.

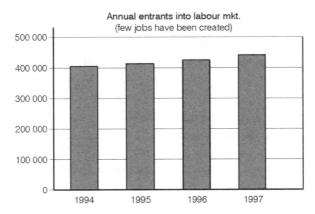

Figure 3   *Annual entrants into the South African labour market (note that few jobs have been created)*

Aside from all our inherited social problems, the traditional economic engines that drive South Africa will need to be replaced. We can no longer rely upon mineral extraction to boost our exports. In addition, manufacturing primarily for the domestic market behind the luxury of high protectionist walls is outdated. These are yesterday's economic engines. Almost 60% of our production remains in the primary sectors — mining and agriculture — while industrial support functions (machinery, transport and telecommunications) are responsible for just 5%. The balance is comprised of food, clothing and other consumer goods. These traditional sources will no longer suffice. South Africa will have to reinvent itself as a powerful exporter of manufactured goods, rather than being largely a minerals exporter.

Only exports of manufactured and semi-manufactured products truly benefit from the rand's contrived depreciation. Approximately 50% of our exports are commodity based and do not benefit from a falling rand. It is time to stop believing optimistic economists who claim that a falling rand will be more than made up for by a major export boost. Time and again this claim has been proved wrong.

Even our manufacturers have a long way to go before they become export competitive.

Given our fiscal constraints — including being over-borrowed as a country, being perilously close to a debt trap, and having a labour force which expands by approximately 3% annually — South Africa must develop new markets to pay its way in the world.

Many have the illusion that new jobs will be financed by government through massive public works programmes and housing construction. Unfortunately, growth built on the back of government spending is destined to be shortlived, and to create an even more severe budget crisis and an even deeper level of government debt, over the medium to long term.

According to many economists, the South African economy has been running out of steam ever since 1964. There has been no economic growth in per capita terms over the past 34 years and no growth in the number of jobs for the past decade.

With the old mining steam-engine running out of power and with no new approach adopted to replace our reliance on mineral exports, it should come as little surprise that we find ourselves in the midst of burgeoning unemployment and economic stagnation, as the increases in the cost of living continues to impoverish millions of older South Africans. Continuing along this path is a recipe for disaster.

A Crisis

Whatever honeymoon the new South Africa had is over. Consider the investment world's stinging vote of no confidence in 1996 —

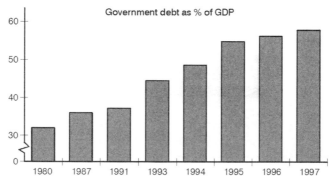

Figure 4   *South African government debt as a percentage of GDP*

reducing the South African rand's net worth by 30% in dollar terms and by over 40% in terms of sterling.

By July 1998, the rand had crashed to new lows of R6.50 to $1 and R10.60 to £1 — wiping out another 30% of South Africa's net worth in just the first six months of 1998. The appointment of

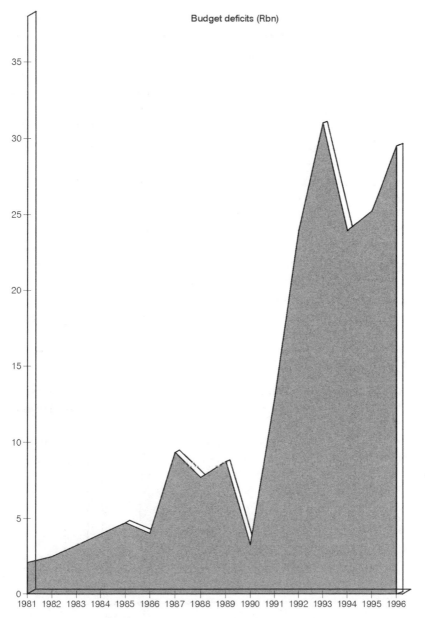

Figure 5 *South African budget deficit (in billions of rands)*

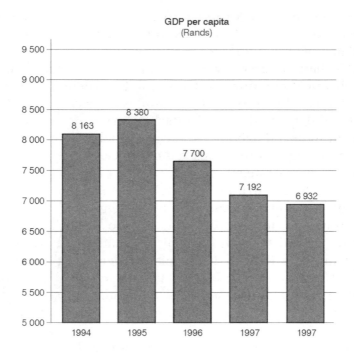

Figure 6   *South Africa: GDP per capita (in rands, adjusted for inflation)*

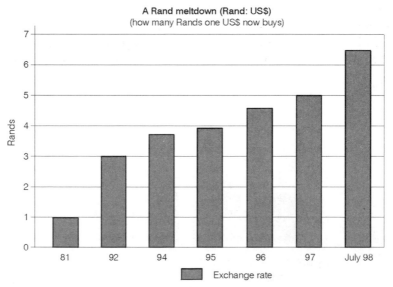

Figure 7   *A rand meltdown (how many rands US$1 now buys)*

labour minister Tito Mboweni to be the new governor of the Reserve Bank in 1999 will almost certainly provide foreign speculators with yet another reason to abandon the rand. After all, he is the first career politician to head the Reserve Bank and most observers question the level of independence he will bring to the Bank. Adding to the scepticism, is the fact that his Labour Ministry did more than any other government department to create an inflexible labour regime — unhelpful to job creation and working against the goals laid out in Gear (the government's macroeconomic strategy).

Moreover, South Africa still has no game plan to attract sizeable flows of long-term domestic and foreign investment. Our disincentives to foreign investors are so great that we were recently ranked second last of 48 nations by the World Competitiveness Report. I am left wondering how serious the South African government is in attracting foreign direct investment for the purposes of job creation. Our over-regulated labour market continues to push manufacturers out of the country.

In the past five years alone, South Africa has had net job losses equivalent to at least 5% of its formal sector workforce, raising our unemployment rate to 40% according to most estimates. A case in point is the gold mining industry, once our largest employer, which has reduced its total employment figure from 550 000 people in 1988, to 300 000 in 1998. Ever since 1980, the population has grown over 1% per year faster than GDP, resulting in a falling per capita income. GDP per capita achieved a high of R8 380 in 1991, but by 1993 had reached a 30-year low of R6 816.

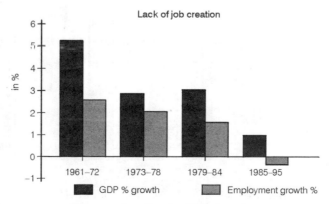

Figure 8 *Lack of job creation*

Gear

Gear has done little to generate jobs, while the prime overdraft rate of 22,5% (July 1998) has successfully stifled any hope of real per capita economic growth. Just muddling along with 1–2% economic growth (GDP) for another few years translates into a need to generate at least 425 000 new jobs per year, in order to just absorb the annual number of new entrants into the labour market, let alone make any dent in the unemployment statistics.

In 1997 and 1998 our formal sector contracted by an average of 100 000 jobs.

Reality

To make matters worse, there is considerable sheltered employment hidden throughout our public sector — an unemployment time-bomb if privatisation ever gets moving. Given the recent relaxation of exchange controls many of South Africa's largest companies are also eager to expand and diversify abroad. By reducing their investment plans within South Africa, reliance on direct, long-term foreign investment to generate jobs will play an increasingly important role.

South Africa requires new ideas and strategies if Mr Mandela's miraculous and peaceful revolution is ever to deliver better lives for all South Africans.

Staying aloof is not the solution to our country's problems. Many in South Africa believe it is not helpful nor politically correct to criticise the government or our country in public in any

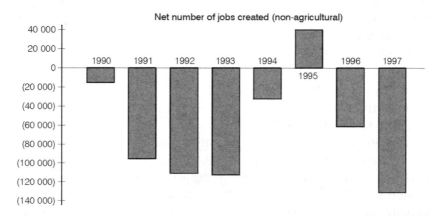

Figure 9 *Net number of jobs created in South Africa, 1990–97 (non-agricultural)*

way, and that it is better to go direct to cabinet ministers and to discuss matters privately. One is told that their doors are open and that one will get more done in this manner. This policy has unfortunately not been successful. It is my hope that this book may make some small contribution towards bringing about the changes required in South Africa.

> The economic and financial crisis that has developed in South Africa can only be solved by a government which has the moral strength to incorporate into the economic and financial ministries top men (and women) from the private sector. They must be chosen from all the talent in South Africa. South Africa needs a government heavily loaded with private sector expertise. One thing is certain: ministers who have so little experience of the private sector that they are inordinately dependent on bureaucracy for advice cannot save this country from the present situation. Bureaucracy does not have the background and the experience required for the solution to our problems.

These words are as true today as they were when A. D. Wassenaar, the former Sanlam chairman, wrote them in his book *Assault on Private Enterprise* in 1977.

Many South Africans believe that terming our country's current situation a "crisis" does a disservice to our nation. However, it is becoming overly apparent that we have an economic and financial crisis that continues to grow day by day. Our public sector has never been as overspent (over-borrowed) as it is at present. At the same time the private sector is unable to generate enough employment growth to reduce the numbers of unemployed South Africans (currently running into millions) in any meaningful way.

In the words of A. D. Wassenaar, far from agreeing with the view that it is a disservice to the country to talk about our crisis, I wish to ask on the contrary whether it is not unjust to the country and its people to continue with what is virtually a conspiracy of silence and to endeavour to hide the fact that a crisis exists and that in fact it is a very severe crisis. South Africa must extricate itself financially from a mess created by decades of overspending coupled with little or no job training and education for the vast majority of South Africans. As each day goes by, more South Africans find themselves unemployed or victims of the crime wave that engulfs our nation.

Solutions must be found today, a blueprint drawn up and then implemented with vigour. Procrastination on tackling any of these problems will only make matters worse. We need to create 400 000 new jobs per year. What are we doing about it? It is time for fresh ideas to be considered in order to put this country on the road to economic prosperity. We are digging an ever deeper hole for ourselves as the formal sector continues to reduce the number of jobs at an alarming rate of 100 000 annually. The time for excuses is over.

It is important to stand up to the realities we face. Rather than always being politically correct, as so many influential people are, true patriots need to stand up and be heard. The man in the street cannot afford a prime overdraft rate of 24%, let alone 15%. Sadly, South Africa will be fortunate if its economic growth rate in 1999 exceeds 1%. It is time to call a spade a spade.

For those who believe South Africa is now one of the hottest emerging stock markets in the world and that this will save the day, it is worth noting that the most influential US economic forecasting and consulting service, DRI/McGraw Hill, which is part of Standard & Poor's rating agency, recently ranked South Africa as the "riskiest" of the ten emerging markets it examined, based on 50 variables ranging from government policies to economic and political risk. Argentina, Poland, Mexico, Turkey, India, China, Russia and Brazil were all rated as less risky than South Africa. The study, published in July 1997, cited as a major negative the fact that economic growth was declining while unemployment was rising. In addition, the report stated that "South Africa's mineral and agricultural output is also stagnant or declining, and consumer debt has reached dangerous proportions."

Accountability

Why is it that our currency depreciated by almost one third against the dollar and pound in 1996 and already by a quarter by mid 1998? There exist fundamental reasons why the rand will continue to head south over the next few years. Blaming it on speculators, and Asia and other emerging markets is pointless. In fact Latin America (a major emerging market) has been unaffected by Asia or so-called currency crises affecting emerging markets. There are reasons why South Africa consistently ranks amongst the least competitive nations in almost every international survey. Back in 1996 in my capacity as an advisor to the Namibian government on their export processing zone (offering a wide range of investment incentives such as no import duties or taxes), it was disturbing to meet South African policymakers who were quite content with, and complacent about, South Africa's unattractive investment regime.

Why is it that the new Labour Relations Act discriminates against small employers, who are held to the same standards and must pay the same wage rates as our country's largest conglomerates?

Unless we want to continue being ruled by special interest groups and their elite group of beneficiaries, it is our duty as the South African electorate to confront our political leaders on the decisions they continue to make.

Our leaders enjoy many perks, but it should also be required of them to be held accountable and to offer us suitable answers as to why they adopt particular policies while discarding or ignoring others.

We as the electorate need to question our leaders regarding where they derive their economic policies from and the empirical evidence of these policies' succeeding in other parts of the world. It is our duty to learn from other nations and to be knowledgeable about other countries' reasons for success. In so doing we can demand answers from our leaders as to why they do not wish to adopt many of the most successful economic policies that have been shown to work over the past quarter century.

Although many of our government officials are intelligent individuals, it should concern us that they are not trained experts in the economics field. They seem to have discarded the successful policies implemented by many fast-emerging and developing countries in Asia, Latin America and Eastern Europe, in exchange for their own new and untried solutions. Despite the present problems in Asia, which result largely from speculative property mortgages and over eager banks, these economies have generated millions of new jobs over the past 30 years and have become some of the world's leading exporters.

It is high time for our leaders to be less arogant in assessing South Africa's economic policies. We can learn from success stories the world over. South Africa's investment incentives are woefully weak in relation to other countries and as a result we have precious few foreign currency reserves to protect the ever shrinking rand.

South Africa does not need to reinvent the wheel in order to solve our massive unemployment and currency crises. Botswana, Chile, the Czech Republic, Ireland and Singapore are but a few of the countries we can learn from. By contrast we in South Africa offer foreign and domestic investors tight labour laws, including a 1% labour levy (read tax), a 43% corporate tax rate, a currency diminishing in value and high import duties. In the face of massive unemployment and a severe lack of foreign currency reserves, it is rather curious to have a tax system and investment policy that rewards the purchase of machines over hiring humans.

Nationalisation and Privatisation Questions

Why is it that privatisation continues to move forward rapidly in Russia and other former Communist bloc countries while South Africa's privatisation policy continues to be implemented ever so slowly?

Many believe that implementing privatisation policies just means the selling-off of state assets. Forty-six years of National Party (NP) rule led to an inordinate amount of nationalisation and not just of industries such as steel, petrochemicals, air and rail transportation, telecommunications, television and electricity. Perhaps even more harmful was the NP's stealthy controls of everything from coal and sugar to corn and cement.

To this day our life insurance industry is compelled to invest a prescribed proportion of its assets and the assets of pension fund monies in government stock. It is an infringement on the private sector and free enterprise to compel the insurance industry to switch its funds into investments that might deprive its policy holders of the best returns on their money. Our government should not have the right to direct the private sector as to where its money should be invested.

Government should not be able to count on the insurance industry to continue to bail it out of any deficit or revenue shortfall. Providing cheap money to government through the funds of insurance policy holders is a great disservice to policy holders, whose funds could be better invested.

That compulsory investment in government stock is tantamount to partial nationalisation is not generally appreciated. The insurance industry is nationalised to the extent that the provision for investment in government is above zero.

Brainwashing

We in South Africa have lived with state-controlled corporations and nationalisation for so long that we rarely question whether it is in the best interests of all South Africans for our state to be operating in so many areas, and in an increasing number of cases actually competing with the private sector, as with airlines and telecommunications (radio and television). We have been brainwashed into believing that government is also best suited to operate such services as waste removal, railways, and the electricity and telephone systems.

It is time to realise that bureaucracies made up of civil servants do not operate in the same cost structure as the private sector — they have the luxury of ignoring the effect of competition on cost. There is an important distinction between the delivery of services undertaken for no profit, as in the case of many state-controlled enterprises, and the delivery of services at the lowest possible cost. The assault on the private sector by our governments, which we have endured for much of this century, has more often than not led to the delivery of services at a far higher price than would have been the case if the private sector had provided such services. The charges paid by the public for their telephone calls are only half the equation. The annual expenditure of Telkom, South African Airways (SAA), and other state-controlled enterprises is funded by each and every South African. This is in addition to paying our telephone and airline bills. It is sad but true that our state-run airline (SAA) continues to operate at a loss at a tremendous cost to taxpayers.

The state-controlled Industrial Development Corporation, originally established with the best possible intentions to "plan, stimulate and finance industrial development," has over time functioned as a state-controlled bank, financing new state-controlled enterprises such as Sasol, Foskor, Soekor, Alusaf and Columbus Stainless Steel. As such it has become more of an empire builder — an investment and industrial conglomerate often in competition with private enterprise.

Can we not learn from successful countries such as the United States, where the cost of a cross-continental telephone call or airline flight remains a fraction of the cost we have to endure in

South Africa? In numerous countries, local authorities have privatised waste removal and water supply services while the airways of radio and television have no government controls. Government does not compete in these sectors, nor does it take more than its fair share from the private sector. Taking our television industry as a case in point, our state-owned SABC does not only compete with the private-sector run stations, but worse still, it takes a sizeable slice of advertising monies spent by the private sector.

The private sector is in effect handing over its advertising monies to bureaucrats who have no training in cost containment or successfully competing in a free market. Where this advertising money ultimately ends up or how it is spent remains a frightening thought. At least when the private sector receives such advertising revenue, we know that the goal of the enterprise is to grow larger and more profitable, thus being able to hire more workers who may then also add to the growth and purchasing power of our economy. Sadly this is not the objective of a state-run bureaucracy.

Exchange Control

Exchange control is an even worse form of nationalisation of the man in the street's savings and investments. If better returns can be had by diversifying one's portfolio abroad, forcing South Africans to invest for their retirement in less stable investments does a tremendous disservice to all citizens. Our corporations and individual investors are constrained by government's policy of outlawing many forms of foreign investment.

In Chapter 6 I will show that the financial markets are every country's new master. The current bogey-man for South Africa's volatile and increasingly poor exchange rate is our government's policy of exchange control. It is time to get rid of this socialistic and outdated policy if we want to be favourably viewed by the world's investment community and have a hope of attracting sizeable numbers of new investors and manufacturers to our shores. The rand is headed only one way and that is south, as long as exchange controls remain in place. That is the fact whether we like it or not. Between January and June 1998, our nation's net worth has been reduced by a quarter in dollar and pound terms.

Growing Bureaucracy

Although our nation's finances and economy are in crisis mode, we have had no problem adding additional layers of bureaucracy to our new political system since 1994. We now have nine provinces, each with its own legislature, provincial cabinet members and a Premier, in addition to an expanded civil service at provincial and local levels.

At national level we now have a Parliament comprising 400 MPs and an additional chamber known as the National Council of Provinces (NCOP) with 90 members, which in 1997 replaced the Senate. Whether the NCOP will ever develop into more than a dumping ground for old or unwanted politicians who just reflect the National Assembly in terms of their voting patterns remains to be seen.

This is not to mention the growing national civil service — unfortunately most of our civil servants have not been trained to fully understand the importance or function of the private sector.

As such it is incomprehensible why we allow our civil servants the authority to decide upon an ever growing number of important issues that have a direct impact on the private sector, price structures, profit levels, the flow of funds across our borders, investment criteria and the capitalist system.

The civil service in South Africa has grown out of all proportion ever since the National Party took over the reins of government in 1948. Between 1937 and 1966, while the White population increased by 70% and the total population by only 87% the Civil Service grew by 276% (Afrikaanse Handelsinstituut document — J. J. Stadler). Today our public sector employs more than 1.5 million South Africans and constitutes 20% of our GDP — an excessive amount. In fact, in terms of government's budgeted expenditure in 1996, the public sector itself enjoyed some 50% of the pie after taking into account the interest payments on the country's debt. Another way of looking at government's excessive cost is that it currently spends a third of all monies spent in South Africa — over 30% of GDP.

We in South Africa continue to vest enormous power in our ministers and bureaucrats — in many cases in persons not trained for and not equipped to carry out the task.

The effect of concentration of power in a bureaucracy has rarely been better formulated than by Ludwig von Mises, a renowned economist and Nobel Laureate, who observed: "[Bureaucracy] is imbued with a fanatical hostility to free enterprise and private property. It paralyses the conduct of business and lowers the productivity of labour. By heedless spending it squanders the nation's wealth. It is inefficient and wasteful. It lacks unity and uniformity; the various bureaux and agencies work at cross purposes. Poverty and distress are bound to follow."

To make matters worse, as the civil service grows and increases its powers, the private sector's extreme dependence on the goodwill (permissions and concessions) of various ministers and bureaucrats has led to a private sector unwilling to offend in any way the authority on whose goodwill it depends so often for so much. As A. D. Wassenaar stated back in the late 1970s: "As a general rule it can be said that [in South Africa] spokesmen for the private sector are loathe to criticise, are liable to understate their case, are prone to agree with and are unwilling to challenge authority."

The stronger the government's hold on power the more valid the above statements are. That is why we in South Africa have every reason to be concerned.

Freedom from excessive regulation, responsive government, lower taxation levels, freedom of currency movement (no exchange controls), a practical range of investment incentives (unlike those in Gear which few firms have qualified for) — these are just a few of the policies that have permitted far poorer nations to consistently outperform South Africa economically. Our backward and uninspired investment regime continues to lose us huge foreign investment projects. Many other developing nations have developed highly focused action plans to generate long-term foreign investment to sustain their high economic growth rates. South Africa barely has a game plan at this stage.

Creating an Enduring, Strong Democracy

In order for South Africa to enjoy an enduring strong democratic tradition, we require a political party system that provides a credible and viable alternative ruling party. It is in the best interests of all of us to have a strong opposition party which can put pressure on the government of the day to meet the difficult challenges facing our nation. The current weak alignment of opposition parties should be a deep cause for concern. In order to ensure good government, a country also needs good opposition parties.

How do we create a viable opposition to a seemingly *de facto* one party state that may rule over South Africa longer than the National Party's 46-year blazing trail of socio-economic disasters? Our history of such dominant political parties has not been encouraging. The legacies that have been left include excessive unemployment, unequal education, inflation rates of well in excess of 20%, the absence of action regarding many economic policy matters such as privatisation, a debt standstill, a world-wide sanctions campaign which made our country the world's leading pariah, a currency whose value is now just one sixth of what it was in 1979 (in terms of the US$), not to mention the R11 bn of taxpayers' money that was squandered on the futile Mossgas oil drilling effort, and an estimated R70 bn spent on a destabilising military campaign in neighbouring countries throughout the 1980s.

Viable opposition parties which can one day assume the mantle of power are crucial to the creation of a healthy democratic country. Without such a viable opposition an attitude begins to arise amongst the populace of: "Why care? Why do anything? Why bother since no one else can run the country or get voted in?" Apathy grows.

It is my hope that the contents of this book will provide a wake-up call to all South Africans and simultaneously stimulate debate. My only objective is to create a dynamic plan that best serves the interests of all South Africans, and then to persuade others to implement it! South Africans want action, not words. We should demand a clear vision from our political leaders on how they plan to achieve the rapid economic growth required over the next 10 to 20 years — a level of growth that is necessary to dramatically cut unemployment and raise sufficient government revenues to fund such programmes as the building of 3 million new housing units and the creation of equal education for all.

Improving the Way of Life for the Majority of South Africans

I make no apologies to those I will offend with the contents of this book. Silence is not the answer — education is. More educated voters will lead to a more demanding electorate and a more responsive government.

This book is not designed to serve as an indictment of the present policies being followed in South Africa. In many instances the transformation of the ANC from an exiled movement to a ruling government has been remarkably fluid and has set an example for other nations to follow. Therefore I trust this book will be seen for what it is: a pragmatic search for a better way of life for all South Africans as the 21st century approaches.

Holding our Leaders More Accountable

Members of our present and future governments should not be treated as untouchables, no matter how courageous their leaders may have been or how many years they may have struggled to achieve leadership positions. By voting them into power we have sufficiently rewarded them for their years of struggle and sacrifice. The longer we wait to demand results and answers to the harsh realities our country faces, the deeper the hole will become which we have dug ourselves into.

By describing the tough challenges and problems facing our country, many of which require immediate action, this book attempts to hold our leaders more accountable and to provide a checklist for each and every one of us to judge the performances of our elected politicians.

It is our role as the electorate to ask tough questions and to demand answers of the people we put in power. They are our servants, not the other way around.

We are the shareholders of government — the current management team is only temporary, and can be replaced by a new team with new ideas every five years if need be.

We the people must be respected by our tenants — they are our temporary tenants: we own the houses our ministers live in at Groote Schuur and next to the Union Buildings in Pretoria. Until we confront our politicians with tough questions and demand specific answers, they will continue to ignore us, while hobnobbing with the same special interest groups at the various functions so many of our politicians seem to attend so regularly.

It is not my purpose to ascribe blame to any political party or any one person, but rather to lay out the bare facts, many of which were inherited from previous governments. As a concerned South African, my motivation for writing this book is define the issues we need to address and the road we need to take in order to ensure economic prosperity, and not economic peril, for all in South Africa.

Between 1993 and 1998 fewer than 50 000 additional jobs were created in South Africa's formal sector, while population experts tell us that the population continues to grow by at least 2.5% per year. The harsh reality is that we need to create at least 500 000 additional jobs per year for the next decade and a half, if we are to seriously overcome our unemployment problems and the looming socio-economic disaster.

Population

Back in 1989 there was one black child born every 28 seconds, and one white child born every 12 minutes. The black population alone is expected to rise to 40 million by 2005, many of whom will move to the urban areas in search of work. According to some economists, the unemployment rate in the year 2005 will be 55% of the economically active population, or 9.8 million people, given a continuation of the present rates of economic growth.

Unemployment should also be one of the fears of whites for the future — but then few other countries have so protected the employment of white workers.

Can we not learn from others around the world who have experience in successfully transforming economies? We must build our South African economic recovery in line with the harsh demands of our new masters — not some political party or leader, but rather the capital markets of Wall Street, London, Hong Kong, Frankfurt and Tokyo.

Countries where a small rich and successful elite lives behind high walls and electrified security fences are not those that inspire confidence with foreign investors.

We need to change our elite old-boy business club attitudes, insider dealings and outmoded economic policies. With more openness and responsiveness on the part of our economic planners, we have a chance of creating a successful and viable economic base which will provide employment to the vast majority of those who desire jobs.

With the implementation of far-sighted policies, given a bit of luck and correct timing, there is no reason why the way of life of all South Africans should not improve dramatically. The need to continue building eight-foot-high walls will hopefully disappear, and we can produce a safe and secure society, and, importantly, one that is at peace with itself.

However, to get from where we currently are to such a position will require sacrifices, including the eradication of preferential treatment for certain companies and industries. Protectionism must be a thing of the past. Hidden monopolistic tendencies cannot be tolerated if we are to gain the respect of the international financial community which can make or break us. We must be seen to be doing everything reasonable to attract foreign investors and to build up our export levels, without relying on such reprieves as rising gold or platinum prices, which are temporary by nature and which have recently fallen to their lowest levels in years. A new engine must be developed to absorb the millions of newcomers to the labour market.

Power of the People

Although I remain but one lone voice, I do hope that those South Africans who agree with me concerning the symptoms of our national problem will use this book as a means of judging our political, business, and labour leaders, even if they dispute some of my proposed remedies. If this book assists in any way in clarifying the demands we should make of our political leaders, then I will feel I have contributed something worthwhile. Our politicians and national leaders must be held far more accountable than in the past. We must demand specifics — policies and strategies must be clearly spelled out.

Our votes should never be taken for granted. We the electorate own and control South Africa. We must ask our politicians specific questions and demand specific answers. Slick electioneering and advertisements on billboards should no longer suffice. However, we must also know which questions to ask. We must reassert our role as owners of South Africa. The questions contained in the Appendix at the end of this book need to be answered by all our elected officials.

We the electorate hold the power in South Africa and are the final judges as to whether or not our leaders have succeeded in their temporary tenancy of the Houses of Parliament and in the Union Buildings of Pretoria.

However, one voice is puny and on its own will not be heard above the normal political infighting and squabbling. The electorate's voice, when it speaks as one and demands action — is a great roar that scares each and every politician worth his or her salt. Only we, the people of South Africa, can change our country. We must demand action and change. It is up to us alone.

This book is written not so much for the elite of South Africa, who in one way or another will use their connections, experience, and adaptability to ensure their own success. Rather, it is writtten for the ordinary people.

South Africa has within itself the ability to transform both its image and its role. It could become the industrialised powerhouse of Africa — so desperately needed if the African continent is to undergo a major economic renaissance. With resources beyond its needs, South Africa is at present a crippled giant. Once its economic shackles have been removed, it could become to Africa what Japan has been to the Pacific Basin — the dynamo that energises and drives languishing countries to become economically viable.

Whatever my critics may wish to knock me down for, they will recognise that my comments are designed to improve the lot of all South Africans, with the intention that black South Africans should be the major beneficiaries.

CHAPTER ONE

Our Inheritance

"Yes, it is the dawn that has come. The titihoya wakes from sleep . . . the sun tips with light the mountains of Ingeli and East Griqualand. The great valley of Umzimkulu is still in darkness, but the light will come there. For it is the dawn that has come, as it has come for a thousand years never failing. But when that dawn will come, of our emancipation, from the fear of bondage and the bondage of fear, why, that is a secret."

ALAN PATON — CRY THE BELOVED COUNTRY

THE NEW South AFRICA has inherited a context in which no real economic growth per capita has occurred since 1964, no real job growth has taken place for a decade, an extremely unhealthy level of national indebtedness exists, and a crime wave threatens to destroy hopes of a prosperous future.

The National Party's highly protectionist tariff policy, which encouraged import substitution through high customs and import duties, led to an abnormal sense of complacency amongst many South African manufacturers who enjoyed the protection of high tariff walls.

South Africa's status as a pariah nation and its isolation from the global marketplace through financial sanctions and disinvestment, led to the tightening of exchange controls, creating a hothouse effect for the Johannesburg Stock Exchange as our conglomerates were forced to reinvest their profits in South Africa.

While the National Party's Verwoerdian policies gave inferior education to blacks and the party spent, on black education, as little as one-eighth of that spent on white education, the level of black skills was kept so low that today South Africa has a severe lack of skilled professional managers and workers. The situation has been exacerbated over the years by the so-called "brain drain", the emigration of highly skilled whites.

The old economic engines based on mining have been running out of steam for the past few decades as gold output, in particular,

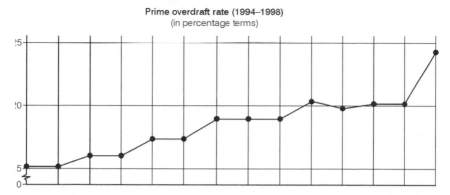

Prime overdraft rate (1994–1998)
(in percentage terms)

Figure 10 *Composition of population groups in South Africa*

has dropped to below 500 tonnes for the first time since 1956, from 607 tonnes in 1987. The numbers of people employed in gold mining have been reduced by half between 1987 and 1997.

With the gold price sinking to an 18-year low of $282 per ounce in January 1998, this negative trend is likely to continue. South Africa can clearly no longer rely on the gold mining sector for a reprieve from either its unemployment crisis or a weak balance of trade. Our country is the world's largest producer of gold, but remains more exposed than any other country to a slump in the gold price, as its deep-level mines are now the highest-cost producers in the world. As such, the South African gold mining

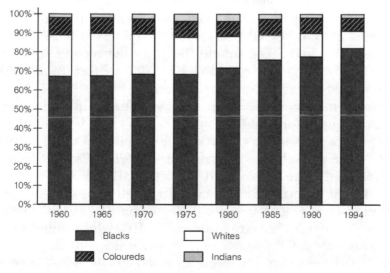

Figure 11 *Gold price (in US$)*

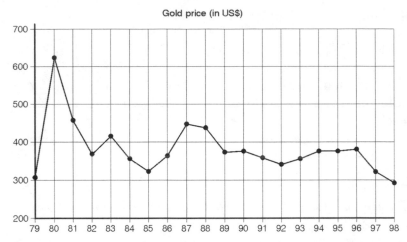

Figure 12   *Gold mining industry employment*

industry is facing a major crisis, with analysts expecting the industry to report its worst losses ever by mid-1998, with a number of marginal mines possibly being forced to shut down, creating further unemployment. A total of 69 000 people are employed by South Africa's nine most marginal mines. By early July 1997 the plummeting gold price had already claimed its first South African scalp with the closing of Randgold's Benoni mine.

Almost 60% of South Africa's gold mines will be classified as "marginal" or loss makers if the gold price remains at or below $320 an ounce. At a price of $320 or below, as many as one third of the 313 000 jobs in the gold mining industry could be in jeopardy. It is expected that 100 000 miners will be laid off between 1998 and 1999, should the price not recover to at least $320. Their only reprieve may be a far weaker rand, which translates into a higher rand gold price.

To make matters worse the pending reduction in interest rates (which has been forecast for some two years now by a number of South Africa's economic gurus) may all come to nothing as South Africa's foreign exchange reserves and export levels recede due to a lower gold price. Since gold exports make up approximately 25% of total exports a $20 sustained reduction in the gold price will result in at least a 0.3% to 0.4% reduction in South Africa's annual economic growth rate in GDP, while lobbing off approximately R3 bn worth of exports, which will increase the country's dependence on foreign capital inflows to finance the larger current account deficit.

With almost no significant labour-intensive foreign direct investment attracted to South Africa in the latter half of the 1980s and early 1990s, and a population growth rate amongst the highest in the world at 2.7%, it is little wonder then that our current ANC-led government inherited a situation with an unemployment rate fast approaching 40% — if it is not already at this level.

Even the recent economic growth rates in 1994–97, which varied between 1.8% and 3.0%, have brought little comfort, as a net loss of jobs has been reported in the formal sector for 1995, 1996 and 1997 (130 000 in 1997 alone). In fact over the past seven years total employment in the formal non-agricultural sector has declined by more than 420 000 workers.

According to the Development Bank of Southern Africa approximately 365 000 people enter the job market annually, while only 82 000 new jobs were created between 1990 and 1995.

Table 1 *South Africa's inherited mess*

- Falling real per capita income.
- Growing unemployment — the unemployed are the fastest growing constituency in South Africa.
- Low rate of economic growth.
- Unsustainability of traditional pillars of primary exports (gold and minerals) and cheap labour.
- Failure to develop a broad-based manufacturing sector primed for exports.
- South Africa's isolation from technological advances in many fields.
- Rapid urbanisation with few jobs to satisfy this migration.
- Heavy government indebtedness.
- Little room to raise additional revenue as society is already overtaxed.
- Low levels of direct foreign investment.
- Persistence of high inflation expectations.
- Obsolescence of the capital stock.
- The heavy tax burden on individuals (nothing is being done about this, while the corporate loopholes continue to lose billions for the South African treasury).
- The excessive dissaving of the public sector.
- The unsustainable size of the fiscal deficit before borrowing.

- The uncompetitiveness of the private sector in world markets.
- The continued anti-export bias in South Africa's foreign trade structure.
- Weakness of South Africa's current account of the balance of payments.
- Low levels of foreign exchange reserves.
- Shortage of skilled labour.
- A high cost of labour combined with levels of training.
- High non-wage labour costs such as labour unrest, strikes and stoppage.
- Poor underlying productivity growth.

A new approach must be adopted that will generate the level of fixed investment and foreign exchange required to create new jobs and capital that will allow us to pay off our huge government debt. This will ultimately allow government to invest more in South Africa, rather than paying 25 cents out of each rand of tax it collects, in the form of interest payments on government debt, into the coffers of wealthy foreign banks, pension funds and unit trusts.

Continued government debt at the astronomical levels left behind by the National Party government will erode South African living standards for the foreseeable future. It is imperative that this debt be eradicated as it saps our annual budget of some 20% of its expenditure. Just the cost of servicing interest on government debt will surpass R40 bn in 1998. The cost of servicing the debt has in fact tripled over the past six years alone, and may well be the biggest sole item of expenditure in the next budget. While the present government inherited this situation, it is imperative that this debt be paid off as soon as possible because it continues to cripple South Africa's ability to spend money on priorities such as alleviating poverty, improving health care and education, and investing in the human resource potential of our country.

Disparities

The worst vestiges of the apartheid legacy is the vast disparity — along racial lines — in the incomes and living standards of our country's citizens. South Africa's inequality in income distribution as measured by the Gini coefficient is amongst the highest in the world, and heads the list of 36 developing nations with a score of 0.68 (the range is between 0 and 1, with 0 representing perfect equality and 1 perfect inequality).

The disparity of incomes and living standards is further reflected by the infant mortality rates and maternal morbidity rates (women who die as a result of childbirth and pregnancy): 130 infants per 1 000 born in the former Transkei area die, while among urban whites the figure is closer to 15 per 1 000. The number of women dying as a result of pregnancy and childbirth is more than seven times greater amongst blacks (based on 1989 figures). South Africa's tuberculosis rates are amongst the highest in the world, a sign of poor living conditions. Tuberculosis almost exclusively affects non-whites.

The disparity in the lifestyles of blacks and whites remains so stark that to this day one feels as if is one is entering entirely different countries when passing from a black to a white neighbourhood. On the outskirts of my native city Cape Town, which lies on the south-westernmost tip of Africa and is surrounded by the most gorgeous beaches and mountains, the squatter camps of Crossroads and Khayelitsha have some of the worst third-world conditions imaginable. The white suburbs less than ten miles away exceed even the luxurious standards of many first world countries' wealthiest neighbourhoods.

These two South Africas are so far apart in terms of lifestyle that no overnight quick-fix is possible. While we have certainly steamed ahead on the political front to a non-racial South Africa, much remains to be done. Our journey has in fact barely begun. Unfortunately the satisfaction of travelling along this road will only be truly felt once we embark on the economic journey leading out of serfdom. Although under a new constitution, blacks now have the right to vote, this does not in any way ensure that they will begin to enjoy the fruits of prosperity in the near future.

In short, the huge drain on resources caused by the need to prop up apartheid structures, such as artificial and uneconomical homelands and multiple levels of bureaucracy, along with the effects of sanctions and the resultant economic stagnation and negative growth rates over the past decade, have all conspired to place the vast majority of South Africans on the brink of economic disaster.

A prosperous future for South Africa is woven into the cloth of rapid economic growth. One can only hope that those in a position of power understand that the vote alone does not assure the transformation to a happier South Africa. Economic prosperity is the most important guarantor of happiness, stability and contentment.

Unisa's Bureau of Market Research has gone so far as to say that if the labour-capital ratio of the late 1980s is maintained, an annual economic growth rate of as much as 8% to 9% will be needed just to absorb the number of new entrants into the labour force. This is due to the fact that more and more companies are investing in mechanised systems, rather than manual labour.

In order to alleviate poverty and thereby raise the living standards of the vast majority of South Africans, our country has little choice but to devote its efforts to sustained job creation, through high economic growth brought about by boosting export levels and attracting long-term foreign and domestic investment. The domestic South African market cannot grow sufficiently quickly to sustain economic grow rates in excess of 5% beyond a few years. In fact, inflationary pressures seem to rear their head well before economic growth even approaches 4%. If manufacturing for a growing export market takes place hot-house inflationary pressures will take longer to appear.

Import substitution, inadequate training and education for black South Africans, along with sanctions, only served to weaken South Africa's job creation potential. South Africa's share of world industrial exports fell by almost 60%, from 0.6% in the mid-1950s to just 0.25% in the early 1990's.

The country's level of gold and other primary exports (minerals and largely unprocessed raw materials) has remained fairly static over the years, while gold itself as a percentage of exports has weakened considerably. It is clear that the manufacturing sector in South Africa needs to be developed with as much of an export bias as possible for the country to begin to sustain the level of economic development required to begin to seriously tackle its rate of unemployment and underemployment.

Informal sector

South Africa can no longer take solace in the informal or grey economy and claim that we do not have an unemployment crisis. The grey economy is a smokescreen for those who wish to claim that 1.75 million people are employed, but do not show up in the employment statistics.

By glorifying the informal sector, many of our leaders are in fact reflecting just how weak our formal sector is in terms of job creation. Much of the employment occurring in the informal sector is survivalist. Certain reports indicate that as much as 80% of the sector is barely scraping through (*Sunday Times*, 5 July 1998) and that average salaries are below R500 per month.

Lack of Long-Term Direct Foreign Investment

Sadly, the majority of foreign direct investment is oriented purely towards the domestic market and in many cases does not lead to direct job creation. Rather it represents the purchase of an existing South African company by a foreign company, which would prefer to enter the South African market without the headache of a start-up operation or having to compete with the handful of entrenched companies which dominate at least 75% of all South African industry.

The difference between foreign long-term investment in South Africa and that in Latin America and Asia is stark. In Asia a majority of such investment is export oriented, and has focused on the establishment of factories and processing plants with international markets in mind. Not only do such plants and factories create many new jobs in these developing nations, but they also generate considerable foreign exchange earnings for the countries concerned.

We in South Africa need to achieve a higher standard of living. This depends on the capacity of South Africa's firms to achieve high levels of productivity and to improve such productivity over time. Increasing the level of foreign investment we receive will help boost our nation's productivity levels and help command premium prices for our exported goods in overseas markets.

In the first quarter of 1997 South Africa's current account deficit again increased to R1.9 bn due to a drop of 5.5% in export levels over the previous quarter. Clearly the potential boom expected by those optimists who were happy to see the rand depreciate by some 30% between the end of 1995 and mid-1996 has failed to materialise. If anything, the lesson we need to learn is that many South African firms are not organised enough to generate sizeable increases in their export volumes, and in many cases their goods are uncompetitive relative to world markets. By attracting world class manufacturers to South Africa and using South Africa as an export base, our weak balance of payments, lack of foreign

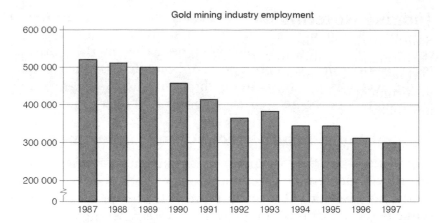

Gold mining industry employment

Figure 13   *Prime overdraft rate, 1994–97 (in percentage terms)*

currency reserves, low productivity and unemployment problems will all be positively affected. We could kill four birds with one stone.

Developing a Misery Index

It is high time that we in South Africa defined a misery index in order to gauge the performance of current and future governments. If we add together our prime overdraft rate, inflation rate and unemployment rate, the sum total will provide us with a simple manner in which to judge to what extent government and Reserve Bank policies are benefiting South Africans. By August 1998 the sum of the different components of the misery index amounted to a massive 65% (unemployment at 35% inflation at 7% and a prime overdraft rate of 23%). Compare this to South Africa three years ago (since unemployment figures are unreliable we will stick to the 35% figure, which is overly generous, as the unemployment rate was certainly lower in 1995). Back in 1995, the prime overdraft rate averaged 14% and the inflation rate was down to 7% — resulting in a misery index of 56%. Although many purists will dismiss this misery index (which shows that South Africans are worse off in 1998 than in 1995) as an overly simplistic measure, it correlates with the most important economic measure of per capita income, after adjusting for inflation. By comparison, the United States has a misery index of 15%–16% (July 1998).

Judging Government

South Africans should use such an index to judge the performance of all future governments. It is a simple yardstick and never lies. If the misery index does not come down during a government's term of office it should be as good an indication as any that we are worse off as a nation than before that government took over.

South Africa's unemployment levels show little sign of improving — in 1996, when the economy recorded a respectable 3% growth rate, employment increased by 0.2%, not even a blip on the radar screen. The only reason the figure was positive at all is due to the large number of government workers who were hired throughout that year. The trend is most disturbing, since almost one out of three working South Africans is now employed in the public sector, even though government has expressly stated its commitment to reducing the size of that sector. This compares with one in six UK workers and one out of seven in Germany and the US. Only France comes close to us in terms of public-sector employment, and given its economic difficulties there is no good reason why we should imitate France.

Also disturbing is the fact that the public sector wage bill keeps rising, with the average salary in 1996 growing by 11.7% to average just over R4 000 a month — more than R500 above the average wage paid by the private sector's largest component, manufacturing.

Pressing Concerns

Although South Africa remains one of the world's 25 largest economies, it ranks a distant 60th in terms of per capita income and 93rd in human development terms (Nattrass, 1996). Just how wide the gulf is between black and white income levels is best illustrated by assuming that whites and blacks lived in separate countries. In such a case white South Africa would rank as high as 24th in terms of human development, and black South Africa only 123rd.

Inequality

While white per capita income is some 9.5 times higher than that of blacks, currently the main reason for income inequality in South Africa are not only discrimination and historically poor black education, but more recently also the lack of available jobs. The massive wage gap between those workers who are skilled and those who are unskilled (and do not have any union representation) adds insult to injury. Without sustainable job creation the level of inequality will only rise, regardless of what government attempts to do in terms of improving education and redistributing income to the poor and unemployed. Government simply does not have sufficient resources to reduce the inequality to any considerable degree through welfare payments and the like.

The lack of job creation in South Africa is evident when one considers that South Africa's economic growth between 1980 and 1995 averaged just 1% per annum while population growth remained at about 2.5% per annum. It is generally accepted that an annual 4% economic growth rate is required simply to absorb new entrants into the labour market. With economic growth of just over 3% for both 1995 and 1996, and just 1.7% in 1997, growth remains insufficient to absorb new entrants. Between 1970 and 1990 the proportion of the workforce without formal jobs rose from 19% to 40% (Nattrass, 1996).

According to some estimates the increasingly capital-intensive nature of investment in South Africa over the past two decades has had the effect of squeezing out the creation of some 2 million jobs. Not only has the South African tax system favoured capital investment through the various tax breaks available to businesses (such as depreciation of assets), but at the same time the cost of hiring labour has become more expensive relative to its productivity levels.

The establishment of legal black trade unions in the late 1970s and early 1980s has largely been responsible for the fact that workers in the formal sector have experienced a real growth in their wages (after inflation is taken into account). At the same time wages in the informal and unregulated sectors have declined in real terms.

Disturbing Reality

Back in the 1960s more than 80% of new entrants into the labour market obtained formal sector wage employment, while in the past few years less than 10% have been successful in finding employment. Increasing numbers of South Africans have been forced into the informal sector, where many of them eke out a living. In 1989 it was estimated (Hofmeyer in Maasdorp's book) that average income in the informal sector was less than R500 a month. Given the poor working conditions, the lack of security which comes from an irregular income, and the low average income, it is possible to say that the majority in the informal sector would have preferred formal sector jobs. In many cases workers in the informal sector are engaged in low-level activities which do little better than provide a subsistence income. Many of these workers should be regarded as unemployed.

The Central Statistical Service unemployment figures most likely underestimate the size of South Africa's economically active population as they do not take into account those who are not actively seeking formal sector employment, such as women in the informal sector who make a bare living from the selling of vegetables. 1994 official data suggested that 57% of the labour force was employed in the formal sector when in reality the figure may now be well below 50%. *Based on current trends and using government statistics it is estimated that no more than 43% of the economically active population will have a job in the formal sector by the year 2000.*

Informal sector

Those who defend our nation's intolerably high unemployment rate and low level of labour absorption in the formal sector by pointing to the growing informal sector, need to be reminded that average informal sector income is, in fact, minimal and well below that of black workers in manufacturing.

The lack of job creation has led directly to the marginalisation of a growing percentage of the South African population. The total number of jobs available in the formal economy in 1980 exceeded the number available a decade later. With the labour force growing by 400 000 per year, the result has been a dramatic decline in the percentage of the South African labour force with jobs in the formal sector (down from 82% of the economically active population in 1980 to 57% in 1994). Youth unemployment is particularly severe, with only one in 14 school leavers (i.e. 7% of school leavers) able to find a job in the formal economy. An indication of the desperate lack of job availability is the example of a recent (1994) advertisement placed for the filling of 11 000 new positions in the public sector which garnered close to 2 million applicants.

Although many point to the growth in the informal sector as having picked up this slack, the reality is that the unemployment rate has soared — the proportion of the black workforce not earning regular formal sector wages has grown from 37% in 1980 to 55% in 1992. Back in the 1960s as many as 97% of school leavers could expect to find jobs in the formal sector. Formal sector employment levels grew by an average of 2.5% between 1946 and 1975. In fact, excluding low-wage sectors such as agriculture and mining, the growth rate averaged 4.2% per annum. By contrast, total formal sector employment grew by just 1% during the years 1975–90, and the high end wage sector by just 0.5% per annum.

Perhaps most disturbing is that between 1975 and 1991, the share of income earned by the poorest 40% of South Africans fell by a quarter from a 5.2% share down to as low as 3.9%. (McGrath in Maasdorp, 1996).

Poverty — The Ugly Facts

Poverty remains worst in the former independent homelands (the Transkei, Bophuthatswana, Venda and the Ciskei) reaching a record of 77% in 1991. By 1991, 49% of households throughout South Africa (including all the homelands) were living in poverty. Even the white population's level of poverty grew at a disturbing rate — trebling from 3% to 9.5% between 1975 and 1991.

Thirty-one million people, or 70% of all South Africans, earn less than R301 a month and are classified as poor. Blacks form 95 percent of this group. A total of 75% of the poor live in rural areas. Some 53% of the South African population as a consequence consume a little less than 10% of South Africa's total consumption. This compares to the top 10% of South Africa's households which enjoy a full 40% of the consumption.

All South Africans should be aware of the stark reality facing the country. As true patriots the wealthy cannot afford to cocoon themselves from the ills that surround them — the poverty has spread throughout South Africa and will destroy our country if something is not done about it. Sadly, the bold attempt to combat the cancerous growth of poverty, as evidenced in the Reconstruction and Development Programme (RDP) has largely failed — although not for lack of trying. Government unfortunately lacked the expertise and resources necessary to implement such a giant programme. Unfortunately, those who have the expertise (i.e. in the private sector) have in most cases continued to widen the income disparity in South Africa and were not brought on board to assist in the implementation of the RDP.

Is there any point in beating the best in the world at rugby or cricket, only to be beaten and trounced by man's oldest enemy, poverty? For South Africa to be a true champion we need to defeat poverty comprehensively. The dismantling of the RDP Ministry under Jay Naidoo underscored the growing shift away from redistribution in favour of macroeconomic growth (as outlined in the Gear plan) as the best means of redressing the legacy of apartheid and the mismanagement of the South African economy over the years. However, Gear has yet to deliver and is in serious need of revision.

First World or Third World?

Whether we like it or not, South Africa cannot be considered a first world country, and we do ourselves a disservice when we construct policies based on such an unrealistic viewpoint. Far too many citizens are impoverished and illiterate; millions lack jobs or sufficient housing, sewerage or running water; and the vast majority of citizens over 18 are not trained for anything but menial blue-collar jobs.

In order to reduce our third world component clear policies must be implemented. Sadly the following areas are indicative of a third world country moving in the wrong direction:

- our Minister of Justice, by publicly welcoming home a man who stands accused of fraud, does nothing to endear South Africa to the outside world and helps to label us as yet another corrupt third world country. If anything, it indicates that we are sliding in the wrong direction, perhaps becoming ever more like African nations, whose track records over the past 30 years leave much to be desired and are very little worth emulating;
- no action has been taken on non-payment of rates, water and electricity accounts. By any measure this is typical of many backward or third world countries. Until the rule of law is respected in South Africa, it will be some time before we can hope to avoid being labelled as just another third world nation and be seen as on the right track to first world status;
- the number of ghost or phantom workers in the public sector continues to be a problem in certain provinces. A number of

provincial administrations have collapsed or are in bad need of attention. This is particularly true in the Eastern Cape and the Northern Province;

- corruption is rampant in a number of public service departments throughout South Africa. In June 1997 it emerged that the housing minister had awarded a R42 m contract to one of her friends, while officials at the Independent Broadcasting Authority had cost taxpayers hundreds of thousands of rands on lavish spending on a wide range of items that showcased their luxurious lifestyle, but had little or nothing to do with their actual jobs. It seems that few of these officials knew how to carry out their jobs, and as such spent most of the time entertaining themselves and their friends at the taxpayers' expense. Reports of massive fraud in the magistrates courts are even more disturbing;
- the Abe Williams scandal relating to welfare payments was uncovered in 1996. A team sent out to investigate the country's social welfare system found that R230 m out of a total budget of R3.2 bn was lost each year through fraud in the welfare system;
- we need to stop the chaos occurring on South African university campuses, especially at former black universities such as Fort Hare, which was recently temporarily closed; and
- numerous other examples can be cited, such as the huge number of bank heists and jail breaks, and allegations of immense fraud at the Johannesburg Licensing Department and Deeds Offices. The blatant cronyism at work in the awarding of new contracts by the housing minister, maladministration of the Petroleum and Energy Fund, and the millions wasted on an AIDS play by the health minister — all do not help to distinguish South Africa from the rest of Africa.

CHAPTER TWO

Crime is Out of Control

CURRENTLY, A SERIOUS CRIME is committed every 17 seconds in South Africa, a murder every half an hour, a housebreaking every two minutes, and an assault every three minutes. At present only 77 people are arrested for every 1 000 crimes committed. A mere 22% of reported crimes are ever prosecuted. Our prisons cannot even cope with those who are convicted. With more than 4 in every 1 000 citizens in jail, South Africa qualifies as one of the nations with the highest proportion of people in jail.

Crime at this level generates high levels of fear and insecurity among our population. Needless to say foreign investors and tourists are put off South Africa by continued reports of Johannesburg, in particular, recording the highest murder and rape rates per capita in the world. Over a million cases of serious crimes were reported in South Africa in just the first eight months of 1994, with 61 murders being reported for every 100 000 people during 1996 — nearly seven times that of the USA and more than 10 times the worldwide average.

What measures have our leaders come up with to crack down on this? How are we ever to attract meaningful investment to create jobs when stories of murder fill our newspapers like daily weather forecasts?

Millions of innocent South Africans now effectively live jailed inside their houses, surrounded by their own barbed-wire fences and walls. Meanwhile criminals rule the streets. How healthy is such a society to be bringing up our children in?

In per capita terms, Johannesburg is now the murder capital of the world. Action is needed right now.

During the past few years we have seen the Bosnian tragedy unfold before our eyes, and our hearts go out to the innocent victims. However, many of our very own neighbourhoods, townships and cities are mini-Sarajevos every night of the week.

Lack of work and boredom among many young males is a direct cause of much of the violence. Lack of economic opportunity must, therefore, be tackled — without improving economic prospects it will be exceedingly difficult to bring the crime wave down.

Crime in South Africa must be rewarding, as so many of our citizens appear to enjoy lengthy careers in this underworld. Police protection of the public is poor and the rate of prosecution of criminals is pathetically low.

For criminals — when judging the risks and rewards — the incredibly low chance of first being detected and even then being convicted and kept in prison, is so low (criminals have a 1 in 20 chance of being convicted in South Africa, according to a recent South African Institute of Race Relations study) that the rewards of being a criminal in today's society far outweigh any conceivable risks.

Convictions dropped from 1 611 per 100 000 of the population in 1972 to 1 145 per 100 000 by 1992. In absolute terms they have fallen from 390 000 in 1987/88 to approximately 320 000 in 1993/94 — despite the dramatic increase in crime levels.

At present in South Africa only eight out of every 1 000 criminals remain in prison longer than two years.

One of the all-time growth businesses in South Africa over the past decade has been private security companies. What are we paying taxes for if we cannot rely on our own police force for protection? We should not need to pay a fortune for private security. This money would be better spent investing in our economy and in new businesses.

Prisons

Our prisons cannot even cope with those who are convicted. As mentioned, South Africa qualifies as one of the world's most imprisoned nations. South Africa cannot even afford to accommodate the approximately 150 000 virtual population of convicted criminals, let alone the hundreds of thousands who are not convicted.

Parole has translated into freedom, as authorities are too understaffed to police parolees. While a supervising officer should be responsible for about 25 parolees, with only 1 100 supervisors in all of South Africa this translates into a ratio of 1 to 300 parolees. Every day another 115 prisoners step onto the streets of South Africa — an additional 42 000 every year.

Our criminals, even when they are convicted, are often released after a very short stay in jail. They are not rehabilitated while in prison. We should make it a pre-condition of release that prisoners are at least semi-literate and also have a marketable skill. With the scrapping of capital punishment even convicted murderers now roam our country freely.

The police force appears unable to curb the crime that makes South Africa the most violent country in the world outside of a war zone. People do not feel safe when the risk of your car being hijacked becomes a daily way of life, the constant fear exists that armed men will break into your home to steal your valuables, and for women the danger of being raped looms large — which with AIDS could be a death sentence.

Negative Effects

The continued increase in crime has led to a renewed wave of emigration out of South Africa, made up primarily of those with the skills necessary to be able to secure good employment prospects abroad. As *The Star* newspaper has said, whether your name is Domingo, De Beer, or Dlamini the fact is that you could be the next victims of rape, torture or hijacking, or just as likely, murder. As such, South Africa continues to lose many of its best and brightest on a daily basis. No country can survive such a brain drain; or at best it will take generations to overcome the loss.

The brain drain will continue to gather momentum. The first task of any government is to protect law-abiding citizens from crime. If it cannot do that, it should resign or *wakkerskrik* and start making a difference.

Many emigrants and potential emigrants fear South Africa will over time become an ungovernable third world country. This, coupled with fears that affirmative action will cause massive lay-offs and job losses in the white community, certainly does not encourage skilled people to remain in South Africa.

This is not helped of course by the concern many parents have about the lowering of educational standards at schools and the turning of universities into populist institutions so that a degree no longer has value in the marketplace. Health care standards also continue to drop, with many hospitals struggling to provide a decent service. This has resulted in the creation of more expensive private hospitals to service the well-to-do.

Of course, whites must accept that they can no longer maintain the artificially high standards they enjoyed under apartheid. Blacks must be advanced in all fields, but unless the government realises, in the words of President Mandela, that to push whites aside "is fatal, that's suicide", the exodus will continue. South Africa, which desperately needs the skills of the emigrants it is losing, will certainly become a poorer and less skilled country.

At the top of the list of measures to ensure that we retain our most skilled individuals, action must be taken to curb the violence and ensure our citizens a decent quality of life. Living in houses – even mansions – behind 8-foot high walls, in neighbourhoods where one is unable to feel comfortable walking around the block, and where one's children are forbidden from going outside the front gates to collect the cricket or tennis balls they have hit over the wall — does not qualify as quality of life, not even if the bank account is full.

Along the streets which contain many of the most enviable addresses in Johannesburg's northern suburbs, it is a rare sight indeed to see anyone walking or children playing. South Africa is fast becoming a country of walled neighbourhoods where inhabitants lead a jail-like existence which is unhealthy for all concerned. Living our separate lives does nothing to increase our understanding of each other, nor does it build a sense of community or good neighbourliness.

We only grow as a nation when we interact with each other and learn from one another. How many years do we have to wait until women will feel secure driving alone in Johannesburg at night, or be able to enter downtown Johannesburg without fear? Being prisoners in a million-dollar prison cell is not an enviable existence for anyone.

Fighting crime

Fighting crime must be our first priority. If our police force is incapable of cutting the level of crime in the country, then we need to listen to and learn from the experiences of the rest of the world. Solutions have been found elsewhere — many of the answers are known. We do not have to reinvent the wheel with new and untested policies. We should not be so arrogant as to think we cannot learn from others.

If there is no more space in our prisons then we must build more. If South Africa is to attract badly needed long-term investment, we must show that we are capable of living in a civilised manner. Each and every law abiding South African deserves better from our police authorities. We need to regain the upper hand and provide law and order for all our citizens. We must demand results from our government. Realistic targets to reduce the incidence of crime should be set for our Minister of Safety and Security. His job and that of the Police Commissioner should be on the line if, after a certain period of time, they have been unable to make an impact on the number of criminal activities or apprehending more criminals.

This is a ridiculous state of affairs and our government leaders must be held to account. What are we paying for? Surely our taxpayers' hard-earned money could be better spent? We are losing the battle against crime. It is time to review our poor performance and construct a new strategy to clamp down on this ever-growing menace to our society.

Enormous cost of crime

Crime cost South Africa a staggering R31.3 bn in 1995, equivalent to more than 5% of the 1996 gross domestic product and 18% of the government's national budget. (Nedcor study as reported in *The Citizen* newspaper, 12 June, 1996.)

According to the Nedcor project on crime, this figure reflects the cost of goods stolen and includes white-collar crime such as embezzlement. It is believed that the annual cost of crime exceeds even the projected benefits from the Olympic Games, for which Cape Town submitted an unsucessful bid. It has been projected that the 2004 Games might have earned South Africa R30 bn over a ten year period, which would have been wiped out by the cost of just one year's crime!

According to the study in 1995, a staggering 80% of homes in South Africa experienced some form of crime or violence costing R11 bn — Gauteng's entire budget for 1996.

Between January and June 1997 there were no less than 184 armed bank robberies, while in the province of Gauteng the Trauma Clinic which treats survivors of violent crime saw a 20% increase in the number of patients over the year to June 1997. The World Economic Forum recently ranked South Africa alongside Colombia and Russia as countries in the grip of organised crime. All this damages South Africa's reputation and good name.

The number of reported rapes almost doubled between 1988 and 1994 to more than 32 000, while reports of attempted murder rose by 31% between 1992 and 1995, to more than 20 000 cases.

There were 51% more reported murders in 1994 than in 1988, and 25% more cases of serious assault in the same period.

Crime harms all South Africans — it not only leads to an increased brain drain of our most talented, who are able to easily find jobs abroad, but also fewer tourists visit South Africa, bringing in less foreign exchange, and international investment perceptions remain negative, severely hampering job creation. Our own children and grandchildren are no longer free to roam the pavements of their neighbourhoods.

It is high time that foreign expertise is brought in: look, for example, at what was done in crime-ridden parts of the US, for instance in New York, where major successes were achieved in bringing the crime rate down. One hopes that Mayer Kahn, who has been brought in from the private sector to assist in the fight against crime, will be permitted to bring in tried and tested experts from abroad.

The Police Force

Police are hampered by a lack of first world policing management structures, low salaries leading to low morale in the force, and inadequate resources, such as an almost complete lack of the computerised information systems which help police forces worldwide to carefully track neighbourhoods and to allocate resources to areas where crime is most prevalent.

What is being done to combat this crime wave? When few of our government or business leaders are seen in serious consultations concerning job creation in a country with 5–7 million unemployed, what can we expect? It's all a great pity — and crime, rape, and murders will just continue, especially when our Police Commissioner and Minister of Safety and Security cannot communicate with each other in a discreet fashion and resort to the newspapers as their channel of communication. The in-fighting and wrangles between our Minister of Safety and Security and the Police Commissioner continue to undermine any confidence South Africans have that our police force is getting a grip on the crime wave.

Police Commissioner George Fivaz was picked to run the police because he was acceptable to most political groups, because he was "relatively inoffensive" (*Financial Mail*, 11 April, 1997). However, he has also proven "to be relatively ineffective". South African crime-busting efforts have appeared meek at best, and most South Africans feel less secure today than when Fivaz took over the force in 1994. His departure, and replacement with a proven effective leader with a history of fighting crime successfully, should be implemented. The same is true for the Minister of Safety and Security — our President should be setting crime targets and evaluating his Minister's performance; pressure must be brought to bear on reducing our crime levels, and the best way to start is at the very top. If Mufamadi, the present incumbent, does not succeed in bringing down the crime level, give someone else a chance. They could do no worse.

Need for a Dramatic Revamp of Police Management

The staff now at police headquarters in Pretoria number 11 000, up from 5 000 in 1994, while at the same time a 3-year-old hiring freeze has starved the rest of the service of skills and adequate numbers.

Wastage is apparent in police finances, where some R25 m is spent on the police band and at least R8 m on upkeep of museums — despite complaints by the hierarchy that its R9.5 bn budget is insufficient.

Where is all the taxpayer money that we allocate to the Safety and Security Ministry going? Recent reports by McKinsey Inc. and others indicate that a substantial amount of the money is going to fund the salaries of an increasing number of police desk officers who never go out into the field. Reports indicate that more and more policemen are requesting office assignments. It would not be surprising to learn that there are more police officers who remain inside their office buildings for the duration of their shifts than the number of police out on patrol.

McKinsey Inc. recently indicated that 70% of staff at police stations is not involved in fighting crime — worse still is that many of these paper-pushers are trained police officers. At a particular police station McKinsey found four fifths of police cars were unavailable for policing while at another only one out of every ten policemen was actually out on the beat, with the rest doing administrative work and filling in forms. Their report also indicates that at any one time poor management results in a quarter of policemen being absent.

Other recent facts are also startling.

- Government recently admitted that 198 of the 1 800 members of the police VIP protection service are facing criminal charges.
- A quarter of the 140 000 police officers today are functionally illiterate, while nearly one out of three does not have a driver's licence.

Unfortunately in South Africa the law favours the criminal over the victim. A criminal who is shot in the midst of a crime will nevertheless be given free medical care at taxpayers' expense, while the injured victim becomes another government statistic.

The criminal will remain the winner in South Africa, if we continue to deny our police force larger numbers of recruits, provide poor training and equipment, pay police on the street low salaries, and use antiquated police management techniques which under-utilise existing police capacity. Recent reports of insufficient fuel being available for police patrol cars reinforces the lack of public confidence in our police force. It is no longer good enough for government to pay lip-service to the fight against crime. Rolling out a new crime-busting public relations campaign every six months will no longer suffice.

Police Organisation

Recent reports indicate that 34 422 police officers left the police service between 1994 and 1996. South Africa can hardly afford to continue losing such senior officers. In the past year alone, the head of detective services, head of national security, and the commander of the Eastern Cape, plus five national police commissioners and six assistant commissioners, all left the SAPS.

Between 1994 and 1997 some 300 policemen and women left the service every month, while a hiring moratorium remained in place (which has only recently been lifted).

The fact that the force is under-trained is a huge problem. For instance, less than a third of detectives have had proper forensic training, and more than half of the police assistants are illiterate. According to reports, their statements are often so badly written that they are useless in court.

Morale in the force is at an all-time low. Recently the staff of a particular police station conducted a wildcat strike against their own station commander.

Understaffed Crime Prevention Services

Meanwhile, vacancies in the Justice Department remain unfilled after 12 months. In June 1997, the Justice Department reported that 1 300 new posts needed to be created in order to maintain law and order and cope with its workload.

The annual reports of four Attorneys-General (A-G) tabled in Parliament in May 1997 indicate the severity of a lack of adequate staffing levels. According to the Witwatersrand A-G's office, staffers continue to resign and take advantage of more lucrative offers in the private sector, with staff turnover reaching 75% and vacancies "everywhere". Senior State Advocate posts were not filled for an entire year, while the A-G post itself took 11 months to fill, and at the time of writing the A-G still had no deputy — the post had not even been advertised. According to the report, the skills flight was so severe that as many as 60% of the current professional staff had only joined the A-G offices within the previous two years.

Due to poor pay, bad working conditions and low morale a total of 520 prosecutors resigned between 1994 and 1997, out of a total complement of 1 620 nationwide. During the first six months of 1997 only 29 of 187 vacancies for Prosecutors, State Advocates, and State Attorneys were filled. The buck stops with the Justice Minister — what is he doing?

By August 1997, filling 23 positions of Senior Assistant State Attorney had been intentionally delayed by the Minister of Justice as he sought to challenge a Pretoria High Court ruling declaring the Justice Department's policy of not considering white males for promotion unlawful. It is clear that the Justice Department has done little to boost morale or to provide incentives to the few experienced professionals to remain. It is fair to say that of the Senior State Attorneys or Advocates, who can find work in the private sector, have already left or are expected to leave very shortly. With the shortage of Prosecutors so in evidence it is surprising that so little action has been taken by the Justice Ministry to rectify the situation. The Society of State Advocates has in fact threatened industrial action on behalf of Prosecutors and State Advocates if employment conditions do not improve.

Police Corruption

Police corruption is now so bad that a recent police quarterly report indicated that, proportionally, the police are more criminal than the society they are mandated to police. More police officers have been arrested and charged with corruption during the past three years than the total number charged with such offences between 1948 and 1994. Until the force is cleansed of such bad elements and out-of-control corruption, there is little chance that the SAPS will begin to be effective in the fight against crime.

Corruption is also in far greater evidence, as revealed by the number of police dockets and files which mysteriously disappear.

Society demands that the government not only designs an anti-corruption campaign to root out the bad blood in the force, but that it also imposes draconian punishments.

If criminals are caught but not convicted or incarcerated, police morale will continue to deteriorate. Political will is required if more disheartened policemen and women are not to leave the force.

Perhaps a recent sign during a one-day cricket match between South Africa and the touring Australians said it best: "It's time to get our run rate up to the crime rate."

The three-year police hiring moratorium was only recently lifted — hopefully this will allow sufficient new blood to be brought in to replace the experienced personnel who have opted to depart the force.

Our appalling crime rate must be brought down by our country's best brains. We can learn from abroad, where separate regions and cities have their own police chiefs, who are able to implement customised approaches for their particular areas.

It is therefore encouraging that Meyer Kahn, the well-respected chairman of South African Breweries, has agreed to take on the task of being administrative head of the South African Police Service for two years. All South Africans should be thankful that he is taking on this somewhat thankless task. Let us all hope that he is given enough of a free hand to turn the police force around.

Unemployment and Crime

With the ranks of school-leavers unable to find formal work since 1993 swelling by close to a million, it should come as little surprise that in Johannesburg crime is arguably so rampant that for their own safety at night residents regularly speed through red traffic lights as though they were little more than yield signs. Law-abiding citizens in Gauteng now drive without their licence plates, in defiance of the lack of crime prevention and police presence in Gauteng.

Measures to combat crime

Since cities are at the nerve centre of South Africa's out-of-control crime wave, it is imperative that crime prevention be brought closer to home and away from a national head-office mentality. Regional and city police chiefs should therefore be appointed with the authority to oversee crime prevention strategies, which will need to be customised to each region.

In an increasing number of countries, including the United States, city police chiefs have been given the necessary authority to combat crime effectively. New York is the clearest example of the success enjoyed in this regard. High technology was implemented in New York to assess on a daily and weekly basis those areas where crime was most likely to occur. Historical data was fed into a computer system which tracked the various neighbourhoods — in other words, a scientific prevention strategy was co-ordinated, based on timely information concerning every neighbourhood.

Provincial governments should be responsible for developing such regional policing strategies to combat crime in their provinces.

Prisons — Finding solutions

- As 91% of prison inmates in South Africa reoffend within 10 years of their release it is imperative that our prisons do a better job of rehabilitation — only one out of eight prisoners in South Africa is regarded as rehabilitated after serving a sentence. Prisoners can be trained to perform certain industrial tasks which will provide them with a far greater chance of obtaining formal employment upon their release.
- A total of 51 279 prisoners are under the age of 25. Boot camps in the United States for such juvenile offenders have produced excellent results. Such camps (patterned after basic military training, and usually lasting some six months) are in fact far less costly than regular prisons, and are specially designed for first-time juvenile offenders.
- The cost of maintaining well over 100 000 prisoners is clearly far too high for South Africa — it is suggested that alternative management structures be looked into, including privatisation

of prison services, as well as the possible sale of the prisons themselves to the private sector, then leasing them back.

- Alternatives to prison such as community service orders have become increasingly popular in Germany, the UK, Canada, the US and Greece. These sentences are generally for white-collar crimes and exclude rapists, burglars and murderers. Compared to the daily cost of R68.15 to keep someone in prison, monitoring someone on parole or under probation costs as little as R14.74.

- In the US a new law known as "Three Strikes and You're Out" is proving effective. Any criminal found guilty three times is locked away for life. Repeat offenders in the US must now think carefully about the risks of crime.

- Clearly SAPS training and recruitment must be overhauled. Police officers in the US receive good pay for the dangerous work they perform — this ensures highly motivated personnel and attracts top-rate individuals to the force. Entrance level examinations must first be passed to enter into the police academy, which in many cases is a two-year programme of practical training. During this period trainees are regularly given practical experience and sent out on the beat. South Africa could do a lot more to strengthen our training and recruitment and to bring them in line with those countries with superior police forces. The police academies throughout the US have ensured the long-term success and professional management in evidence throughout much of the US police system.

- The gap in SAPS training to combat crime is obvious, considering that the police under apartheid were often not deployed to control crime, but rather to suppress political activities.

- Taking the inflation rate into account, the SAPS has in fact been spending a diminishing amount of money — 5.4% less in real terms during the 1996/97 fiscal year than in the previous year. More targeted funding is required.

- A regionalised extradition treaty should be instituted between South Africa and all of its neighbours.

- Border control duties should be shifted from the police to the South African National Defence Force.

- Bail for repeat offenders should be severely restricted and no bail should be permitted to those accused of murder.

- Ban firearms — to purchase firearms, background checks should be required. All gun shops should be linked up to a central computer which provides a database list of all previously convicted criminals, as well as criminal suspects. With proper enforcement this should prevent previously convicted criminals walking into a gun shop and buying a gun.
- A national referendum should be held to find out what the majority of our citizens wish to do about capital punishment. But

the facts speak for themselves: a moratorium was placed on the death penalty in 1989, and between 1989 and 1995 our murder rate rose by 61%, armed robberies by 119%, and rapes by 80%.

Solutions do exist. We need to be proactive in solving our crime problems.

CHAPTER THREE

A South Africa in Danger — The Need for Change

As THIS BOOK WAS DUE to go to press, my beloved South Africa continued to shoot itself in the foot as it attempted to overcome its many severe socio-economic problems, in particular growing unemployment and a growing wave of crime.

It is February 1998 and I am about to bring a delegation of foreign investors to South Africa. However, members of the delegation are growing weary of recent developments in the country.

With 21 ghastly murders already reported in Cape Town since the New Year, it is becoming ever clearer that South Africa's crime wave continues to spiral out of control. At the same time there is talk amongst senior South African bankers of hiring a mercenary military group (Executive Outcomes) to protect bank security vans against alleged highly trained MK gangs staffed by former ANC military personnel. (MK was the name for the ANC military wing during the apartheid era.)

As though this is not discouraging enough, I have just received three phone calls from US executives who are concerned about what they hear of the new Gauteng premier whose record (according to allegations) does little to inspire much confidence, given that he is alleged to have misappropriated funds. One of the callers also mentions that he has just heard that Peter Mokaba, South Africa's Deputy Minister of Environment and Tourism, reportedly had a convicted criminal — who was on the loose — attend his birthday party.

Meanwhile I have just read the *Financial Mail's* usually funny "Did You Hear" column. However, this past week's column includes a very sad and tragic joke. The magazine light-heartedly reports that posted outside a big house in East London is the following sign: "To all criminals — if you want to find out if there is life after death just enter our grounds."

The phone rings again: "Have you heard of the latest

development in South Africa?" the caller from Ireland asks. "What can it possibly be this time?" I retort. "I thought I had just caught up on all the bad news over the past few days."

The caller tells me of the large number of resignations of senior staff from the Ministry of Public Enterprises headed by Stella Sigcau. The caller, who is due to come out to South Africa as part of a business delegation asks me two simple questions: "Is this not the Ministry that is tasked with overseeing the privatisation of South Africa's major parastatals and is looking for foreign investment? Oh, and by the way Anthony, do you feel confident that Stella Sigcau, the Minister, has the appropriate financial background to work with global investment banks such as Goldman Sachs and Merrill Lynch in attempting to sell off numerous government entities such as Transnet?"

Hopefully by the time you read this book either the Ministry will have been disbanded (let's pray) or someone will be appointed to head it based on merit, a far-fetched dream, despite the fact that there are many South Africans (both black and white) with international experience and the perfect background in accountancy and investment banking to take up such a post.

Sadly, none of this inspires investor confidence abroad. Without foreign investment, South Africa will never be able to dramatically reduce its growing unemployment figures.

I ask myself: "How am I to respond to foreign businessmen in my delegation, which is due to leave in under a week, when they confront me with the following statement: 'Anthony, tell us how can we convince our Board of Directors in the US or UK to invest in a country where the money our firms might make is not safe at any bank, where we are unable to walk around downtown Johannesburg alone, where the majority of wealthy South Africans are attempting to schlep as much money out of their own country as they possibly can, and where high tax rates and few (if any) competitive investment incentives greet us? Not to mention a declining currency that hits new lows almost monthly.'

A pharmaceutical executive called my office earlier in the week complaining about the fact that his company's patents are under threat in South Africa. In fact, he tells me that the latest news from Washington concerning the US pharmaceutical companies is that PHARMA, their US trade association, has now filed a formal complaint with the US State Department. In essence they want South Africa to be black listed for not honouring pharmaceutical companies' patents (which the new South African law threatens and undercuts.)

In fact, the next step (as of February 1998) is for the US Trade Representative (both a Cabinet-level appointee and a separate government department) to file a formal complaint against South Africa, with the World Trade Organisation. At that point the US will already have black listed South African.

Such negative publicity cannot help South Africa attract any form of foreign investment. Some of the largest US and UK companies, such as Eli Lilly, Merck & Co. and Glaxo Welcome, are affected and very concerned.

I wish I had more positive news to report. The truth hurts. Something must be done.

Any Light at the End of the Tunnel?

However, there must be some light at the end of the tunnel. The doomsayers who speak only of growing unemployment and a crime wave that is out of control must be proven wrong over the next few years. Sadly, at the moment most statistics concerning crime and our economy paint a very negative picture. Any realist must realise that South Africa faces a daunting task — and at present we are losing the battle.

It is not good enough for our leaders to keep deflecting criticism on the management of our country away from themselves and to always be defensive about our problems. Shouting "Racism!" when international observers criticise the lack of job creation, slow economic growth and our crime wave does not help our cause, but rather we lose much credibility in their eyes. President Mandela caused jitters among international investors when he scapegoated almost every conceivable non-ANC entity, and whites in particular, at the 1997 ANC Mafikeng conference. It is time to grow up and to take some responsibility.

The Lesson of Zimbabwe

Just as Robert Mugabe must find a scapegoat while the economy of Zimbabwe crumbles and food riots spread, sadly South Africa may be headed for a situation where government's non-delivery will just be blamed on apartheid — not only in 1998 but even 20 years from now. Foreign observers wonder whether we Africans will ever take responsibility for our actions. Are our leaders just so arrogant that they believe they can do no wrong? Impartial observers often wonder in amazement whether it is always some secret conspiracy that prevents African countries from succeeding.

Poor old Mugabe — he has had 18 years in office and look what kind of a legacy he has left. A currency that has lost half its value in just two months during 1997, while inflation is running at 24% and nearly half of the country's 12 million people are unemployed. Meanwhile Mugabe sets a wonderful example of a non-caring despot by spending some Z$2 m on his wedding in 1997 and by building a Z$1 m house for his new wife, who has still not occupied the house almost a year later.

But then again, he has often put his own interests above those of his countrymen. One can only hope that South Africa's political leaders do not fall into the same trap. As unemployment continues to rise in South Africa, let us hope that our government will be willing to admit to at least some of its failures and be prepared to re-examine its failed policies. A government in self-denial is dangerous.

Government's credibility

South Africa can no longer afford to have its leaders spouting untruths to the rest of the world. Some of our leaders may live in glass houses, whiz back and forth to work in the comfort of an air-conditioned BMW or Mercedes Benz, and indeed get paid to put a positive spin on everything, but the world and perhaps more importantly the growing million of jobless South Africans are rapidly losing patience with South Africa's leaders. Government's credibility is eroding rapidly.

The stinging vote of no-confidence we received over the past two years as our currency lost more than 50% of its value in terms of both the US dollar and British sterling should be reason enough to realise that we are staring into the abyss. We may well fall over the precipice — unless we learn how to solve our problems rather than just being arrogant, while continually defying the facts and claiming that everything is just fine.

The time will soon come when the majority of South African citizens will no longer tolerate a situation where unemployment just grows by another 1 million every three to four years. While school-leavers cannot find a job and turn to crime, household debt in 1998 (as a percentage of personal income) has shot up to around 70% — an increase of 27% in just two years. South Africans are becoming increasingly indebted. With interest rates at a 13-year high in July 1998, the number of bankruptcies and foreclosures is set to rise to new heights in 1999.

The utopia promised by our government's much-heralded Gear economic plan has been shown to be pie in the sky as far as the dismal delivery of new jobs is concerned. In fact, as of February 1998, Gear has not only created no new formal sector jobs since its inception, the economy has shed close to a quarter of a million jobs since Gear's inception some two and a half years ago. By its own goals Gear is now more than 700 000 jobs behind in its plan. Is our "miracle" of 1994 going to unravel? Did we win the battle only to lose the war against poverty and unemployment?

Government is already rueing the day that it decided to announce the Gear targets. Employment in South Africa has slumped to its lowest level in 16 years amid signs that the economic growth rate in South Africa will remain well below 2% for both 1998 (in which GDP growth of 1% is expected) and 1999.

Gear is admired by many businessmen and government leaders even as you read this book. However, as government muddles along, Gear will become increasingly discredited. One wonders when our leaders will wake up.

Gear is a woefully insufficient blueprint to create jobs in South Africa. Whereas Poland has 3 million small and medium-sized enterprises that by mid-1995 generated 50% of its GDP and 60% of its jobs, by comparison South Africa's micro-enterprise sector accounts for only 10% of our GDP and 16% of our employment. This potential engine room for creating new jobs remains hampered by inefficient government policies and corporate indifference. Excessively high interest rates only exacerbate the problem.

Unemployment and Crime Bring South Africa to a Crossroads

This is no time for complacency in South Africa — we are at a crossroads. Our country is in crisis, whether we like it or not.

Our leaders can no longer afford to be so arrogant as to believe that in fact everything is just fine, as some of them would have us believe. They must really take the average South African citizen for a total idiot. International markets vote with their money — their harsh vote of no confidence is unmistakeable.

How are we ever to attract meaningful investment to our country when stories of murder fill our newspapers like a daily weather forecast? Spiralling unemployment fast approaching 40% has led to a dramatic increase in crime throughout South Africa.

A Lack of Vision

The longer South Africa muddles along with no vision of how to solve the country's unemployment crisis, the more precarious our country's long-term future becomes. Unless imaginative solutions are implemented to combat our enormous unemployment problem, South African's standard of living will continue to drop while our streets are ruled by criminals.

Given our enormous national debt, exorbitant interest rates, an education system in disorder, high taxes, ever-growing unemployment, draconian labour laws that are enough to put off any foreign investor, internationally uncompetitive investment incentives, a rand hitting all time lows on an almost weekly basis, and a gold price at its lowest levels since the 1970s, it is truly amazing that our government should be so complacent.

The need for a viable opposition

But then they can afford to do so. Sadly, there is little effective political pressure brought to bear on our government. Yes, the ANC must be the luckiest political party in any democratic country. In other countries it would be a sitting duck to lose an election in 1999, given its woeful track record on the most basic of government tasks i.e. protecting its citizens and overseeing an economy that creates jobs. If a government cannot even protect its citizens' well-being, what use is it?

So long as there is no viable opposition to the ANC-led government, whose members continue to fight among themselves (about privatisation, Gear, etc.), South Africa will continue to stare into the abyss.

South Africa cries out for a truly healthy democracy — where a ruling political party must perform for fear that it will be voted out at the next election if it does not deliver on its promises.

The maladministration South Africa has had to endure over the past decade has brought our country to its knees. The rand has lost 90% of its value since 1981, almost half of this loss in value occurring during 1996 and 1998 alone. But the positive spin consultants in South Africa would have us believe that a rand that hits new lows almost every month is a good thing for

South Africa. If this was so true why is a free-falling Indonesian rupee or Thai baht seen as such a disastrous thing by the rest of the world?

Investors do not wish to invest in a country where the currency is unstable and, at worst, in free-fall. In defence of these positive spin consultants there is something to be said about a rand that is no longer at R6.51 to the US dollar (or worth just 20 US cents), but perhaps worth as little as just 10 US cents. At that point our unproductive and (in many instances) over-priced labour will be relatively cheap and attractive for foreign investors.

The only problem is that our inflation rate will balloon, as South Africans will have to pay ever higher prices for imported goods. But then there will always be those who will argue that a weaker rand boosts our exports.

These are the people who believe that South Africa's exports are so large that exports alone will save South Africa — a very myopic view and a fantasy, given that the rand has already depreciated more than 50% in sterling and dollar terms in just the past two years, and what little improvement we have had in exports has translated into zero job growth in the formal sector. In addition, exports have not grown at the same pace the rand has fallen. South Africa today is in fact far poorer and worse off than it was two years ago as measured against most stable currencies, particularly the US$ and British sterling.

But then many of these positive spin masters obviously do not care that their own net worth has already depreciated by 50% in US terms. I sometimes wonder in amazement what they are smoking. Who in their right mind wants to lose 50% of their net worth in just two years? The only answer might be that many of these people are in executive positions which permit them to fly abroad often and to schlep as many rands as they can lug onto Boeing 747s in order to deposit these funds into foreign bank accounts. It is as though many of these executives are in a race to see who can schlep the most money abroad. This of course they do in private, while in public they proclaim that a falling rand is in fact a wonderful development.

But certain businesses in South Africa are apparently also more than happy for the rand to depreciate to the detriment of the rest of the country, although such businesses would never admit it.

The Old Game of a Falling Rand
No Longer Works

As the gold price falls to an 18-year low in US dollar terms, perhaps the South African Chamber of Mines and its members would like the Reserve Bank to play that great old game we saw in the 1980s — a falling dollar gold price but a rising rand gold price. Wow, what a great business to be in, where regardless of an industry in turmoil these lucky South African mine owners actually report higher profits thanks to the good old rand taking a dive yet again. And of course the share analysts who work on the Johannesburg Stock Exchange (JSE) will be only too happy to report that another good year in mining was had with a 20% growth in earnings. How many of these analysts will see through this deception and realise that the 20% earnings rise was in fact a negative 3% earnings slump (a mild disaster) when viewed by the rest of the world.

The big problem for our rich corporate friends in 1998 is that this game does not work so well any more. Today many of their shareholders are foreign institutions which do not enjoy a continually falling rand as much as the South African executives seem to. A falling rand cuts into the rate of return enjoyed by a foreign institution, particularly when invested in shares listed on the JSE and quoted in rands. These foreign institutions will dump their shares as soon as the returns no longer achieve a consistent rate of return of at least 10% in dollar or sterling terms. Foreigners dumping their shares in our mining houses will send the rand share price southwards in a big hurry.

We are now part of the real world. With our access to international capital, we can no longer play the games of old. Perhaps this accounts for the massive ownership shake-up among our mining houses during much of 1997 and 98.

Disturbing Reality

Yet our political leaders continue to dream that Gear will solve everything. Sadly our government has shown itself completely helpless in implementing an economic strategy to foster job creation in South Africa. Consider the fact that there are already some 350 000 school-leavers wishing to enter the job market annually, with less than 10% able to find employment. Increasing numbers of South Africans have been forced into the informal sector where many of them eke out a living.

Unemployment is spiralling. Our problems are so severe that even if by some miracle our economy actually created 350 000 new jobs in any one year (which is a pipe-dream given current policies), this would barely break even with the number of new jobseekers. Our unemployment rate will only begin to fall when more than 350 000 jobs are created in any one year.

The lack of any job creation policy is absurd and a disservice to all South Africans. Well, what can we expect when there is no cabinet minister tackling job creation? Former Labour Minister Mboweni was certainly not a minister focused on "labour creation".

Nevertheless, we in South Africa continue to place an increasing amount of power in the hands of our ministers and bureaucrats — in many cases persons not trained for, and not equipped to carry out, the task. It should therefore come as no surprise that South Africa has chosen to adopt Germany's outdated labour policies at a time when that country's unemployment rate is at record levels not seen since Hitler.

Keeping Foreigners at Bay and Throwing a Few Scraps Tokyo Sexwale's Way

Without large-scale labour-intensive investment, South Africa has little hope of generating 350 000 to 400 000 jobs per annum. Nevertheless, we remain saddled with an uncompetitive and out-of-date investment and tax policy which continues to lose us huge foreign investment projects on an almost weekly basis. But then the international investment community knows that South Africa is not really serious about job creation. The whole of 1997 passed us by without even a jobs summit being held, while we enjoyed an anaemic economic growth rate of less than 2% when a minimum of 5% to 6% was required.

Add a spiralling crime wave, a falling currency and unfriendly labour laws and it is not surprising that our unemployment rate continues to rise and serious foreign investors take their projects elsewhere.

To make matters worse potential foreign investors rightly ask why they should consider investing when many of our politicians are busy spending their time cutting private, underhanded and preferential business deals — as happens in the rest of Africa.

Our largest companies are scared of foreign competition and are only too happy to maintain the status quo, so they can continue to enjoy a captive market in South Africa, compelling consumers to pay large premiums for goods that in other parts of the world sell for a fraction of the prices here.

How then does one account for De Beers giving Tokyo Sexwale a deal of a lifetime (interests in up to six diamond mines) or the South African Chamber of Business (SACOB) blocking moves to create attractive foreign investment legislation for export processing zones which have worked so well in the rest of the world? At the same time SACOB's public face remains the same as it did a decade ago, no new young blood represents SACOB publicly. Spouting forth about a more friendly tax system is easy. Coming up with practical action plans is less so. It is high time that SACOB become more proactive in solving South Africa's joblessness crisis.

It is an incredibly short-sighted approach. Perhaps the stockbrokers and financial analysts of today may cheer our large companies' forthcoming annual reports, but every year there are fewer South Africans who can afford to buy their products as more of our countrymen and women join the unemployment lines or simply emigrate.

We have a long way to go before we can start convincing potential foreign investors that we are serious about encouraging an open and free market — that we are in fact different to the rest of Africa, where underhanded deals and politicians who are only out to enrich themselves are the norm.

Historians are likely to look back on those in leadership positions today and judge them on their responses to our critical needs as we approach a new millennium. The report card so far is unfavourable, to say the least.

Boosting Exports and Making GEAR Work — Outlining a Solution

It is time for bold new thinking if South Africa is to ever attain the goals laid down by government's macroeconomic Gear plan and compete more effectively in the global economy. Without large doses of foreign direct investment (FDI) South Africa does not at present have sufficient internal capacity to generate 400 000 new jobs per year nor to grow GDP at 6% per annum on a sustained basis — we are deluding ourselves. Developing countries in Asia and Latin America which regularly achieve such high growth rates all rely on large inflows of FDI.

Rather than just talking, such countries have all developed highly focused detailed action plans to successfully compete for and attract FDI into their countries.

With some 4.7 million people officially unemployed and a further 1.4 million likely to be unemployed by the year 2002 based on current growth rates, South Africa faces an economic and social crisis. Nearly half a million jobs were lost between 1992 and 1994 according to the Central Statistical Service, coupled with an additional 104 000 jobs lost in the private sector between June 1995 and June 1996. Even in 1995 when the growth rate reached 3.5% the number of recorded jobs barely inched up by just 0.6%. By 1997, we had lost more than 116 000 jobs in the formal sector. South Africa is bleeding.

To make matters worse, South Africa has a high proportion of sheltered employment buried throughout the public sector — an unemployment time-bomb. Also, the gold mining industry, once the largest employer of labour, has reduced its total employment figure from 550 000 people in 1988 down to 300 000 in 1996.

The Need for a New Ministry — A Ministry of Foreign investment

South Africa clearly needs a government heavily loaded with private sector expertise, preferably with international experience. Why is it that South Africa remains among a small minority of countries with only two ministries devoted to fostering foreign investment and economic development? Besides the typical Minister of Finance and a Minister of Trade and Industry, the vast majority of successful countries have established specific ministries devoted to attracting FDI, which are staffed largely with individuals with a strong background in the private sector and training in international finance and tax issues (See Chapter 7 on Export Processing Options for further details).

These countries and numerous others have shown that their commitment to attracting foreign direct investment goes beyond fluffy speeches and *ad hoc* trade missions. How can South Africa possibly compete against countries which not only have shown their seriousness in attracting FDI by making cabinet-level appointments, but in addition have put their money where their mouths are by developing very comprehensive investment policies to stimulate both foreign and domestic fixed investment?

South Africa — a Lesson in How to Scare Off Long-Term Foreign Investment and any Job Creation

Sadly, this may soon be the title of a new Harvard Business School case study. As a former South African who recently advised the Namibian government on establishing an export processing zone (EPZ) (offering a wide range of tax and investment incentives resulting in over R400 m in approved foreign investments and generating at least 8 000 new jobs), it is depressing to have to inform my countrymen just how pathetically uncompetitive South Africa's foreign investment regime is.

On 23 November, 1997, the *Sunday Times* business section highlighted yet another case in a growing list of instances in which our country has lost huge foreign investment projects. In this case a R1.4 bn fertiliser plant will now be built in Jordan rather than in South Africa, due to Jordan's better investment incentives, including EPZs.

Why is it that Costa Rica, the Ivory Coast, the Dominican Republic, Malaysia, Malta, Mauritius, the Philippines, Mexico, China, Thailand, Singapore, and numerous others have succeeded in attracting vast amounts of long-term foreign investment (often well in excess of 7% to 8% of their GDP) while investment in South Africa remains at less than 2.5% — the vast majority of which is in fact short-term passive portfolio investment creating few, if any, jobs? It is foreign investment which spurred the creation of millions of new jobs in these countries. Their EPZs, freeports, and related tax and investment incentives are vital to this process.

Mauritius, after suffering from tremendous unemployment as recently as 1980, offered EPZs and related foreign investment benefits. It now has full employment and in fact must import labour or discourage foreign investment in labour-intensive processes. Mauritius' EPZ exports grew sixfold between 1983 and 1989 to US$600 m. The Dominican Republic's EPZ exports trebled to US$710 m between 1986 and 1989, and the Philippines' EPZ exports doubled during the same period.

Costa Rica's EPZ resulted in employment growing fivefold between 1986 and 1990, while in the Dominican Republic it tripled, and in Jamaica it doubled. Export growth resulting from countries offering either EPZs or competitive foreign investment incentives are truly phenomenal: after more than a decade Singapore still offers multinationals a 5% tax rate for setting up regional headquarters in that country, while training subsidies can still be found throughout Asia.

Let's get serious

Foreign business executives can be forgiven for believing that South Africa does not care about attracting foreign investment. A case in point is the United States, where South Africa has no trade consul or investment representative for the entire western region of the United States (which comprises approximately 10 states, including California, which alone is the seventh largest economy in the world), although we do staff an entire consulate with political and other functionaries.

It seems that some of our political leaders are arrogant enough to believe that South Africa remains a huge bright spot on the investment radar screens of many of the leading foreign multinationals. The reality is that given the high growth rates in such economies as Brazil, Malaysia, the Czech Republic and China, there exists little desire in the boardrooms of the world's leading companies to risk investing in South Africa where crime, an unstable currency and tough labour unions stand at the welcoming gate.

Like it or not we are not at the centre of the universe — we are tainted by the continent to which we are attached, our own dismal economic performance and unattractive investment policies. We will have to be incredibly aggressive if we are serious about attracting the necessary large-scale FDI required to make a sizable dent in our unemployment numbers.

It should concern us that our government remains one of very few developing nations with no separate cabinet appointment or presidential envoy mandated to attract foreign investment. Rather we rely on *ad hoc* trade missions, led by people who are not trained experts in the workings of the private sector, or such fields as economics, international investment and taxation.

Whatever honeymoon the new South Africa had is over. The dramatic depreciation in our currency has had many negative repercussions, not the least of which are the perceptions abroad that South Africa is not a stable economy in which to invest for the long term and that even if a foreigner could make a R100 profit by manufacturing widget X, it may not be worth all the effort when at the end of the day it will translate into a measly $15 or £9.

A Highly Focused Game Plan is Needed

Other developing nations — rather than just talking about investment – have developed highly focused action plans to allow them to successfully compete for and attract FDI into their countries. However, South Africa has no game plan to attract sizable flows of long-term investment. Perhaps our government and the many vested interests in South Africa which currently make a nice living want to keep it that way. It certainly seems so. Otherwise, South African policy makers must just be plain stupid in offering such an unfriendly welcome to potential foreign investors and scaring off any potential job creation.

How else does one account for South Africa even losing out in the B league for foreign investment (against our own neighbours and countries like Jordan), when we should be competing in the A league against Chile, Malaysia, Brazil and others? Many of our tax holidays are poorly conceived and remain uncompetitive by international standards — for example, the length of the tax holiday period is too short (three years), concessions do not take into account international tax rules, and they appear to be an *ad hoc* move on the part of government with no long-term commitment.

South Africa currently ranks poorly in comparison studies with other countries' investment friendly tax systems. In terms of our country's competitiveness compared to the rest of the world, in 1996, the World Competitiveness Report ranked us second last of 48 nations.

How can a country with few significant investment incentives, a tax rate which remains excessive for foreign investors and corporations, ever higher labour costs and high import duties, expect to attract the large-scale manufacturers so desperately needed to set up the labour-intensive, export-oriented factories required to absorb the growing numbers of unemployed?

Our over-regulated labour market continues to push manufacturers out of the country, while we experience rampant and growing unemployment.

One of South Africa's largest manufacturers, Pepkor, which admits that it can no longer manufacture certain products profitably in South Africa, has moved certain South African plants to Malawi. Even Swaziland is eyeing new incentive schemes to attract foreign investors.

Lesotho has already drawn a sizable number of Taiwanese and other investors away from South Africa. Recently 24 factories alone have created 16 000 jobs in Lesotho

Our job creation and foreign investment policy-makers continue to ignore the international rules of the game and will not succeed in attracting any substantial long-term foreign investment — translating into no meaningful job creation in South Africa.

We should ask ourselves who in government is responsible for job creation or generating long-term foreign investment? It seems no minister can be found!! Although Gear is designed to catapult the South African economy forward and create as many as a million jobs over a five-year period (1996–2000), no government minister seems to want to take responsibility for meeting the employment targets. More than likely the reason is that Gear's job creation targets are, and have always been, just a pie in the sky.

Export-driven Industrialisation

South Africa needs to generate substantially more foreign exchange by developing an export-driven culture. The best of both worlds would be to couple such export-led industrialisation with labour-intensive manufacturing and then attract foreign manufacturers to establish many of these plants. By so doing we could begin to soak up our unemployed while also generating substantial foreign exchange earnings, ensuring a healthier balance of payments and a stronger and more stable rand.

In the meantime our country's policies are to reward capital-intensive investment with various tax breaks to the detriment of hiring additional labour. The generous tax breaks to invest in capital-intensive machinery, along with the proposed new payroll tax levy, provide a double incentive for every South African company to divest itself of as much human capital as possible in favour of a German machine and other capital-intensive production processes.

Huge Job Losses

Of course not much will be done by our government to rectify the situation. In several months' time President Mandela will once again address the opening of Parliament with the same sad words of a year ago, stating that job creation in 1998 was dismal, and that in fact another net job loss was reported.

In just the past five years, South Africa has had a net job loss equivalent to at least 5% of its formal sector workforce, raising our unemployment rate by most estimates to 35%.

Rather than our leaders learning from the successful policies implemented by many fast emerging and developing countries in Asia, Latin America, and Eastern Europe, these success stories are dismissed out of hand in favour of our leaders' own new and untried solutions.

Government's macroeconomic strategy (Gear) has done little to generate any positive job creation, while the prime overdraft rate of close to 20% has successfully stifled any glimmer of real per capita economic growth. Just muddling along with a 2% to 3% economic growth rate (in GDP) for another few years translates into a need to generate at least 425 000 new jobs per year, in order to just absorb the annual number of new entrants into the labour market, let alone make any dent in the unemployment statistics.

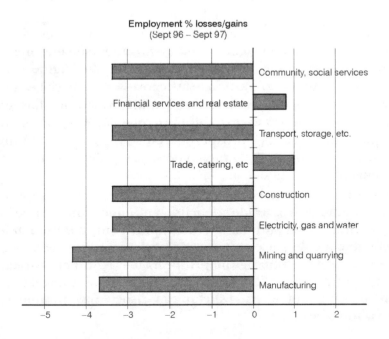

Employment % losses/gains
(Sept 96 – Sept 97)

At present approximately 1 100 people enter the official unemployment figures every day.

New policies must be created if 400 000 new jobs per year are to be generated and a 6% growth rate achieved. EPZs are one of the most effective and proven ways to simultaneously attract long-term foreign investment, generate local jobs and boost exports, thereby generating foreign exchange and a much more favourable trade balance. Throughout the world a common feature of successful foreign investment policies has been a national commitment to removing legislative, regulatory and institutional constraints holding back the free flow of trade.

Until South Africa is able to compete effectively for long-term foreign investment capital, the rand will continue to fall at more than just the inflation differential, while the brain drain will simultaneously roll on unabated. No country can afford to lose many of its best and brightest brains without suffering severe consequences.

It is high time that South Africans begin to open their eyes to the large number of economic success stories the world over. We do not need to reinvent the wheel, but rather become more open minded about particular strategies that will enrich our country.

Historians are likely to look back on those in leadership positions today and judge them on their responses to our critical needs as we approach a new millennium.

South Africa remains Africa's leading economic power and at the same time its sleeping giant. But if we continue on our present course we will soon squander any hope of being the engine which drives an African economic renaissance.

Fortunately, with the right policies and an accountable and responsive government we can still overcome our many problems and pass on a more prosperous South Africa to future generations. But the opportunity to do so is rapidly slipping away. The signs of peril exist.

An enormous national debt, exorbitant interest rates, an out-of-control crime wave, trade deficits, an education system in disorder, high taxes and massive unemployment, the rand at an all-time low, a gold price at its lowest levels since the 1970s — all are on the verge of ruining the prospects for a prosperous future for all South Africans. It is high time that South African citizens stopped sitting around and watching in disbelief as their quality of life diminishes.

We have the ability to solve these problems and to lift ourselves up by our own bootstraps. The big question is: Do we have the will? South Africa clearly has to wake up now. *Dit is tyd vir die slapende reus van Afrika om wakker te skrik.*

Danger 1: South Africa's Burgeoning Unemployment Crisis — Lack of a Viable Job Creation Strategy

It is time for bold new thinking if South Africa is ever to attain the goals laid down by the government's macroeconomic strategy for growth, employment and redistribution (Gear). Without large doses of foreign direct investment (FDI), South Africa does not at present have sufficient internal capacity to generate anywhere close to the 400 000 new jobs needed per year, and has little chance of achieving, let alone maintaining, an annual economic growth rate of (6% in GDP) on a sustained basis. In short, we are deluding ourselves. Developing countries in Asia and Latin America which regularly achieve such high growth rates all rely on high inflows of foreign direct investment to supplement their already high levels of internal savings.

It is interesting to note that just prior to this book's publication, the South African government acknowledged that its employment projections outlined in Gear could not be met.

Given South Africa's high level of government debt and continued budget deficits coupled with few incentives to encourage South Africans to save, our level of internally available savings is only half of what it needs to be. As such we are more dependent than ever before on attracting long-term foreign capital to fund our economic growth and the creation of jobs.

While Gear projected that 126 000 jobs would be created in 1996 and 252 000 jobs in 1997 (along with a 1997 growth rate of 2.9%), reality has proven very different. South Africa lost more than 71 000 formal sector jobs in 1996 and some 116 000 jobs in 1997. By late 1998, these figures put government about 700 000 jobs behind its Gear estimates. The figures would be even worse were it not for some 19 000 new jobs created in the government sector — at odds with the Gear plan of reducing the size of the public sector.

Government's Credibility and GEAR

Government committed itself in 1996/97 to cutting the deficit to an acceptable level of 5.1%. The actual target achieved was 5.6% of GDP.

Even more damaging to investors' sense of confidence is the continuing rise in the employment levels of the public sector. By December 1996 it had grown to 1 913 000 workers. This increase is largely due to the provinces having to absorb the bloated bureaucracies of the former homelands. Given the priority of reducing the size of government and its percentage take of the South African economy, it is therefore disturbing that government's commitment to get to grips with the 50 000 ghost workers identified in 1996 — workers who are paid but who do not exist — continues at a snail's pace.

Clearly, the plan to reduce the public sector by some 300 000 workers over three years (1996–99) was unrealistic.

Meanwhile 1 195 people per day are added to the official unemployment figures.

South Africa clearly has to wake up and smell the coffee. Just muddling along for a few more years with GDP growth of between 1% to 2.3% as in 1996, 1997 and 1998, translates into a need to generate at least 500 000 new jobs per year by the year 2000, to even begin reducing unemployment in any meaningful way.

Even Namibia and Lesotho are ahead of South Africa in terms of job creation (in the period 1994–97). We are in fact losing in the B league of investment and job creation when we should be competing against Chile, Malaysia, Brazil, and others who are in the A league.

While Cosatu (the largest trade union group in South Africa) and business fight it out over new labour legislation, there is little to celebrate in Gear's first, second or third anniversary — growth is hardly evident, the number of unemployed has risen still further, and the income gap is widening. If anything, the gap is also widening between the government and its alliance partner, which might be the only positive sign yet that Gear will lead to a new South Africa.

In many respects there are no greater opponents of the Gear plan itself than the ANC government's own alliance partners, Cosatu and the South African Communist Party (SACP). The lack of consensus within the government's own structures has led to increasing uncertainty as to whether Gear will ever truly be given a fair chance of implementation. With the recent crash in the value of the rand in June–July 1998, our government leaders have finally distanced themselves from the SACP and Cosatu.

The Ministry of Labour has done nothing to create an enabling environment for employment growth, although Minister Mboweni acknowledged (*Sunday Times*, 29 June, 1997) that "it has policy instruments that can create an enabling environment for employment growth." Unfortunately, all the attention of the Labour Ministry appears to be directed to protecting those who currently have a job and require improved benefits, such as maternity leave and fewer working hours. What legislation has the Ministry enacted that focuses on unemployed workers or that highlights ways to increase the size of the labour market and create more available labour?

Belatedly, in late 1998, we should be privy to a first-class public relations performance — a jobs summit which has taken at least 18 months to organise. Hopefully more will come of this assemblage of political, labour and business leaders than some puffed-up speeches for prime-time television. But I for one remain very sceptical — where have these leaders been for the past three years?

Danger 2: Crime

As mentioned in Chapter 2, it is the ANC government which has a duty to protect all South Africa's citizens. The government's failure to act with any sense of urgency will only continue to reduce the likelihood of more direct investment taking place. The perception that crime is out of control and that government remains inept in dealing with the problem will haunt job creation for some time to come, unless radical steps are taken. As citizens we should no longer accept a further deterioration in our living standards — being virtual prisoners in our own homes is untenable.

Danger 3: The Population Explosion

South Africa's population continues to grow by some 2.5% a year, and this translates into more and more South Africans flooding into the major metropolitan areas, pushed by rural poverty and attracted by apparent urban opportunities. South Africa's population is expected to increase by one third from its current level of 44.7 million to 65.7 million by the year 2020 (according to the Development Bank of Southern Africa). In 1995, South Africa's population was 62% urbanised, but up to 82% can be expected to live in towns and cities by 2020.

The demand for housing has reached in excess of 3 million units, and it is estimated that at least R7 bn is needed each year for the next decade to eliminate the housing shortage and to keep pace with demand (Human Sciences Research Council, 1991).

Back in 1991 the South African Chamber of Business predicted that the economy would have to grow by at least 8.4% a year for an entire decade in order to wipe out unemployment. It is sad but true that since this projection was made, it will now take far longer than a decade to wipe out unemployment, even if we were to have such a high growth rate.

Health care

Government spending on health care, which reached 10.7% of budgeted expenditure for the 1997–98 financial year, is more than double that spent by middle-income countries and on a par with many industrialised nations. It is critical that this money be targeted at the most desperately needed regions of the country — in urban areas there exists one doctor for every 700 people, while in rural areas the ratio is three times greater. In the former homelands the figures are as bad as one doctor for between 10 000 and 30 000 people. At present close to 70% of whites are members of medical aid schemes, as opposed to just 7% of black South Africans. Many of our largest hospitals are operating under desperate circumstances. For example, it was recently reported that deaths at Groote Schuur Hospital in Cape Town were occurring as a direct result of the reduction in its staff numbers — which have declined by 31% between 1995 and 1996, while patient numbers grew by approximately 25% during the same period. Reports indicate that in three months in 1996 at Tygerberg Hospital, 16 babies died from a bacterial outbreak due to cockroach infested wards, overcrowding, a severe staff shortage, and poor hygiene.

Commenting on the need to close as many as 500 hospital beds at Groote Schuur, Red Cross and Tygerberg hospitals in Cape Town (a 15% cut), Professor Johan Terreblanche, Groote Schuur's head of surgery, stated recently "We're faced with problems that are mindblowing ... my advice is don't get sick, injured or run over because you are likely to end up at one of our academic institutions. Despite the best will in the world we will treat you badly. You could sit slobbering for five days with a broken jaw because we don't have the staff to see to it." (*The Argus*, 1997).

Another case in point is that of Dr Timothy Visser, head of internal medicine at Conradie Hospital, who is responsible for 60–80 inpatients per day and 150–200 outpatients per day, with only a few medical officers to assist him.

It is clear that the Western Cape's three academic hospitals are in danger of collapse. A total of 4 500 academic hospital posts will have to be terminated by 2001–2, due to the 31% cut in health expenditure in this region. Since the University of Cape Town and Stellenbosch University produce a third of South Africa's doctors, if their intake is reduced due to health budget cuts it will go a long way to health care standards reducing in South Africa. It is apparent that highly skilled doctors have little reason to remain in the public sector — or for that matter the country — when they are unable to perform their jobs properly.

For the necessary improvements to take place on the ground, clear distinctions must be drawn between the functions and responsibilities of the national and provincial health administrations.

Population issues — AIDS
It is shocking for many South Africans to realise that 6% of the population is infected with the HIV virus — representing 2.5 million people. 10% of males between 15 and 45 years of age are infected, and 14% of females within the same age bracket are HIV positive. These figures represent an increase on 1.8 million people infected with the deadly virus in 1996.

Danger 4: Lack of Skills —
The Brain Drain and Education

President Mandela continues to show his concern for the brain drain — highly skilled people leaving South Africa. On 9 July, 1996 he commented: "To think that you can just push whites aside is fatal, that's suicide." His comments were prompted by a report by the Central Statistical Service that indicated that three times more professionals emigrated from South Africa than were immigrating to the country.

Some three quarters of South Africa's chartered accountants leave the country soon after qualifying, and only a third at most return, according to research conducted by Deloitte & Touche. Although many find temporary or part-time work in such countries as the UK, accountants cite crime as a primary reason for leaving South Africa, along with the very high levels of taxation.

The South African data concerning emigration figures is so weak that the figures regularly reported in the media are mostly worthless since they only reflect those few South Africans who state officially they are emigrating. For instance, official South African records indicate that between 1984 and 1993, 28 965 emigrants left for the UK as against 33 640 British immigrants arriving in South Africa. By comparison, for the same period UK data indicates that immigrants from South Africa were 100 700 and emigrants to South Africa were 52 600. While the South African data recorded a gain for South Africa of 4 675 people, UK data records a loss for South Africa of over 4 800. Australian figures indicate that almost 60% more South Africans immigrated than were recorded by South African authorities.

Many South African emigrants do not declare to the South African authorities that they are leaving for good, and most often leave the country as tourists, never to return on a permanent basis. According to Kaplan and Lewis (*Business Day*, 23 April, 1997), "between 1974 and 1994, the number of South Africans who declared that they were departing as tourists exceeded the number of returning tourists by more than 511 000 persons — or more than 25 000 persons a year. Many of these effectively emigrated."

While our emigration data is near worthless, the saddest fact concerns those who are emigrating — in most cases our most skilled and highly desirable workers. In some cases emigrating today is easier than it was 10 or 20 years ago, when fewer South Africans were abroad and as such the personal networks were more limited in terms of trying to get a job abroad.

High emigration and high interest rates have in the past two years halved the number of new homes sold. Only Cape Town's southern and Atlantic suburbs buck the trend — but this is largely due to "internal emigration" by Gautengers to Cape Town.

A grim residential property market has resulted in the industry perhaps sitting on as much as R200 m of unsold inventory.

Many recent buyers in Johannesburg have found their mortgages higher than their homes are actually worth. Prices in real inflationary terms have dropped by as much as 20% over the past two years in the middle-priced housing market (between R150 000 and R400 000).

Danger 5: The Bloated Public Sector

In total 1.5 million South Africans are employed by government. This includes national and provincial departments (1 162 000), statutory bodies (70 000), the South African National Defence Force (120 000), and local authorities (26 000).

Believe it or not, the current employment figures exclude 135 000 vacant and unfilled public sector jobs. An audit needs to be performed to cut government employment drastically — our public sector expenditure must be brought down to the low teens (from more than 30% of GDP at present to 10–12%). Pen pushers in back offices have rarely done much for the good of our economy.

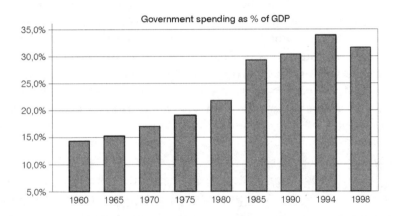

Over the past decade, the public sector has grown by close to 20% — an astounding figure when one realises how bloated the bureaucracy was back in 1987. The frightening reality is that government over the past two decades has remained the fastest growing industry in South Africa — outpacing manufacturing and mining. How can this possibly be healthy? Our public sector wage bill now comprises close to 50 % of the non-interest portion of the budget (i.e. the expenditure remaining after interest payments are accounted for). This is ludicrously high — we can't afford it. The exact figure for public sector wages is R70.6 bn in the 1997/98 budget, and R77.1 bn is budgeted for 1998/99.

The history of the current bloated bureaucracy can be traced to the National Party's victory in 1948, at which time the Afrikaner establishment set out to make the civil service its fiefdom and powerbase. Public service jobs also proliferated in order to enforce the growing labyrinth of apartheid-related laws and regulations. By the late 1980s an estimated 43% of economically active Afrikaners were employed in the public sector.

Employment growth in the formal sector has stagnated for over a decade, and private sector employment has fallen over this period. Our unemployment figures mask the problem of underemployment or temporary employment, where large pools of South Africans find themselves earning income on only a sporadic basis.

South Africa's finances suffer from a "high cholesterol syndrome" in that we have experienced overspending by our governments for decades. In the interests of all future South Africans we need to bring our "high cholesterol" under control. The debt standstill in the mid-1980s, which for the first time ensured that South Africa would default on its loans, has already provided an experience as close to a financial meltdown or heart attack as any country would care to experience. To continue our high intake of pork belly projects and fat government expenditure is asking for disaster in the same way that some heart attack victims continue to smoke and eat fatty foods. It is just plain irresponsible.

Cost of government workers

Ill-conceived and overly generous severance packages in the public service has cost more than R1 bn over the past three years, and according to Public Service Minister Zola Skweyiya, have achieved little more than the loss of the most talented workers. The Minister has since admitted that "the best people are leaving the service and you are left with the ones you wish would go." If all this sounds like a bad dream, consider that the same is true of many other areas of government, including the parastatal organisations such as the SABC, where Zwelakhe Sisulu lived through his own nightmare, before departing recently.

Any similar mistake in the real world of the private sector, or in countries where politicians are truly accountable, would have led to the immediate firing of the minister concerned and much of his or her team.

Although the previous civil service under the National Party government was nothing fantastic, it is looking increasingly professional when one considers how taxpayers' money is now being spent and the depressingly low standards of competence among many new public service workers.

Although affirmative action is necessary, it must be accompanied by competence. Where a candidate can be found who is from a previously disadvantaged group and who is competent for the job, he or she should be hired ahead of an equally competent white. However, if a concerted effort to find a suitably qualified black candidate for a certain job fails, then the search must be widened beyond race.

Danger 6: Uncompetitive Labour and Investment Policies

Given the high incidence of crime, an unstable currency, the lack of competitive investment incentives in relation to our neighbours as well as other countries worldwide, it should come as no surprise that very little "bricks and mortar" (job-creating) investment has occurred in South Africa since Nelson Mandela's Government of National Unity came to power. With an annual 3% increase in entrants to the job market, South Africa's low 1% GDP growth rate for 1998 remains woefully insufficient to even absorb the number of new entrants into the labour market, let alone the growing numbers of the unemployed.

If South Africa cannot attract foreign investment with a goodwill ambassador and leader of Mr Mandela's stature, how will it perform in the future when we will no longer enjoy the leadership of the world's most famous statesman?

How can a country with few significant investment incentives, a tax rate which remains excessive for foreign investors and corporations, and ever higher labour costs and high import duties, ever expect to attract the large-scale manufacturers so desperately needed to set up the labour-intensive, export-oriented factories required to absorb the growing numbers of unemployed?

With at least three unemployed workers lining up for every one labour union job, it is indeed amazing that the cost of labour has risen to become one of the highest of all emerging markets. Millions of South Africans would work for a competitive free market price, if only given a chance through well-formulated

economic policies, which take into account other countries'
experience.

Unfortunately, the pro-union tone set by the recent Labour
Relations Act of 1995 has done little to encourage either local or
foreign investors to consider establishing labour-intensive
factories and related operations.

Labour and economic growth

The South African labour market remains one of the most rigid.
While unemployment remains excessively high, the gap between
what unionised and non-unionised workers now earn has reached
the highest level anywhere in the world. These union wages are in
many cases very high in relation to world productivity standards,
making South Africa an unattractive investment location for
labour-intensive manufacturers who have to compete on the
world market, and can select another jurisdiction in which to
manufacture just as easily as choosing South Africa.

With no new jobs being created — in fact the formal sector has
been shedding jobs for the past three years (a net loss of almost
500 000 over the past seven years) — inequality among the
"haves" and the "have nots" has increased, due to the lack of low-
wage jobs available to poorer South Africans, who are therefore
not employed and receive no wages at all.

Is it not better that poorer South Africans achieve some
employment, even at a relatively lower wage, than none at all?
This would at least reduce inequality, given that millions of
potential South African workers receive no wage income at
present. Creating large numbers of relatively lower-wage jobs will
dramatically improve the poverty situation in South Africa. We
should not lose sight of one of the major disincentives to job
creation in South Africa — the cost of employing workers, which
only seems to go up and remains out of line with improvements
in productivity.

South Africa continues to move in the wrong direction on the
labour front. Cosatu's demands of a 40-hour work week, double
pay for work on Sunday, and six months' maternity leave, of which
four must be paid, have the effect of dramatically increasing the
cost of labour.

Former Labour Minister Mboweni's recent call for a 1.5%
payroll levy to pay for an increased level of training and
development of employees just adds to such costs.

This provides an incentive to South African companies to divest themselves of as much human capital as possible in favour of capital-intensive production processes.

It would behove the labour ministry to review what methods successful countries have employed with regard to the idea of a payroll levy. Malaysia, for instance, compels those companies employing more than 50 people to pay 1% of their wage bill towards upgrading the skills of their workers. The companies receive this money back once they have trained their workers. In Singapore companies receive tax credits when they have met certain criteria, such as the training and development of their workers. In other words, in other countries companies are not penalised in order to persuade them to train their workers but in fact are rewarded (often in the form of tax credits) when they produce qualified people with specified skills.

How government believes that paying more overtime and levying a payroll tax will foster an environment where companies will wish to hire additional workers is amazing — *bid jou dit aan!* [Can you believe it!] Basic economics tells us that if you want less of something, either tax it or raise the price of the product.

Possible further job losses
Our neighbours, including Namibia, Botswana and Lesotho are either in the process of adopting or have already adopted a wide variety of attractive incentives such as free trade zones to encourage foreign investment, including South African manufacturers, in their countries. It is not just the South African manufacturers they attract that should concern us; as important are the large number of prospective foreign investors who may decide to forego investing in South Africa in favour of setting up shop quickly and cheaply next door, especially given the wide range of fiscal benefits that are on offer across our borders.

Danger 7: Lack of a Viable Opposition

Many observers believe that we in South Africa will enjoy attributes of a *de facto* one-party state for the next few decades. Their reasoning may well be sound given the evidence that the ANC continues to enjoy an overwhelming 55%–63% support base nationally, judging by elections in the last four years. The notion that South African opposition parties are more often than not destined for years in the political wilderness (i.e. perpetual opposition) does not bode well for the creation of a strong alternative to the current ANC government. Commentators argue further that the charisma of Mr Mandela and many of his ANC colleagues makes it most unlikely, for a long time to come, that the ANC will splinter.

Our opposition parties remain weak and fragmented, and thus pose little threat to the ANC, allowing our government to meander along with half-baked policies which will take years to implement. Look, for instance, at the slow pace of privatisation. Good governments require good oppositions.

Putting pressure on government to perform
We will have only ourselves to blame for a *de facto* one-party state and the many disadvantages that such a political reality might bring.

A fully functional democracy that holds its leaders to the highest moral standards and keeps them fully accountable ensures that corruption is rooted out as fully as possible.

We need to build a grassroots democracy that does not just pass on power from one regime to another.

If our current crop of opposition parties does not come up to scratch, and does not appear credible or have a likely chance of recapturing power for at least 15 to 20 years, we have a problem. Our democracy will not function optimally in these intervening years. Our present government will not be put to the ultimate challenge and not be forced to take hard decisions or make correct policy choices.

A *de facto* one-party state feels little pressure to effect change immediately as it need not perform within a given time-frame of one election cycle. As we have seen with the National Party, any ruling party that remains in power for more than a few election cycles breeds excessive amounts of corruption. Many observers would even argue that it has taken our current government less than four years to reach levels of corruption only found in the third world.

Danger 8: Taxes and duties

Already we as South Africans are among the most highly taxed people in the world. Unless we wish to thwart economic growth further and drive ever more entrepreneurial young talent from our shores, we must challenge the belief that ever more revenue can be collected by hiking up tax rates further. The disincentive to work already exists. Given the levels of taxation, many South Africans are effectively working for the Receiver of Revenue for five full months per year. From 1 January to 1 June of each year we are working to pay off our tax bills of the previous year.

Collecting tax revenue is already difficult given an understaffed and undertrained South African Revenue Service. Imagine the difficulty of collecting taxes in the future when the general populace reaches the point where it feels that taxes will only reduce government debt and the interest on it which continues to accrue. Government must be seen to be performing for the good of the population, otherwise taxpayers will increasingly be tempted to work clandestinely and not disclose much of their income. Such a situation is seen in Russia today, where government tax receipts are less than half of what they should be. To make up the increasing revenue shortfall, Russia continues to borrow heavily from the IMF and the World Bank. South Africa can ill afford the fiscal chaos and the related underground mafia types that seem to cast an ever-increasing shadow over the Russian economy.

Our new Revenue Service is understaffed and ill-trained. It is therefore not surprising to learn that the Revenue Service is five to ten years behind in its tax assessments of some of our country's largest companies. The recent resignation of the head of the South African Revenue Service does not inspire much confidence.

Making matters worse, of course, is the failure of the Masakhane Campaign aimed at ensuring that ratepayers pay their rates, taxes and rent. This defiance by the electorate speaks volumes for its disenchantment with available lifestyles and job opportunities. For most people, little has changed and they see no reason why they should all of a sudden begin to pay the rates and taxes that they successfully boycotted under the previous government.

Customs duties

The rumours circulating about the proportion of goods introduced illegally into South Africa have a direct relationship with the draconian customs and import tariffs levied on importers to South Africa. Why do Hong Kong, Mauritius, Taiwan and Malaysia not suffer from similar problems? Perhaps it may have something to do with them not levying import and customs duties on a wide variety of products? Our import tariff system is so complex that few trade lawyers in South Africa can either figure out all the different tariff categories or keep abreast of the updated tariff rates, which constantly change. We need to dramatically reform and simplify our tariff structure still further, in line with other successful nations. (This has already happened on a limited scale and government should be encouraged to continue.) Let us reduce the workload of the customs officials who seem overwhelmed by their complicated task.

The United States has a very simplified tariff structure compared to us. Could we not learn from others?

Danger 9: Small Businesses are Over-regulated

Successful small businesses tend to double their size at least every few years, far quicker than the old conglomerates of yesteryear. Co-ordinated financing and credit policies must be implemented if we are ever to realise the potential of this sector. Small businesses in South Africa already employ the largest proportion of workers and are best positioned to generate the vast majority of new jobs so urgently required.

We can no longer rely on the corporate giants and mining companies. We must, therefore, empower our small businesses to compete with the best in the world. High import duties and customs costs have to go if manufactured products in South Africa are to be competitively priced on world markets.

Small businesses should no longer be overly burdened with government paperwork which adds nothing but additional costs to their business. Red tape must be streamlined. Businesses employing less than 100 workers should only need to fill out a handful of government forms per year. We must let our small businessmen focus on what it is they do best — improving their products and perfecting their services. This is in the best interests of our country. As these small businesses grow and become successful they hire many more workers.

To stimulate investment in small business a wide variety of investment incentives can be created to establish private equity pools, allowing the risk to be shared between a wider group of individuals.

Mentor programmes in the US take advantage of the wealth of talented retired people, who assist young companies and entrepreneurs to avoid the pitfalls of mismanagement and help steer these growing enterprises along the straight and narrow.

Danger 10: Protectionist Policies and Outrageously High Prices

Domestic investment capacity alone cannot create 6–7 million jobs in the next decade, nor can it sustain growth rates of 6%, yet South Africa shows little interest in cultivating long-term foreign investment in any serious manner. In fact foreign investors can be forgiven for thinking that the few large monopolistic companies in South Africa (together with the unions and government) are content to keep foreign investors out, while protecting inefficient and unproductive domestic industries which mandate the South African consumer to pay a hidden tax every time he enters a store.

Whereas a cotton shirt might cost $12 in New York, a South African must pay R145 at home for the same shirt in a Truworths or Edgars store. The message to foreign investors is that the monopolies in South Africa can continue to rip off the South African consumer. These hidden taxes that we as South African consumers must pay every time we purchase clothes and a variety of other items makes us one of the most heavily taxed people in the world. Many of us are paying more in hidden taxes (i.e. because of the tremendously high prices levied by our manufacturers) than we pay in income tax. As consumers we need to put our foot down and refuse to be ripped off in this way. But we must organise ourselves far better if we wish to effect change in this area.

Fuel prices have a hidden tax that continues to be called upon by government to meet its revenue targets. The fuel price rose three times in 1996, a process which will most likely be repeated in 1998. Taxing fuel is a very regressive form of taxation, affecting most lower income citizens far worse than the upper income bracket. The upper income bracket more often than not passes on their fuel costs to their employers — a perk many executives and managers enjoy.

At present the attitude in South African economic circles appears to favour the rich getting richer at the expense of the average South African consumer. The large domestic companies enjoy a captive domestic market which ultimately pays for any wage increases.

It is also foolish to expect the Nedlac forum of big business, government and the labour unions to favour the consumer or to seriously tackle the country's unemployment problems. Big business will continue to meet the wage demands of Cosatu (the largest trade union federation in South Africa) as long as it enjoys a captive local market which allows any wage or tariff increase to be passed directly on to the consumer at the Pick 'n Pay check-out register. With no threat of outside competitors undercutting their prices, big business and organised labour will continue to undermine the free market and milk the South African consumer for all he or she has. That is why Nedlac should be scrapped immediately. It serves little if no useful purpose.

Danger 11: South Africa's Huge Debt

More than one fifth or a full 21% of the 1997/98 budget goes towards repaying interest on government debt. Our total government debt amounted to a staggering 58% of GDP at the end of 1997.

South Africa, many economists believe, is notoriously close to falling into a so-called debt trap, where our interest repayments just become larger and larger, swallowing up all other available resources.

Ross Perot said it best about interest payments due on government debt: "Debt is like a crazy aunt we keep down in the basement. All the neighbours know she's there, but nobody wants to talk about her."

The more we continue to allow the debt to grow the more impoverished we as a nation will become.

We must ask ourselves and our government, what does interest buy us — does it spur new business to provide new jobs? Does it

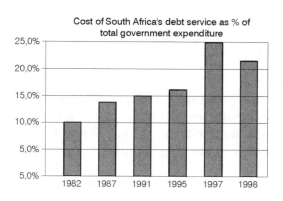

Cost of South Africa's debt service as % of total government expenditure

help people out of poverty? Does it maintain our roads and related infrastructure? Does interest put more police on the streets? Does it build classrooms or new homes? What do we get in return for all this interest we are paying? One out of every five rands our government spends goes towards interest repayments. How wise is it for government to be borrowing ever-increasing amounts of money abroad in foreign currencies that continue to batter our rand currency into a pulp? Just in the past three years South Africa has borrowed more than R10 bn in yen, dollars, and pounds sterling. Our total foreign debt stands at more than US$21 bn.

As a result of the rand's 50% depreciation against the dollar and pound during 1996–1998 the cost of our foreign borrowings has risen dramatically. The overall repayments have risen by as much as 50% in rand terms.

It is time to face up to our debt. We have to do it now, as no developing nation can afford to pay R30 bn in interest a year, and have nothing in return. Without a resolve to eradicate this wasteful expenditure, no future government of South Africa will have the ability to successfully implement equal education standards, meet housing construction targets, or indeed afford to provide adequate services in return for taxpayers' funds. It is unfair to future generations of South Africans to be mortgaging their future to finance a lifestyle which we haven't earned and can't afford. Something has to give; the status quo cannot continue.

Interest on government debt operates like a stealth tax on all citizens. Not only do we spend the second largest portion of our annual budget (after education) on interest payments on this debt — when these unnecessary expenditures could be better directed for the upliftment of the poor — but even more disconcerting is the fact that the high interest rates we currently have to pay are also based on the lack of commitment to reducing our debt. Since the market will view favourably any serious budgetary commitment to reduce our government debt, it is most likely that interest rates will subside, in accordance with reform of our pork belly approach to increased government expenditure. The markets' lack of confidence in our government's commitment to cut our annual deficit and thus our growing debt is apparent in the exorbitant interest rate levels. The prime overdraft rate reached 24% in 1998.

All South Africans currently suffer from these high interest-rate levels — our mortgage rates are out of control, destroying any

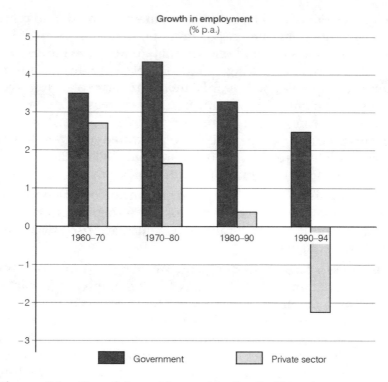

Figure 14   *Growth in employment in South Africa (percentage per annum)*

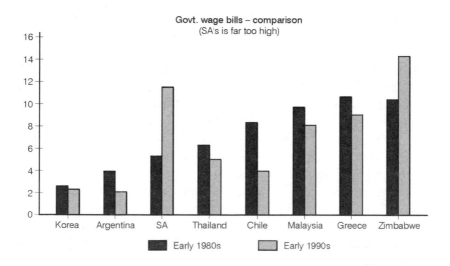

Figure 15   *South Africa's high government wage bill: an international comparison*

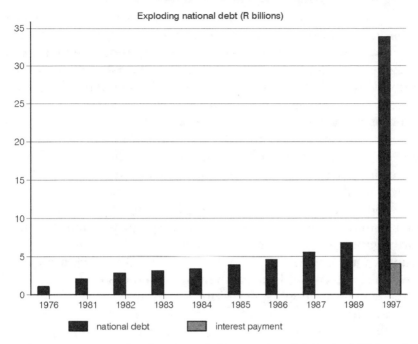

Figure 16 *South Africa's exploding national debt (in billions of rands)*

chance of the average South African affording the purchase of a house. At the same time, interest rates on student loans squeeze most families, while excessive credit card and car loan rates prohibit many purchases and dampen our country's economic growth. Many companies do not see any increase in demand for their products and thus do not hire new workers.

The middle class is thus being continually impoverished. In most cases a growing number of families require two incomes just to get by. Where the two incomes are roughly equal, it is sad but true that almost the entire income brought home by one of the spouses will go to pay the tax authorities.

Priority

We are the shareholders of South Africa — we own the country, and have over the years passively allowed special interest groups, along with government bureaucrats, to overspend as they see fit, with little or no accountability or public outrage from the electorate.

Our priority must be to reduce our huge interest burden, which means that our annual deficits must be reduced considerably. The only two ways in which an individual can reduce a deficit are to either reduce spending or to generate additional revenue. In any business the same principle applies. Government should no longer be able to sneak around this problem by borrowing further or by printing more money. These approaches will continue to drive us into an abyss and will only compound the problem by unnecessarily delaying tackling the problems head on with bold new economic policies. It is up to us to set the priorities which our leaders must carry out.

We should be voting in our political representatives based on their commitment to perform — to carry out the mandate they have agreed to, which is in line with the best interests of our country. Our leaders should not be permitted to back away from these tough decisions because they are scared of getting scratched in the face by an angry special interest group.

Government is not a candy store in which candy can be doled out to every special interest. It is our candy, our money, that is being doled out to fund many of these projects. To begin with, our government should be focusing on reducing our growing annual deficit and our nation's total debt. Revenue can be raised by implementing such well-known and successful policies as privatisation, which, besides raising revenue from the sell-off of state enterprises, also reduces the government's payroll. Given its current high level of expenditure on so many parastatal workers, few believe that privatisation will not be in the best interests of the majority of South Africans. And even Russia, Poland, Hungary and the former Czechoslovakia have successfully implemented privatisation reforms more quickly than we have in South Africa.

Disposing of R50 bn of state assets could transform the current level of the government debt-to-GDP ratio from around 58% down to 45% and reduce interest payments by at least R5 bn per year.

Danger 12: The Catchphrase — Benefication

South Africa mirrors the pattern of numerous other resource-rich countries, whose economic growth is slow and even stagnant once their resource-based industries have reached maturity. It is imperative for South Africa to develop new sources of long-term development that will produce vast new job opportunities and lift per capita income. Encouraging labour-intensive manufactured exports is certainly one solution for which there is empirical evidence the world over — it successfully improves a country's economic growth and stimulates the creation of thousands, if not millions, of new jobs (for example exports from Malaysia, Taiwan, South Korea, and Mauritius to Chile, Argentina and China).

The benefication of South Africa's minerals is currently the catchphrase in South African industry — although it often sounds good in theory, in practical terms few jobs are being created. Take the Industrial Development Corporation's (IDC) (i.e. government-funded) Alusaf Hillside smelter, the cost of which amounted to R5.5 bn, and which will create just 900 jobs, or Samancor's Columbus Stainless Steel project, which for all the hype surrounding it will create even fewer jobs, and cannot guarantee sufficient exports to ensure a sound balance of payments. The plummeting global stainless steel prices have also pounded Columbus, which has in addition been beset by technical and quality control problems. According to estimates, it is currently losing R1 m a day.

Capital intensive

Meanwhile the IDC in its capital-intensive wisdom, will be spending R35 bn of taxpayers' funds on ten mega-projects over the next four years. It is doubtful whether the return on investment is much in excess of government's average borrowing cost of 15% per year. As such, is it not in the interests of all South Africans to use these funds to pay our debts? Could such funds not go rather towards paying down our government's average debt or building houses for the poor?

If the taxpayers had a chance to decide as to where these billions of rand should be deployed, it is highly doubtful whether they would wish to subsidise and fund many of our country's wealthiest mining and industrial groups.

The IDC's recent Saldanha Steel project, which requires some R4.7 bn of funding, will create just 600 jobs, with the IDC's R750 million investment in the project translating into R1.25 m per job created. Taxpayers should demand better use of their money. The export earnings that will be generated will probably be small, relative to the earnings that could be generated from fully functional free trade zones — a concept which has been proven to work, costs far less to implement and creates far more long-term employment.

In the end the IDC uses taxpayers' funds to help subsidise and fund these giant capital projects to the benefit of mega-companies such as Highveld Steel and Anglo American. Do they really need to be subsidised or assisted in this manner? How does the South African taxpayer benefit? Few jobs are created, and by the time sizeable exports will have been generated, new houses could have been built and government debt reduced years earlier. The state should get out of these areas of investment, and leave them to those who know best. The IDC at present acts as little more than a financier of mega-projects — a bank on behalf of our biggest and wealthiest companies. It is truly amazing that this is allowed to go on, but then again few citizens might realise that they actually own the IDC. We are told that the IDC plans to spend a total of R188 bn over the next ten years. Could this money not be better spent?

The bottom line is the IDC is a state-owned development agency, which along with other state-owned organisations continues to systematically plunder taxpayers' funds in order to invest in heavily capital-intensive investments to the benefit of a small group of industrial and mining companies.

Selling off taxpayers' interests in Sasol, Iscor, Alusaf, Columbus and the Saldanha project, would alone generate some R20 bn in income to pay off our burgeoning debt. The capital channelled into these investments has reduced the availability of tens of billions of rands which could have gone directly to more job creation in the form of housing construction.

Government has also protected the investments made by the IDC and its conglomerate partners by providing tax incentives such as Section 37(e) of the Income Tax Act and tariff protection for the products manufactured by these projects. This has gone even further with the provision of forward cover on foreign loans through the Reserve Bank. How much more help does the innocent South African taxpayer need to provide to the IDC and the big conglomerates? South Africa cannot afford to spend such billions. Let big business do it alone if these mega-projects are such wonderful deals. The South African taxpayer does not need to be dragged into deals which, without subsidies and assistance from the IDC, would not be viable.

Danger 13: Relying on Mining as Our Economic Lifeline

Our gold mines are losing their glitter too. South Africa's gold production has fallen precipitously since the mid-1970s from 1m kilograms, down to just over half a million kilograms (522 tonnes) in 1995 — the lowest for nearly 40 years. South African gold mines are now the most expensive gold mine producers worldwide, with the weighted average production cost of gold in South Africa reaching in excess of $320 per fine ounce versus the equivalent of just $240 per fine ounce in Australia, Canada and the US (our costs are thus a third higher than other key producers). Production costs shot up by 19% in 1995, or double the rate of inflation, the results being a 38% decline in the profitability of every kilogram mined and a 36% fall in the dividends paid by the mining companies.

We enjoyed a rapid rise in the gold price during late 1995 and early 1996, when it soared to $405 per ounce. It has since sunk to between $280 and $300 per ounce. In 1980, according to the Chamber of Mines, the profit-to-revenue ratio for South African gold mines was of the order of 75%, but this has been falling ever since, reaching an all-time low of 17% according to 1995 figures. Roger Baxter, the chief economist of the Chamber of Mines in Johannesburg, estimates that even based on a gold price of $340, the number of marginal mines has doubled since 1994 from 7 to 15. The precarious nature of the industry is obvious when one considers that these marginal mines employ some 150 000 workers and produce 190 tonnes of gold, accounting for 37% of production and of the gold mines' labour force.

The burdensome labour agreements and other restrictions continue to hamper South Africa's gold mines. Industry-wide standard agreements on the wage rates of miners also unfairly penalise the older and more marginal mines which must compete with the larger companies. Paying higher wages is a worthwhile goal, but not if it means that an entire mine must close and all its miners must lose their jobs.

According to most experts, no new South African industrial empires will be created on the profits of gold mining within South Africa. Capital costs continue to rise as the industry must mine ever deeper with mine shafts in excess of 4 kilometres now being planned.

With our unemployment problems the last thing we need to

hear is that the gold mines have shed some 200 000 jobs since
1987 and that further reductions are planned among the
remaining 330 000 workers. Freegold, South Africa's largest gold
mine, announced back in early 1996 that it was planning to lay off
some 10 000 miners, and only swift negotiating appears to have
prevented this for the time being.

Clearly we can no longer rely on the mining sector to absorb the
continual and growing wave of new entrants into South Africa's
labour market. We have a problem and it must be solved NOW!

Danger 14: Our Enemy is Complacency

Although some will point to the number of new companies from
abroad establishing a presence in South Africa (mostly for sales,
distribution and marketing purposes), the fact is that regardless of
the current level of foreign direct investment in the country South
Africa is not an attractive destination for capital. In fact, if one
excludes from consideration foreign portfolio investment in
South Africa, long-term capital flows have remained negative
since July 1996. Ideally South Africa needs long-term foreign
direct investment (FDI) which involves physical investment in
factories and people, rather than portfolio investment which can
flow out as swiftly as it came in. Far fewer foreign firms have come
to South Africa and created sizeable numbers of new jobs than was
expected. For every dollar that has been invested in South Africa,
this country should have seen four or five times that amount — it
is not enough to compare our performance in 1998 to the old
days of apartheid in the late 1980s. This is mixing apples with
oranges: we all know most foreigners with their heads screwed on
properly delayed any meaningful investment until after the
transition. We need to compare investments in South Africa to
investments in Latin America and other developing regions since
1994. The comparison is distressing, as we have performed
miserably in terms of foreign direct investment.

The ja-broer (yes-man) syndrome

Many South African leaders surround themselves with yes-men —
who owe their jobs to the leaders themselves and rarely, if ever,
contradict their patrons. It is high time that our business and
political leaders' inner circle consisted of fewer ja-broers and
more individuals who are unafraid to speak their minds, partly
because of their experience and partly because they can readily

find gainful and more profitable employment elsewhere should they upset their leader and be asked to leave. If the truth hurts, so be it. The political correctness that currently exists undermines healthy debate in South Africa. The recent sacking of two top bank economists for their outspoken views is therefore cause for concern.

Danger 15: The Reserve Bank

Job creation and employment strategies for South Africa will remain frustrated and unachievable as long as the Reserve Bank continues its costly campaign of keeping down inflation at the expense of providing even the slightest stimulus to the economy. Is it not high time that Reserve Bank officials give up their obsession with "official statistics", which may be inaccurate, and take note of the situation on the ground? Activities on the street paint a truer picture of the South African economy.

House prices in South Africa (excluding parts of the Western Cape), the extension of mortgages, the number of businesses hiring new workers, the number of new businesses being established, the level of new construction — these statistics have all fallen considerably after taking inflation into account. One recent study of the cost of disinflationary policies to South Africa's GDP growth rate ranges from R9 bn to R13 bn for the years 1990–95.

Currently South Africa has the highest real interest rates (the prime overdraft rate at 24% less the rate of 7% inflation) in almost two decades. This will successfully stifle any economic growth beyond 1% for 1998 and most of 1999. High interest rates, we are told, are necessary to protect the rand. What is more important to the majority of us — economic growth and jobs, or a stable rand? At present the rand remains incredibly vulnerable to further speculation.

The longer that South Africans continue to stuff their pockets with travellers cheques and jump on Boeing 747s to leave the country with as much money as possible, the more reluctant foreigners will be to invest in South Africa for the long term. It is only once South Africans of their own free will invest in their own country, rather than taking their money and running, that meaningful levels of long-term direct foreign investment can be expected. Therefore, exchange controls must go as quickly as possible. South Africa would be better off if all our exchange controls were abolished and we had a weaker rand than if we continue to artificially bolster the rand with more than half our exchange controls still in place.

Although history will always honour the greatness of Nelson Mandela – the true father of our new nation – let us do everything in our power to prevent history's footnotes recording that having barely escaped civil war, South Africa plunged into a ruinous period of anarchy and corruption, where few job-seekers could find employment.

CHAPTER FOUR

A South Africa that Reforms its Politics — Holding Our Leaders Accountable

SOME MIGHT SAY: What is wrong with having an ill-informed public so long as the brightest members of the society understand the challenges ahead? This misses the purpose of a true democracy. How can we question and challenge our current and future leaders and demand of them solutions to ensure our country's future prosperity, when the vast majority of the voting public remains ill-informed and blindly follows one party or another? Political parties and their leaders need to be held accountable.

We need to be able to measure politicians' performances between elections. If they can be shown to be fulfilling not just their own promises but, more importantly, also our demands for progress and change, then they rightfully deserve to serve another term in office. However, if we as the electorate do not know what questions to ask, what issues to raise, what targets to set, then we do not have any criteria with which to judge the performances of our elected officials.

Of course, each of us has issues we feel more passionately about than our neighbours and friends. As such, we assign more or less importance to different issues and to government policies as they affect our lives. This is normal.

Fortunately democracies such as the United States do not rely on blind faith in their leaders. Neither is the US government run purely by a band of bright Ivy League graduates. The highest office in the land is owned by the people of the country, they are the real landlords of the White House. The White House was bought and paid for by the US electorate and their president is merely a temporary tenant.

The issues that come before government are not dreamed up by policy advisers — rather they are mostly in response to the needs and desires of the voters who put the politicians into power.

The US media are so pervasive and powerful that in 1974 one single newspaper (or two reporters) could bring down a sitting president — Nixon. Americans are notorious for holding their leaders responsible and demanding action from them.

The more informed the electorate, the more realistic their demands and often the more appropriate their responses. The job of elected leaders is after all to respond to the demands of those who elected them.

The Role of Media

In South Africa our television news and current affairs programming remains incredibly weak and limited. Of course, if and when the airways are opened up to the free market, new programmers would meet whatever needs or desires existed among the viewing audience.

Increasingly television and radio are the communication media of choice for governing a country. By this I mean that the majority of housholds now receive most of their information concerning the major issues of the day through their TV set or radio.

Although the media in South Africa is purportedly free and fair (and this is most certainly true in the case of the printed word), our public at large remains oblivious of many of the crucial issues of the day.

There are those who say that Africans do not like debate or dissent and wish to quash the implementation of such programming. I believe that they misrepresent our culture. Debate is healthy — it opens up new ideas and frontiers. Competition is more healthy than unhealthy. President Kennedy set 1969 as the final date to get a man on the moon not because he dreamt up the idea, but because he knew that America was in the fight of its life to win both the space and technology races.

Our government–sponsored television service provides few actuality or current affairs programmes. It is an indictment us, the electorate, that we have few such programmes.

By comparison both in the UK and US entire channels are devoted to news and topical economic, business, political and social issues 24 hours a day.

How can our leaders be held accountable when our reporters and journalists often remain under-utilised, reporting on soft stories about the opening of a new school or the unveiling of a new football stadium?

The evening prime-time news in South Africa continues to lack any substantive interview format. The lack of television programming addressing the key issues facing our country's future limits the electorate's understanding of these challenges. Many more programmes along the lines of Professor Dennis Davis's *Future Imperfect* need to be produced.

Many politicians would have it just that way. They are scared by the US political system, where all elected officials are held up to close scrutiny and questioned on many issues. South Africans do not need 64 TV channels to be well informed, but an electorate that does not know which questions to ask and at the same time permits its leaders to avoid answering tough questions — such a country is under-performing as a true democracy.

Lessons for creating a healthy South African democracy

Looking at the US for a moment, the genius of George Washington wasn't so much in winning the American War of Independence against the British (in fact he lost almost every battle he fought against the British), as in serving his two terms in office and then retiring. After being the Commander in Chief of the US army during the War of Independence, he was so popular at the time of his first election to the office of President of the United States that it is often said that he could just as easily have been crowned King of America or have served as the country's ruler until the day he died.

The inspiration that led him to give up the mantle of power after serving two terms in office is what set the precedent for all future American leaders to be nothing more than willing servants of the people. How different this is in comparison with many of the so-called democratic countries in Africa, such as many of our northern neighbours, whose leaders cling to power until they are ultimately overthrown, killed or die in office. Perhaps that is Africa's fate: that the electorate must live with its leaders until a coup or death removes them from office. Recent developments in Kenya and the Congo support this viewpoint.

Understanding our leaders

We need to hold our leaders accountable by having a better understanding of their job descriptions, and the challenges that face them. This will allow us to monitor their performance from an educated point of view, and at the same time we can better understand the problems they may be encountering and be able to sympathise with them if we are better informed. We will also be better able to judge whether they are successful at implementing the policies we have entrusted them to carry out.

Their job description is for them not to enrich themselves at our expense, but rather to serve us, the people who put them in power. If they do not measure up we should be free to replace them according to the rules of our democratic constitution. (Shape up or ship out.)

Remember the days of Simon van der Stel, the 17th-century governor of the Cape: when the Dutch settlers grew dissatisfied with him, he was recalled to Holland. Unfortunately, the 1830s saw *trekboers* (Boer farmers) resorting to every conceivable means of expressing their grievances, but with no power to affect government policies they ultimately took the radical step of entering the interior of an unknown continent.

The New South Africa's Political System

Unfortunately our new electoral system of proportional representation allows many MPs to ride into Parliament on the backs of one or two party stalwarts. Under the previous constituency-based system these candidates would be compelled to go out and campaign in the field — in their constituency, where they would be forced to address the concerns of their fellow citizens. To make matters worse, since no Members of Parliament are currently directly elected, there are vast areas of South Africa that have no real voice or real representation in the national legislature, as the majority of members hail from a few large cities. At present many of our MPs are among the most out-of-touch and unaccountable politicians South Africa has ever elected.

That is not to say that any decent citizen who is elected to Parliament and who receives all kinds of perks, such as free airline tickets, free use of a car and an apartment or house, as well as a supply of complimentary tickets to rugby and cricket games, also wouldn't lose touch with reality. The best of us probably would lose touch in a hurry!

These people work for us, remember, not for all the special interest groups which are so busy taking up the time of our elected officials on a daily basis in the hallways and offices of Parliament.

No matter how high their office or how lofty their titles, Members of Parliament and Members of the Provincial Legislature should fly in economy class, get in line at the airport, lose their luggage, eat a bad meal, and stay in touch with how we ordinary people live. Then when there's a recession in South Africa (a distinct possibility for 1999) or a certain industry is being discriminated against or part of the country is suffering a drought, it won't take them months to figure it out. The person sitting right next to them on the aeroplane will let them know in no uncertain terms.

Our hotch-potch political system

Since South Africa has selectively chosen elements from the British Westminster political system and the American Congressional system of governance it is important to understand what form of governing structure we currently enjoy. Our hotch-potch system of government is unique. We reinvented the wheel somewhat unsuccessfully.

Unlike in the UK, where MPs are at least accountable to their constituents and are voted for directly by name, in South Africa the majority of people do not even know who more than 80% of their MPs are. No more than a very small minority of South Africans probably even know which MP has been assigned to their district or constituency once elected. (The idea is that once in Parliament, MPs are assigned a constituency they must represent, but little action appears to have taken place in this regard.)

I hope you are one of the few who knows the name of the MP who is supposedly responsible for your area, because I have not met many educated South Africans who do. You are certainly in the minority.

Worse still, only MPs are picked to be in the Cabinet — unlike the US, where the brightest brains and experts in particular fields are chosen for the Cabinet — whether it be Henry Kissinger, Robert Rubin (a Wall Street banker with impeccable qualifications, now serving as the Treasury Secretary) or Madeline Albright (who has a PhD in International Relations and has many years' experience in international diplomacy).

No, in South Africa many of our politicians just disappear once elected, and confine themselves to three-hour lunches and the parliamentary backbenches, never to be heard from again, while pocketing more than R240 000 annually plus perks, which bring their packages up to R300 000 per annum.

The Cabinet

In South Africa the President appoints his cabinet exclusively from the inexpert ranks of Members of Parliament. At the same time we have done away with directly elected MPs who represent particular districts or constituencies. As such we have numerous MPs who have never been properly tested or held accountable. Their qualifications have not been scrutinised by the voting public, since our MPs are hidden from view by riding into Parliament on a party list. However, once they make it into Parliament these individuals are generally the only candidates who are considered as potential cabinet ministers.

In the United States the elected President rarely appoints members of his cabinet from the ranks of Congress (the House of Representatives and the Senate). Rather, the President in most cases turns to the country at large, seeking to appoint experts to fill the various cabinet positions.

The President is able to handpick his cabinet from the best minds of the country — those men and women with the necessary knowledge and experience. He rarely selects party politicians — most often he appoints experts to each cabinet post. Often he appoints people with no political experience and does not expect them to play political games. It may well be this simple fact that has led to much of the success of the US economy, to the absence of nationalisation and to increased privatisation.

In South Africa it would appear that the idea of appointing the most qualified experts to even a minority of the cabinet seats would be akin to breaking with a sacred political tradition. The ancient Westminster superstition that all Ministers serving a Prime Minister must be politicians and must subscribe to the political code of the party is outdated. On the rare occasions that an outsider has been appointed to the cabinet — such as Derek Keyes, a past Minister of Finance who was appointed in accordance with the US-based system — their performance has been excellent. Historically no South African Prime Minister or President has seemed concerned at the appointment of politicians from the private sector with little or no experience to oversee such portfolios as finance, trade, privatisation, minerals and energy, and transport.

In South Africa we also have a penchant for moving our Ministers between different cabinet posts. It is indeed both startling and astounding that there exist so few bright men and women in South Africa that we must rely on a small number of super-versatile and brilliant individuals to handle the various cabinet portfolios.

Perhaps the reason behind this may well lie in the fact that our Presidents understand that the practical day-to-day work of his ministers is carried out by the civil servants comprising their ministries. In effect it is the bureaucratic heads of the relevant departments who make many of the policy decisions and usually only provide the Ministers with information that coincides with what the bureaucracy thinks. The heads of the civil service departments found within each ministry largely make the important decisions. Unfortunately, the main task then of a minister is to present decisions and policies to Parliament and to the public — not to make actual decisions.

It is therefore somewhat frightening to realise that the vast majority of the civil servants themselves have little or no experience in the private sector — and as such do not understand, and cannot be expected to understand it. South Africa should have learned its lesson under the National Party: relying on our bureaucracy to come up with the best policies for our economy, or the well-being of all citizens, is indeed wishful thinking.

At present we in South Africa have a political system that has unfortunately not taken the best from either the Westminster and US-based systems as it was supposed to do. Rather, what we have is an unhealthy hotch-potch of selected features, many of which comprise the weakest aspects of both systems. At least under the true Westminster system MPs and cabinet members are directly elected and held to account by their district or constituency.

Demanding Action Today

Our cabinet members both nationally and in the provinces should be spending more of their time out in the field. The Minister of Health can best tackle the overwhelming bureaucratic problems within her juridiction by listening to the nurses and doctors in the hospitals who are on the front lines fighting needless bureaucracy every day. What good does our Minister of Education do behind a desk in Cape Town or Pretoria while our schools receive a larger and larger slice of the national budget and simultaneously the pass rates among black matriculants does not improve?

The answer to improving education is not just to throw more money at it and to expect improvements. Education already comprises the largest single item of expenditure in our annual budget. We're throwing money at education and not reaping any benefits. Now our Minister of Education is quoted as saying that the education budget will have to be increased by R23.58 bn to R58.81 bn if education equality is to be set at the level of former white education.

This increase would take spending on education from 6.9% to 10.5% of gross national product (GNP) — more than double the world average. The percentage of GNP we currently spend on education is already higher than the averages for Africa (5.9%), the Americas (5.4%), Asia (4.3%), and Europe (5.5%).

Of course the standard of education offered to all sectors of the population must be equalised, but what has happened to the savings one expected from eradicating the needless duplication of 11 different education departments as recently as five years ago? Surely once these apartheid relics had been dismantled, destroyed and streamlined into one department some measure of savings should have ensued? Somehow no savings have resulted; more and more funds are demanded.

How can we be getting value for our money in education by spending two percentage points more of GNP on education than anywhere else on the globe? Something is wrong with the way our education system is funded, organised and implemented. Who is ever held to account for this? To make matters worse, thousands of qualified teachers are being permanently laid off in urban areas such as in the Western Cape.

What is all this money being spent on, and why do we not see any results for all the billions spent? Pass rates remain inadequate, and only 40% of our schoolchildren ever complete secondary schooling. Of course historically disadvantaged communities deserve as much help as possible, but practical solutions will not come from our bureaucracy. Our Minister of Education should be consulting with those in the front line, with our teachers and parents — they are the ones who see the problems on a day-to-day basis.

Regional and Provincial Powers —
An Oxymoron

The US system of congressional districts and the Westminster system, which closely parallels the US House of Representatives, do a far better job of having representative Members of Parliament for every city, town or village.

Proportional Representation

Proportional representation, as found in small countries such as Israel, has been shown to be workable. But in a country as large as South Africa, with its highly diverse geographical regions and rapidly evolving social and economic structures, our political leaders need to be far more in tune with and accountable to the electorate.

Proportional representation can work very well if mixed with a healthy dose of local constituency politics, as in Ireland, where a number of parliamentary seats are allocated to various regions.

In South Africa this would mean for instance that in the event the Johannesburg northern suburbs comprised 5% of the population, then 5% seats in Parliament would be assigned to this area. As in Ireland, parties would nominate their candidates for each area. Given the present 400 seats in Parliament, this would mean that 20 seats would be allocated to the northern suburbs. In the event the ANC won 50% of the vote in the northern suburbs constituency, this would entitle it to ten seats. In this manner residents of the northern suburbs would be able to identify their MPs easily and to hold them accountable. At the following election voters could then send a very direct message to their MPs.

Both the National Party and its successor, the ANC, have sought to govern South Africa in a very centralised manner. Thus the current provincial government structures remain at best semi-autonomous, and at worst have to refer back to national government for approval of all key aspects concerning expenditure and undertaking new projects in their provinces.

With the creation of provincial parliaments we have succeeded in adding billions of rands to our public spending at a time when we can ill afford it.

At present the provinces have little or no revenue-raising ability and are thus unable to autonomously decide on their budget priorities. They must still kowtow to central government for their revenue handouts. This contrasts with the United States, where each of the 50 states has the autonomy to raise revenue through taxes, and provide investment and tax incentives (trade zones, tax holidays) to attract investors. States are run as separate governments with the autonomy to institute or change their laws and court systems. Whether we in South Africa need to go that far is questionable given the added bureaucracy, duplication and wasteful spending it will no doubt create.

Empowering the Provinces

There is a great deal to be said for empowering the people of the provinces with the muscle to implement economic policies to stimulate investment and job creation. After all, who knows more about a province's potential, as well as the problems it may be facing: some faceless bureaucrat in Pretoria, or the local political leaders, Chambers of Commerce of the region, and the men and women living in the province?

The faceless bureaucrat in Pretoria most often has little or no motivation to understand the needs of a particular province, whereas the locally elected leaders, both in politics and in business, would certainly lose much of their credibility if they did not respond adequately to the demands of those living in the province who had elected them to positions of influence.

Unfortunately, what we have in South Africa today is a Pretoria-controlled governing structure disguised as a mixture of the US and Canadian federal systems, with provincial Premiers instead of governors. When one looks at the powers of these elected provincial leaders it becomes clear that their ambit is rather narrow. In fact it is all too easy for provincial and local leaders to blame the lack of progress in their regions on the centralised government which holds the purse strings and which in almost all economic policy matters must not only be consulted, but must agree to any new policy that a province may wish to implement. At present the central government remains afraid of devolving any real power to the provinces in case this leads to unhealthy competition — a term I do not understand.

Healthy competition

If the civic and business leaders of Cape Town are of the opinion that the city and its surrounding region will benefit from the creation of a duty-free port within the Cape Town harbour and that such a structure will create thousands of new jobs, why should this concept not be implemented?

Central government's answer is that Durban, Port Elizabeth, East London and other potential free port areas would be unfairly affected, if not marginalised, and thus central government continues to refuse to agree to the implementation of any such free trade projects that a particular region brings to its attention.

If we agree that it is provincial and local leaders who know best, then why do we give central government a veto over any legitimate attempt by a province to create jobs and increase trade? Central government should not have to contend with criticism from a region that it is guilty of favouritism for permitting one province or another to implement certain incentive-style policies to attract investment.

Private enterprise has been shown to defeat communism the world over. Then why is our central government afraid of competition? Let Durban and Cape Town each have the power to implement those policies it feels are best to stimulate its own region. No doubt if Cape Town's free port concept proves to be successful, very quickly Port Elizabeth, Durban and East London will wish to follow suit. Competition is healthy. Cape Town's waterfront success has already been duplicated in Randburg and Durban. If the free port proves to be a failure, the Western Cape leaders will be held to account and will most likely have a tough time explaining the failure.

The provinces at present are unable to fend for themselves as they do not have any revenue-raising ability. Until such time as our provincial governments have financial responsibilities in line with other elected governments, it will be impossible for them to be free to implement any large-scale fiscal policies that may lead to increased investment and job creation.

By giving more powers to our provincial leaders, we the electorate will have the right to hold our provincial leadership accountable. It is too easy — given the current system — for our provincial leaders to simply blame the lack of progress in their provinces on the fact that many of their good ideas have been blocked or are under review by bureaucrats in Pretoria. Why do we have to pay for an entire provincial bureaucracy when in many cases it does not have enough autonomy to implement the policies that are in the best interests of the region? Perhaps we should question the true role of our provincial leaders at present. The impartial observer may be forgiven for thinking that many provincial government employees are creatures of the central government and have little to do on a daily basis.

The choice is clear. If the national government believes that it knows best for the regions, then why do we need to continue spending billions of rands to fund a complete provincial legislature which also comes with an entire provincial cabinet and its own civil service, all multiplied nine-fold (since there are nine provinces in South Africa, each with such a structure). Alternatively, the provinces must be empowered to perform the tasks that they are best suited to carry out, but then no Pretoria bureaucrat should have the right to block such policies, other than through the Constitutional Court, in cases where the provinces go beyond their constitutional authority.

It is time for our central government to answer these questions and to explain why they are afraid of empowering the provinces and why competition is seen as unhealthy. What are they afraid of?

Excessive Number of MPs

With 400 parliamentary MPs, plus 90 members of the National Council of Provinces, we have nearly as many national representatives as a country the size of the US, with a population almost seven times ours and a land area some 40 times greater.

The National Council of Provinces which recently replaced the Senate has yet to reveal the full extent of its powers or provide evidence of its mandate. Many believe it will serve little purpose other than to rubber-stamp the views of the political parties represented in Parliament.

With such a large number of MPs it has been surprising to hear many stories over the past four years of numerous occasions where not enough MPs have been in attendance in Parliament to vote on a particular measure. Perhaps we should wonder what many of our MPs are doing on a daily basis, given that they have no real constituency to visit continually to ensure re-election. Perhaps that's why so many MPs can be found having lengthy lunches in the Parliamentary dining room or at many of Cape Town's finest restaurants during the months that Parliament is in session.

Attendance in Parliament is so low on some days that the standard joke doing the rounds is that any day now Speaker Frene Ginwala will be left sitting there alone talking to herself.

However, it is not good enough just to throw out the current under-performing MPs in order to replace them with a new bunch who in a few months will perform little better. No. What we have to do is to insist on a more efficient form of political governance, where our MPs each have a sufficient workload and a defined contribution to make to Parliament.

All too often it seems that if an MP is not elected to the post of chair of a Parliamentary Committee, nothing else is demanded of him or her. Surely there are better things we could be doing with all the money we are paying for every MP's car allowance, housing allowance, salary and free travel allowance? Although the figures are hard to come by, Parliament should disclose the average cost to South African taxpayers of maintaining a single MP.

One solution would be to cut the number of MPs by at least half.

Additional Wastage

What about the cost of operating Parliament in a separate city to the national administration, and thus the need for two residences for many government civil service staff who constantly shuttle between Pretoria and Cape Town? What is the enormous cost of operating the parliamentary dining room and the various sports facilities at Ferndale, in Upper Newlands? It doesn't take a genius to figure out why none of these questions are ever asked within the walls of Parliament. We cannot maintain this largesse of public spending — our government in its present form is too expensive. Drastic reforms need to be made if we are ever to bring the share of public sector expenditure significantly down from over 20% to around 12% and more in line with successful developing and industrialised nations.

Our public sector officials need to learn to live within South Africa's means.

A Crisis — Costs are Out of Control

We should not find it strange that the average Member of Parliament now receives a base salary of close to R240 000 (excluding many thousands of rands worth of perks). Our politicians only did what they thought we would let them do — i.e. voted themselves higher and higher salaries. Our leaders, who are quick to blame others for the situation South Africa finds itself in, are increasingly adept at taking care of themselves financially.

What is saddest of all is the way we react to the continual increases in public service salaries: we do nothing.

The combined total spending for Parliament alone, including salaries and related housing, car allowances and free flights, most likely exceeds R3 bn a year. If no such number exists, what better way to get our money's worth out of the Auditor-General's office, than to demand an investigation into the cost of operating this runaway train of bloated salaries, perks, freebies and allowances? Better yet, a complete audit of all government expenditure should be completed within one fiscal year by the Auditor-General, who should remain a non-political appointee.

This would most likely shock the electorate and at least temporarily derail the parliamentary gravy train.

In July 1997 our Deputy President, together with ten Cabinet Ministers, two deputies and 100 other government officials, all descended on Washington DC only five months after seeing their US counterparts in South Africa. This exodus was for the purpose of attending the United States-South Africa binational commission. What the meeting achieved for South Africa in terms of job creation or even private sector investment is debatable. Why the South African taxpayer needs to foot a bill of at least R1.5 m, (*Business Day*, 23 July, 1997) and probably closer to R2 m, for a few days' jaunt in Washington, when the only major item on the agenda was to create another sectoral committee (the seventh) to deal with military issues, is ridiculous!

But do we demand an explanation of such expenses — whether it is a trip overseas, or how we can justify having numerous MPs or many new bureaucracies not only at national level but in each of the nine provinces? Of course not. Who were the academics who dreamed up the structures of all these bureaucracies? I can give you a little clue if you ever wish to identify those "rocket scientists": they have never ran successful businesses and have most likely never created any wealth for their fellow citizens. Who else could have dreamt up a scheme to further impoverish us as a nation by heaping on additional layers of bureaucracy, until one needs a computer programme to figure out who the right bureaucrat might be to talk to?

We will continue to harbour a lot of dead wood in our Parliament as long as the majority of our MPs are not accountable to the electorate and wish to continue enjoying the many perks afforded to them. Under our present system, being an MP can far too easily become a job for life. For example, by remaining one of the top 150 people on the ANC's parliamentary electoral list, an individual is virtually assured of remaining in Parliament until the day he or she dies.

Individual MPs must be seen to perform. Under our current system it is far too easy to use a position as MP to provide jobs for pals who do nothing more than vote occasionally, pocket a huge check every month, and fly for free on South African Airlines. South Africa can no longer afford such waste.

Government Spending and Our Auditor-General

The Auditor-General's recent report on state finances gives cause for concern. A key culprit as far as unauthorised spending goes is the Department of Health, which recorded R58 m over budget. Budgeting in government is extremely inaccurate with the rapid rise in unspent funds growing from 2.1% of total appropriation in 1991, to 10.1% in 1996. Since delivery is seen as one of government's key tasks, the growing level of unspent funds indicated a serious flaw in financial management. Financial systems appear to be very outdated.

According to the Auditor-General's report, local government inefficiency and financial mismanagement is worst of all. Until the necessary political will is found to solve these problems they will unfortunately hinder government's effectiveness and efficiency. Clearly effective training programmes are necessary for many civil servants.

Curbing the Role of Government

Fifteen percent of the total economically active population works for the government. This percentage rises to 45% in the case of high-level manpower. Government's role in the South African economy needs a drastic scaling down. The public sector wage bill is now approaching record levels (approximately 40% of budgeted expenditure), while the total amount of public sector expenditure is just under 20% of our nation's GDP. This excessive expenditure on a bloated bureaucracy cannot continue as it contradicts any serious efforts to curb our nation's indebtedness. Indeed, it is hypocritical to hear talk concerning belt tightening to reduce our nation's debt when the largest job creation industry in South Africa remains the government.

The appointment of a vast number of new commissions from the Youth Commission to the Gender Commission has led to a disturbing number of perks being handed out to commissioners, who in many cases are paid far more than seasoned senior private-sector executives. Providing free cars worth as much as R200 000, along with salaries approaching R350 000, for many public sector employees serving on commissions, is simply outrageous. Many of the commissions should be staffed by currently employed public servants or elected officials, many of whom do not have adequate full-time job descriptions, and do not appear to be overworked.

Billions of rands continue to be spent on salaries for public servants without work. Currently the wage bill and interest payments on state debt come to 58% of total government expenditure. Salaries are still being paid to some 54 000 employees of the state, 20 000 in central government and the rest in the provinces, particularly the Northern Province and the Eastern Cape (*F + T Weekly*, 24 July, 1998).

Having 490 parliamentarians is excessive, as are the huge bills necessitated by the regular travelling between Pretoria and Cape Town. Although both cities enjoy this largesse of spending, the country can no longer afford such an expensive public sector. The duplication of resources between Cape Town and Pretoria is out of control.

Given South Africa's economic situation, hard choices need to be made. The country cannot afford to be giving ever greater wage increases to politicians who in many cases already receive free housing and transportation.

The consolidation of government in one location would send a clear signal that government is also prepared to cut back and play its part in reducing our deficit and spiralling government debt. Increasing MPs' own salaries in real terms (i.e. giving them above inflation increases) does little to inspire confidence of any belt tightening in government.

It has also now come to light that at least 100 (out of a total of 800) local authorities face financial and administrative collapse, due largely to their deep financial trouble and indebtedness.

The failure of the Masakhane Campaign, which has not quelled the rent and utility boycotts, has left many local councils in dire straits. The administration they have inherited from the discredited apartheid system is also an embarrassment, with limited staffing and few revenue collection points.

Looking in the Mirror

We need to look into the mirror ourselves before we cast blame on anyone, since we as the electorate have abdicated our responsibilities as the "owners" of South Africa.

While many South Africans' confidence in our government continues to be eroded, we cannot afford to lose interest. We each have the vote and we remain the owners of our country. The facts can be easily studied, and change can and should be demanded.

As owners of South Africa we can rebuild our country and demand change. However, individually we have no effective voice. Together, the politicians are forced to listen to us and to take notice. Together we can change South Africa for the better — for our children and grandchildren.

Winston Churchill instilled in his government and the military the concept that when the survival of a nation is at stake, any action worth taking is worth taking now and not delayed. He would scribble on his memos "Action This Day!" South Africa needs the same lesson instilled in its government, in Parliament, in Nedlac (the economic and labour forum) and among our people. We cannot wait for a ten-year plan to unfold in order to solve our problems.

It is time to stop bickering and posturing for partisan political advantage. The future of our country is at stake. It is high time to stop avoiding the hard decisions. There is work that must be done. At a minimum we need to live within our means as a country until our economic and financial health has improved.

The Duty of the South African Voter

The longer we remain silent the more likely our silence will be viewed as tacit support and endorsement of the government and bureaucracy's new policies and political agenda. It is each and every voter's duty to understand the economic and political crossroads at which our country currently stands. The policies that are implemented by our government will affect each and every one of us. It is in our own best interests to question our leaders in order to ensure that the policies they decide to adopt are for the greater good of the South African population and do not just

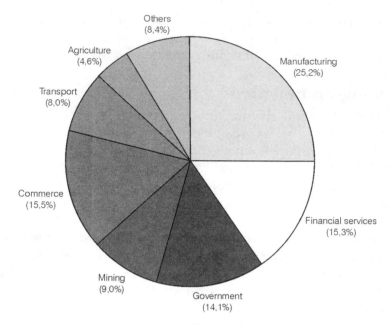

Figure 17   *South Africa GDP by sector (1995)*

benefit a special interest group — be that interest group a particular community, organisation or industry.

Special Interests

All too often it seems as though the special interests have successfully hijacked the political agenda while trying their utmost to distort the facts. One would think that the millions of unemployed workers in South Africa would have some say and, as a group, be at the forefront of a political agenda to transform South Africa. However, on a daily basis we are confronted with trade union representatives frustrating the development of South Africa's economy by threatening nation-wide strikes to stall the privatisation process and continually demanding ever-higher wage increases, while gains in productivity are non-existent.

Who does government listen to — the silent majority, or the vocal minority which belongs to various well-organised special interest groups such as trade unions? The answer would seem to be rather self-evident in, for example, the tortoise-like speed with which the privatisation process has been moving forward. Special interest groups have also helped delay an agreement with the European Union for a large measure of free trade between

Europe and South Africa, which would stimulate an increase in bilateral trade.

The message from government is clear: if you are a well-organised group and vocal — no matter how small you are — we will listen and take note of your views. Without an organised group representing the economic views of the majority of the electorate, the unions will continue to triumph over the masses of unemployed, and the millions of South Africans who would benefit from the implementation of such policies as privatisation.

If we, the unemployed and struggling middle class, wish to retake our country, we need to mobilise support and become far better organised. If no political grouping currently exists or no political party adequately reflects our needs, then it is time to form a new party or group that will be taken seriously and will get our views across. It is time for action now.

Conclusion

Unfortunately, at present the interests of 1.8 million members of a trade union (Cosatu) are held in far higher esteem than the interests of some 6–7 million unemployed South Africans. "Why invest in South Africa?" a foreign investor continually asks, when he can establish a manufacturing facility in numerous other countries without incurring import duties, heavy taxes, exchange control problems, minimum wage levels, the risk of strikes and more. Furthermore, elsewhere the investor may be able to benefit from preferential trade agreements which South Africa is not party to. This is no time for complacency. South Africa must *wakkerskrik* and become competitive, or else.

The message we must send to government is: it is time for South Africa to wake up and compete in the real world for bricks-and-mortar foreign investment if we are to ever have a serious chance of creating jobs for our growing numbers of unemployed. Implementing competitive economic policies is of paramount importance.

Who amongst us loves their children and grandchildren so little that they would be prepared to let these future generations inherit a weaker and more feeble South Africa than the one we inherited? With the rising levels of government expenditure and our huge existing public debt, we appear to be oblivious to the fact that we are mortgaging our children's futures. They will have to bear the brunt of future tax increases to fund the deficit and repay the huge interest bills we are accruing.

Of course the problems described here are not easily solved. One person alone cannot create 3 million jobs and a prosperous South Africa. However, if we work together towards a common goal there is hope that we will be able to steer our ship safely into the port of opportunity, wealth and the fulfilment of dreams. The buck stops with each and every one of us — the South African electorate.

We will be unable to repair our economic engine, re-tool our economy to be competitive or lay a solid foundation for future generations to enjoy, unless we seize back control of the government and related bureaucracies which operate as though they are the sole owners and decision-makers in the country. We must teach them who is boss around here, and force them to drastically cut their wasteful expenditure and get rid of the bad habits and policies they have inherited from 46 years of National Party rule.

Government employees should be encouraged to treat citizens as owners. Any owner of this country who walks into a government building should be treated with the respect and courtesy that an owner should receive. Government workers should also be rewarded if they do a good job, and reprimanded when they screw up.

Over-regulation does not benefit anyone — more bureaucrats must be hired at greater expense to taxpayers to enforce these new regulations. It is time for our government to review the mammoth number of regulations which impede our country's development.

Many of these regulations were implemented close to half a century ago, and are no longer relevant. Let's methodically review our ever-growing number of regulations, especially in the economic field. It would be surprising if we did not come up with perhaps thousands of useless or outdated regulations that are of benefit to no one, and that merely inflate the bureaucracy our businessmen have to deal with.

With regard to all future regulations, we should stop and ask ourselves whether it may not be easier to provide people and businesses with an incentive to do the things the right way.

By treating our elections seriously and requiring our political candidates to lay out their proposed policies and suggested solutions to the problems we face as a nation, we can regain control as owners of our country. We must be educated enough to see through the less than adequate answers to our many questions. The bottom line is: we should not allow our leaders to avoid facing the tough issues — it comes with the territory. Why are we paying our Cabinet Ministers half a million rand salaries if they cannot provide coherent responses to our questions (such as those in the *Appendix*)?

CHAPTER FIVE

An Electorate that Demands the Best — The Need for a Viable Opposition

HOWEVER HARSH IT MAY SOUND, if the National Party fails to reinvent itself as a credible opposition party with a realistic chance of regaining power, it must be relegated to the trash heap of history. We have enough young and capable leaders who deserve a chance to steer our country into the future.

In the event that the current opposition parties fail to improve on their powerbases in any measurable way, it is both our duty and the responsibility of our new breed of leaders to ensure that a viable alternative party is formed that can assist in unseating any ruling government in the foreseeable future. Just the threat of a no-confidence vote succeeding is enough to ensure that the ruling party will appoint the most qualified members to its upper ranks in order to better deliver on promises and lead South Africa along the road of prosperity.

At the risk of offending our leaders, we must feel free to ask tough questions and to seek adequate answers. We will reap what we sow. In South Africa today, we need to sow the beginnings of a healthy political opposition that can appear as a credible successor to the current government, to ensure that the current government feels the pressure of having to deliver on its many promises. South Africa's future depends on it.

The importance of a viable opposition is critical if we are to be the beneficiaries of the best leadership and stewardship of our country over the next few decades, no matter which party is in control of government.

The healthiest democracies rarely retain the same political party in office for longer than a decade and a half, before the electorate turns over the reins to a new party.

Opposition politics

In South Africa our opposition parties have remained notoriously weak for a variety of reasons. Good government requires good opposition. Even the most ardent of ANC supporters should recognise that a strong and healthy opposition is required to keep our government leaders on their toes. A weak, nonviable opposition permits government to be complacent and to procrastinate, so avoiding difficult decisions.

The dismal performance of the Democratic Party (DP) in the last few elections bears testimony to some of the numerous blunders made by South African opposition parties, which have often remained elitist, racially divided or exclusive.

Many believe, correctly in my view, that the National Party (NP) as it is currently constituted will never again rule South Africa and that it may in fact lose its status as the official opposition in the 1999 elections. The DP, which advocates many of the most pragmatic and realistic policies, remains an elitist, white, urban-based English-speaking party, a situation which obscures many of the constructive policies for which it stands. Hopefully DP politicians have learned some of the hard lessons delivered by their dismal electoral performances in 1994. Recent election victories seem to indicate that they have done so.

The Inkatha Freedom Party remains the vassal of one man who, for all his achievements and positive attributes has too often in the past proven unpredictable and disappointed many of his supporters. Inkatha unfortunately remains largely a provincial player, as well as largely Zulu-based, and has not succeeded in building much of a wider following. In fact, even within the urban areas of KwaZulu, Natal, Inkatha's following now appears to be under severe pressure, and is roughly evenly split with the ANC in the cities.

There seems little likelihood of a split in the ANC in the near future: simply put, if a split took place too many former prisoners would be out of work or would not enjoy the high level of remuneration they currently do by sitting in Parliament. It would be foolish of them to risk such a split at the expense of sacrificing their current privileged existence. Besides salaries running into the hundreds of thousands of rands, their perks often include free accommodation, use of a car, a large number of free flights per year, and the list goes on. Thus even if a growing number of black political and business leaders began to feel that our country was not moving fast enough in the right direction, one would not expect them to simply jump ship. Of course, at present there exists no other large, steady, well-organised ship to jump onto, so anyone showing dissent jumps overboard at their peril and will most likely drown (forfeit their political future).

In a *de facto* one-party state, it is better to stay within the ruling establishment, even though one may disagree with its policies or wonder at the slow rate of progress. Why give up privileges to forge a new party to challenge a ruling establishment which can hand out favours to its friends and swell the gravy train, just as its predecessors, the NP, did so fantastically well for over 40 years?

The power of Opposition — for the good of South Africa

To reap the maximum dividends from our ANC leadership and current ruling party, its leaders must be made aware of the reality of being voted from power in the following election should they not perform sufficiently well within a five-year period and meet the expectations and promises it has repeatedly made.

If we do not do this, we will have a new ruling elite that, as with most political parties, doles out favours to its constituency for decades, while acting complacently on policy matters and failing to meet the immense challenges facing our country.

As we see in the world's most successful democracies, it is not healthy for the same party to rule our land for much beyond a decade and a half, otherwise the breeding of corruption and the feathering of one's own nest will exceed even the normal bounds of political indiscretion.

What incentive does an overwhelmingly powerful ruling political party have to tackle the toughest problems in our land, which might often mean confronting part of its own powerbase, if there is little chance of it being voted from office in the short to medium term? It is far easier to do nothing and to avoid the implementation of policies. We have already seen this in the case of labour reform, government debt, reducing the deficit and privatisation.

Zimbabwe — a lesson

Take for example the case of Zimbabwe. The dire economic performance and limited socioeconomic improvements that the majority of black Zimbabweans have seen between 1980 and 1998 bear testimony to the fact that since it was almost impossible for President Mugabe to be defeated at the polls, there was no reason to adopt certain painful policy measures. These measures would have initially caused pain, but in the longer term would have brought about improvements for the Zimbabwean masses who remain unemployed and impoverished. (At present the unemployment rate is 40% while inflation is in excess of 20%. The Zimbabwe dollar has depreciated by some 300% against the US dollar since 1980.) Food riots in 1998 and the cutting off of IMF aid have brought Zimbabwe to the crossroads.

Complacent electorate

An undemanding electorate is no better than a complacent electorate. A complacent electorate unfortunately leads not only to a complacent government, but a government that can afford to spend more time on its own selfish concerns. Absentee electorates have been taken advantage of in numerous nascent democracies, including India and Mexico. Finally we have seen the democratic overthrow of the ruling Congress Party elite in India, although this has taken some 48 years to achieve. The exposure and dismissal of a half dozen Indian cabinet ministers on corruption charges just prior to the April/May 1996 election which brought the Hindu-backed JNP party to power was to some extent responsible for this.

Although our current government certainly has a wide range of support, from the most radical economic dreamers of the Communist Party to liberal idealists, from millions of unemployed South Africans to free-thinking economists, at present there appears little chance of these supporters finding a new home elsewhere. The party political scene remains mostly unchanged since the early 1980s, when the Conservative Party splintered off from the National Party.

Effects of a *de facto* One-party State

As in the case of the National Party monopolising the white vote for 46 years, the mood of complacency and lack of a credible opposition in the early years of ANC rule may prove to have long-term, disastrous effects.

In the same way that a runner or swimmer performs better when challenged by a strong opponent, thus achieving a better time for completing the race, that same athlete will most likely not improve on his best time for the distance if he has no strong opponent to push him to his limits and threaten his victory.

In the same way, if we want to win a gold medal as a country — meaning, among other things, achieving a substantial improvement in our economic and social performance — this will be far easier to achieve if our favourite political party has some credible opponent that could challenge and pressurise it to pull out all the stops and deliver the performance of a lifetime.

At present some 6 million voters remain unemployed. Taking into account their dependants, husbands and wives, one might calculate quite realistically that this large group of mostly impoverished blacks might comprise some 12–13 million voters. This powerful voting bloc should no longer be ignored if the interests of most South Africans are to be considered. We would all benefit from the creation of employment opportunities for the vast majority of our unemployed.

Crime levels will be reduced, thus curtailing the brain drain. Economic output will grow, since more workers will produce more goods and the spending power of millions more people receiving wages will have an enormous multiplier effect on the economy. We should not be so short-sighted and think only of ourselves. We are all affected by the terrible levels of unemployment.

Dilemma

The longer the growing number of unemployed workers experience the absence of a new dispensation and better opportunities (such as better employment prospects and a brighter future), the more likely it is that they will become increasingly disenchanted with the ANC and, over time, begin to demand ever more radical solutions to their plight. Already these unemployed masses and the trade unions represent opposite poles of the black electorate. Cosatu's 1.8 million members have enjoyed the fruits of the ANC's Labour Relations Act of 1996, which arguably entrenches the interests and pay levels of workers beyond what South Africa's unemployment levels can bear, or small businesses and foreign investors are willing to pay. The 1998 Employment Equity Bill and related labour levy bill will only help entrench a more rigid labour policy, making labour more expensive.

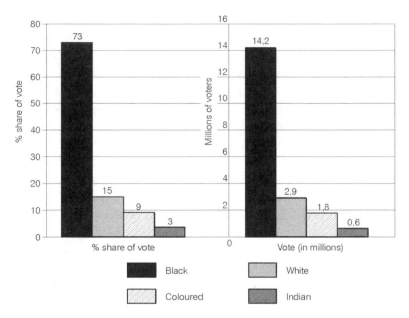

Figure 18 *Composition of the vote in the 1994 general elections*

Economists say that our labour market is in disequilibrium, with wage levels continually rising for those with jobs, while unemployment grows. In 1996, when inflation averaged 7.4%, wages rose 11.2%, due to the power of the unions. In 1997 the gap was reduced; inflation averaged 8.6%, with wages growing 10.7%. An ever-rising cost of labour continues to be a constraint on the labour-intensive investment our country is able to attract; at the same time, workers' rights are so entrenched that in order to legitimately lay a worker off, a tremendous amount of paperwork must first be generated. If anything, this has made owners of businesses even more intent on hiring machines and robots to perform work wherever possible. The increase of late in the capital intensity of South Africa's factories is in fact a direct result of a highly regulated labour market, where smaller businesses are dictated to by unions which are intent on standardising wage levels across numerous industries in South Africa. The banding of workers' wages within particular industries often causes smaller businesses to suffer most, as they do not have economies of sufficient magnitude to be able to afford the new wage increases agreed upon by the large employers and the unions within their sector.

Using the Power of the Electorate

The void that currently exists in South Africa, whereby voters have little opportunity to question their leaders other than every five years at election times, demands an improved medium for South Africans to ask tough questions of their elected leaders.

One cannot rely on politicians in weak opposition parties, no matter how hard working and well meaning they are, to always steer the debate or to get adequate responses to the many useful questions they raise in Parliament.

We, the electorate, have the power to demand the attention of our current leaders. We are their landlords. If they fail to create jobs for us and to improve our lot, we have every right to sign a new five-year lease with another tenant and to give this new tenant in Tuynhuis a chance of being at the helm of government for a period of time.

A New Political Party

If no alternative opposition party appears viable to us, we need to create such a party in order for it to have a chance to govern the country for five years. It is high time to demand far more of our political leaders. But we must first become far more informed and active as an electorate.

We should not vote for our political parties only on the grounds that such parties historically fought hard for their day in the sun, or because we are voting against something. We must know exactly what our leaders stand for — what do they want to do with our country, and in what direction do they wish to take it? What are their solutions to the many tough questions we should be asking them — many of which are raised in this book? (See the Appendix for details.)

Those with viable solutions deserve a chance. Being against something is not good enough. What are they for? Amongst other questions that need to be answered: How do our leaders propose to create 8 million new jobs, stop the rand's decline, root out the criminal element that rules our urban areas and create an educational system that affords equal opportunities for all South Africans, and not just spend more and more of our limited budget on one area?

Our democracy would be strengthened if it had a viable coalition that could perhaps threaten the majority status of the

ANC. Based on the 1994 election, the DP, NP, and Inkatha received a combined total of just under 35% of the vote. Under the current system of political parties, what is needed is a new party that could possibly capture 15–20% of the ANC's voting base, which would reduce the ANC's number of seats in Parliament to roughly 50% of the entire body. However, at present none of the existing opposition parties appear to be correctly positioned to capture such a sizeable slice of ANC support.

We will only have ourselves to blame if we do not address these issues and come up with viable solutions. If we remain an undemanding and ill-informed electorate that does not question our leadership, we deserve a government that one day may become as unresponsive and aloof as the British Governor was in the 1830s, or as secretive and bureaucratic as the securocrats and Nats were during the P. W. Botha era.

It takes guts to build a true democracy, where we have viable opposition parties that serve to threaten the dominant party's control of government. We should heed the lessons of the past — the sad litany of many of our previous opposition parties which failed to attract larger followings. We need to address these hard truths.

Politics — A Viable Opposition

Hopefully South Africa will have a viable opposition one day — we could learn a thing or two from Tony Blair. Successful countries succeed because they have a strong opposition. But South Africa may be staring at two decades of single-party rule — clearly we'll have to wait until at least the 2004 election to see even a slight change in the power structures.

South Africa desperately needs a healthy democracy, but this requires an alternative political party to the ANC alliance of convenience, where constant infighting within the ruling party has led to incredibly slow delivery in a number of key areas.

It should not take the death of a Ronnie Bethlehem to make South Africa sit up and consider the direction in which our country is headed. Every day ordinary people are being stabbed, tortured and murdered. What about the thousands of Robbie Kaplans of this world who are hardly household names in South Africa? Robbie was tortured with a hot clothes iron for two hours, shot three times, and stabbed — all in the relative safety of Linksfield, Johannesburg.

Surely we can expect more as citizens of one of the most beautiful and richly endowed countries in the world?

Politicians often speak out well, but in South Africa today saying anything more about crime just makes our leaders appear even more incompetent. How many new crime initiatives will they announce over the next few years? Come on guys, it's time to do something. If you can't, give someone else a chance. Actions *do* speak louder than words.

It is selfish to give positions of power to people who have demonstrated favouritism and a clear lack of leadership, moral judgement, action, tact and the like.

In numerous countries, when scandals and disasters continue to happen, leaders are fired. But few if any of our government ministers are reprimanded or told to find greener pastures.

New black and white blood must be brought in to tackle our numerous problems. Leaders whose only qualification is that they know how to disrupt meetings and have served time in jail have, in many cases, been shown to be out of touch with reality and sadly ineffective in improving the standard of living for the average citizen.

Sense of Complacency

Businessmen and women who say "What are you complaining about? — South Africa could have had communism and our precious swimming pools could have been taken away." are obviously so interested in currying favour with the black elite that they are *poep* scared to say anything negative. They do this country a disservice; it is high time that they got off their high horses and became true patriots once more. The honeymoon is over — 1999 is here.

It is indeed sad that they dismiss the enormous problems plaguing South Africa and offer no solutions or commentary on the situation. It would appear that government has successfully surrounded itself with *ja-broere* (yes-men) who never criticise any of their actions. The only time they seem to hear negative comments are when they emanate from the unions and the left, who remain in the socialistic slumber of the UK Labour Party of the 1970s.

The temptation to leave South Africa has become irresistible to many South Africans, especially those go-getters who have the requisite skills and those whose family members have been attacked or who have lost a loved one to violence.

South Africa can no longer afford to lose its most talented members. Even huge corporate salaries may no longer be sufficient to keep many young, talented workers — those who have portable skills.

Acepticism is healthy

Who are our education and health ministries attempting to help by importing Cubans as teachers and doctors — are we trying to help uncle Fidel reduce his unemployment rates by importing these Cubans, or are we genuinely attempting to improve our health and education systems? Cuba may have a high literacy rate, but what achievements can it boast in more than 30 years of attempting to develop the country?

Perhaps the only reason our Education and Health Ministers have recruited Cubans is that South Africa is such a crime-infested place that only desperately poor Cuban doctors and teachers who were previously forced to shop for rationed goods are willing to make the trip here. If not, why have Zuma and Bengu not attempted to interest First World nations in sending us their talented teachers or doctors? Let the truth be told: South Africa is an unattractive proposition for any foreigner wishing to settle here — one's life is in danger unlike anywhere else. Murders, rapes and hijackings are among the highest per capita in the world.

time for action

If this is all depressing stuff, it should be: but rather than throwing up your hands and saying, "*Ag man, ja nee*, there's nothing I can do about it," it's time to do something. For too long South Africans have just sat back and done nothing and let the criminals take over. Sitting idly by as our elected officials continue to accumulate frequent flyer miles for flying first and business class, while doing little to improve the lives of South Africans, will no longer cut it.

Whether or not you support the ANC, you should reflect just how fortunate this political party currently is. With no viable opposition to worry about its failure to deliver on numerous promises, it has no cause for concern. In any other country it would be a sitting duck to be thrown out of office in just under a year. But not in South Africa.

Considering the ANC's performance over the past four years and its failure to deliver on such basic issues as the protection of South Africans from crime and violence, it is not surprising that foreigners find it hard to believe that no viable opposition exists in South Africa.

South Africa is in desperate need of talented and skilled, young and vibrant new leadership that can appeal across racial and ethnic lines. While our political process remains divided along purely racial lines with little or no voting along policy lines, South Africa will remain in a sad state of disrepair.

We remain an unsophisticated electorate.

Unfortunately, given the current political make-up in South Africa, there is little hope of a realignment of parties or the creation of a new party overnight.

Realignment Needed and Quickly

Given the infighting occurring within our largest opposition party, the National Party (NP), South Africa seems far from having a viable opposition movement to combat the *de facto* one-party rule that the ANC enjoys.

Many would agree that Roelf Meyer (previously of the NP) was being set up for failure in his quest to define and create a new opposition movement. The NP is a walking corpse with enough apartheid baggage to bring down any political party. Clearly in its present form it is unlikely to ever be a viable opposition. South Africa needs new young black and white blood for that task. Until such time, we will continue to stare into the abyss.

In the 1994 election, the NP garnered more than half of its total votes nationwide from the Western Cape — in essence making it a regional-based party rather than a true national party.

- The NP captured just 3.5% of the total black vote nationwide, while capturing exactly two thirds of the coloured vote, 65.5% of the total white vote, and 50% of the Indian vote.
- By comparison, the ANC captured 81% of the black vote, 27.7% of the coloured vote, 1.7% of the white vote, and 25% of the Indian vote.
- The DP only managed to obtain 388 000 votes, or just 1.7% of the total vote, with between 80% and 90% coming from the

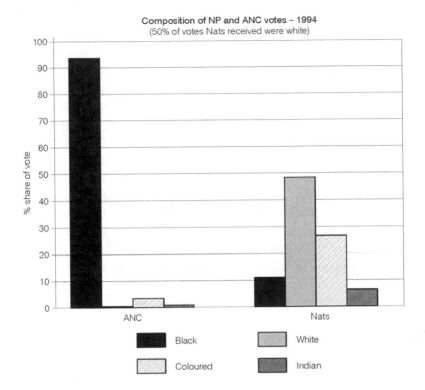

Figure 19 *Composition of NP and ANC votes, 1994 (note that 50% of the NP vote was white)*

white urban communities in Cape Town, Durban and Johannesburg.

- The DP only garnered the support of some 10% of white votes on the national ballot — less than half the figure it sustained in the all-white general elections of 1981 and 1989.
- The DP garnered 18% of the total white vote on the provincial level.

Although the planned amalgamation of Roelf Meyer's New Movement Process and Bantu Holomisa's National Consultative Forum to form the United Democratic Movement (UDM) may provide a new cross-racial opposition party, in all likelihood it will remain a small opposition party, skimming votes off the NP and the DP. The recent defection of 10 NP representatives on the Pretoria City Council to Meyer's movement is encouraging and does deprive the NP of control of the Pretoria City Council. However, this only points to a reshuffling of the anti-ANC vote.

The amount of infighting within the National Party is a clear sign of dissatisfaction among its members over their party's future role in South Africa. The NP has been overshadowed in opposition by the tiny DP which, with just 7 MPs as opposed to 84 NP MPs and a far smaller research staff and budget, has been able to provide a fairly effective voice in opposition, approaching problems with well thought-out proposals on how to tackle such issues as South Africa's crime rate, unemployment, education standards and health services.

More than ever it can truly be said that in its present form the NP will follow the slow death of the United Party, which refused to reinvent itself and ally with other political factions, until it was too late. For the benefit of all South Africans it would be advisable for the NP to clearly set out its strategy.

Given its historical baggage, the NP does a disservice to South Africans by remaining in its present form. By joining others to form a new political movement in which the NP would be only one of a number of groupings, it could provide a glimmer of hope that in the not too distant future South Africans would be able to vote for a viable opposition that might one day actually have half a chance of unseating the ANC. It is only then that South Africa will have, in effect, a healthy democracy.

The NP in its present form will continue to lose its effectiveness as a viable opposition party as its core of support continues to shrink, and the numbers of new black voters appearing on the voting rolls by 1999 and 2004 effectively squash any chance the NP has of building up its support base.

It is possible that the NP may retain power in the Western Cape, but its values do not appeal to blacks, and over time it will lose power if its appeal is unable to cross ethnic divides — which is highly unlikely given its past. The quicker the NP wakes up to the reality that ten years from now it will be little more than a rump party appealing only to those die-hard supporters or those who vote for it out of habit, with no hope of ever regaining a meaningful political powerbase — the better off all South Africans will be. At least then it may be able to face reality and begin to reach out in a meaningful way to other ethnic groups.

But this can only be done by the leaders of the NP themselves when they realise that their party as it currently exists has no long-term future in the new South Africa, given its diminishing white support base. Recent studies by Professor Lawrence Schlemmer of

Wits University indicate that the NP's support base on a national level has shrunk from 20% of the electorate to just 14% which is not surprising given the almost daily revelations in the Truth and Reconciliation Commission of the NP's dirty deeds over the past four decades. The NP must not only focus its attention on groups that are in opposition, but also on those inside the ANC.

Democratic party

At the end of the day a party such as the Democratic Party (DP) which has little historical baggage — and by comparison with the NP is respected by non-white ethnic groups — is in a far better position to be able to establish larger political alliances. The fact that the DP was invited to join the ANC government's cabinet recently is indicative of the respect it enjoys. However, the ploy to invite it into government would have resulted in the stifling of debate on what needs to be done in South Africa. At present the DP is far more effective in opposition; it would only be overpowered in government.

It is true, though, that the DP should be working at expanding its political network and alliances for the forthcoming election in 1999. The DP could steal the NP thunder in this regard, by pre-empting moves by the NP to cosy up to movements such as the IFP and the alliance between Roelf Meyer and Bantu Holomisa.

The DP's main weakness at present is not its policies, nor its history. Rather it is its unwillingness and unsuccessful attempts to move beyond its narrow support base of the white middle-class and business community. It should take a leaf out of the books of such stalwart campaigners as Bill Clinton and Tony Blair, who have moved to the centre to become more appealing without losing the support of their core constituency. With the correct strategy it is highly unlikely that the DP would lose any of its support among white English-speaking South Africans, while capturing an increasingly large slice of Afrikaans, coloured, Indian and black voters.

The DP until now has not shown itself able to break out of its image as the liberal English-speaking party of the white suburbs. Until it does, it will remain a relatively weak political party, despite an energetic leadership which consistently raises its profile by clearly enunciating what South Africa should be doing. Although such opposition leadership serves a useful purpose, it is sad to see such talent go to waste. Perpetual opposition for the next few decades is not an altogether exciting prospect.

Without a new political realignment it appears that for some time to come if you are white or coloured you will continue to vote for the NP and possibly DP; if you are Zulu, for the Inkatha Freedom Party; and if you are black (and non-Zulu), for the ANC.

Room for the Creation of a New Political Movement

It is clear that a large number of voters are dissatisfied with the management of the new South Africa. A recent Human Sciences Research Council (HSRC) report clearly indicates that the level of support throughout South Africa for the ANC has fallen from a high of 63% in May 1994 to around 55% by July 1996. If anything, further slippage has occurred during the last two years. However, most revealing is that this 8% loss has not been absorbed by any of the other political parties. Of ANC supporters, 12% affirmed that they were willing to consider switching allegiances. This translates into 1.4 million of the 12 million votes the ANC secured in the 1994 elections, a new floating vote of predominantly black voters.

At the same time 20% of NP supporters admitted that they had considered supporting another party — this amounts to some 800 000 voters. According to the report, as many as 2.3 million South Africans are dissatisfied with the choice of political party they made in 1994. It is most interesting that in percentage terms white, coloured and Indian voters were far more likely than blacks to abandon their existing party affiliation.

Nevertheless, a loss of one million voters by the ANC is little more than a blip on the radar screen. As many as 72% of those interviewed stated that they would not leave their current party, since no alternative was available to them other than those that currently exist. What is clear, though, is that there is a growing dissatisfaction with the lack of delivery on political promises, as well as a lowering of many South Africans' standard of living as measured by lack of personal safety.

The HSRC report indicates that black South Africans have no comfortable alternative to the ANC, and that despite their increasing dissatisfaction they are still most likely to vote for the ANC, as they find it easier to justify voting for leadership born out of opposition to apartheid than for any of the other existing parties, which are in one way or another tainted by their participation in the apartheid system.

Combining the NP, DP, Freedom Front, and IFP in an alliance will do little more than form a *de facto* anti-black partnership. It is therefore imperative to create a new post-apartheid party that is able to attract significant black as well as white support.

Although the vast majority of black voters will wish to give the ANC another chance at governing South Africa well into the 21st century before switching allegiances, it is clear that a considerable minority may be willing to send the ANC leadership a message that they should not be taken for granted. They may be willing to vote for an alternative party on a provincial level and perhaps on a national level as well.

A minority of blacks and the majority of whites, Indians and coloureds will wish to send a message to the ANC in 1999 that their performance has been less than stellar, and it is imperative to create a new political realignment that will appeal to such dissatisfied voters.

While the ANC continues to wish to be something for everyone, little movement is likely on the job creation and economic fronts. Given the reality of a global free market system, the ANC's liberation allies, the South African Communist Party (SACP) and the unions, have become more of a hindrance in policy formulation than a help.

With unemployment in some townships running as high as 70% and the rural poor being largely ignored, if the majority of South Africans wish to see action, they will need to send the ANC a bold message that its overwhelming majority at the ballot box in 1994 is not nearly as secure as it has assumed, and is in fact under threat — perhaps sooner rather than later.

If we consider that Cosatu's membership has plateaued at 1.8 million, and that support for the SACP is declining, it becomes clear that the ANC continues to pander to a minority of voters representing little more than 10 – 12% of the electorate. Although the SACP would get just 1% of the popular vote in South Africa (according to a survey in *Finansies en Tegniek* 10 July, 1998) as a stand-alone party, it has over 80 of the ANC's 252 seats in Parliament and currently at least five ministers are SACP members.

Although the ANC may have the capacity and leadership skills to solve many of South Africa's problems, it continues to be hamstrung by the views of a minority of its supporters: unionists, socialists and communists.

The lack of a clear vision for the future of South Africa and the lack of accountability among many in leadership roles inspires few South Africans to view the future of this country optimistically. Living standards have not improved for the vast majority of South Africans — and given the tremendous crime wave in the country, those South Africans who do have skills and are well paid are increasingly looking to emigrate, even though they realise that their living standards will drop. But at the same time their likelihood of being hijacked, raped or murdered will be dramatically reduced by moving elsewhere. The costs the South African middle class currently incur in fortifying their homes with additional alarm systems, response units, electric fences and barbed wire has become a huge additional tax that many are increasingly unwilling to pay. So they leave the country. Perhaps government could appease them by providing a tax credit or an income tax rebate for legitimate expenses citizens incur to protect themselves from criminals.

Serving the electorate's needs

It is high time that a new political party or movement tapped into this level of dissatisfaction. What is clear is that no political realignment poses a serious threat to the ruling ANC government unless the various splits, defections and alliances occur within the ruling party itself. Continued ethnic-based voting in South Africa, with no visible change on the horizon, prevents a natural progression towards issue- and value-based voting. The longer parties just hide behind racial and ethnic support, the longer South Africa will remain a *de facto* one-party state and be little different politically from countries to the north.

Rather than voting out of emotional or historical loyalty and fear, it is imperative to give South Africans the choice of voting for those parties willing to tackle the issues by providing realistic solutions to our country's many problems. Like-minded individuals should be encouraged to establish a new party which will appeal across ethnic and colour lines, and not be historically tainted as the current opposition parties are, whether they like it or not.

Sadly, our "democracy" continues to function by squelching dissent. How else can one account for a parliamentary system in

South Africa which prohibits a party member from voting according to his or her own conscience (in contrast with the UK, US, and Canada), whether it be in line with the party or not? Politicians who are elected on a list basis are little more than grateful pawns of the top leadership. They are often too scared to say anything that may offend their party leaders and, unlike in other parliamentary systems, they are unable to cross party lines should they so wish.

Perhaps that's why Jennifer Ferguson left Parliament soon after the abortion vote (she was allowed to abstain). She is just one MP in a long line of some 85 others who have left Parliament over the past three years. Clearly, even our elected leaders appear to be disillusioned with the state of progress in South Africa. Many find serving in Parliament extremely boring, with little or no constructive role or job description.

Political Ramifications: Does Anyone Care about the 6–7 Million Unemployed?

In view of South Africa's dramatic unemployment problems, the need to create jobs is of paramount importance. As a South African citizen, I must relay my surprise at the complacency that continues to prevail among our country's policy-makers regarding the need to create millions of jobs. Politically, the unemployed are now the single largest constituency or voting bloc.

Opportunity for the Opposition Parties

It is quite likely that by the next election a large voting bloc made up of the current 6 million or so unemployed, plus their direct dependants (forming a total voting bloc of perhaps as many as 10–12 million) will feel disillusioned with the lack of economic progress made by the ANC-led government. Projections are that unemployment will grow in South Africa over the next few years, unless GDP growth of 5% is achieved and maintained, which remains unlikely until at least the year 2000.

We are currently unable to achieve even half that rate of economic growth.

If the opposition parties play their cards right, they could be in a unique position to capture a sizeable number of the votes from this group of frustrated voters. A strong argument could be made by the opposition parties that voting once again for the ANC would bring about little economic improvement or job prospects and guarantee a dithering economic policy, ending in failure to deliver on numerous electoral promises, and thus perpetuating the status quo.

However, in order for the opposition parties to have a firm leg to stand on, they should formulate a serious blueprint or working paper proposing the kinds of policies they would initiate to create sustainable economic growth and soak up the growing sea of unemployed.

For the good of the country it is imperative to implement new investment and tax policies in order for South Africa to attract more long-term foreign investors, who not only bring foreign exchange and technology, but also create jobs. (To ensure that political parties receive credit for such policies, in the US, for instance, the parties often publicise their economic policies in book form.)

Capturing More Votes

In terms of this scenario the NP, DP, and Inkatha would be able to rightly claim that their policies for economic growth have never been adopted by the ANC. By the next election these parties would then be in a stronger position to criticise the ANC's lack of economic progress and the continuing unemployment problems.

However, unless the opposition parties adopt and publicise their own clear set of economic, investment and tax policies, these parties will not differentiate themselves from half-hearted ANC policies which have done little to stimulate foreign investment or cut unemployment.

Consequently, what is needed is a clear economic blueprint covering investment and tax policy, that can be shown to stimulate economic growth by generating foreign investment, increased export earnings and foreign exchange, as well as offering greater employment opportunities.

Why There is a Need for a Viable Opposition Party

As long as there is no viable opposition to the ANC-led government, not much will change in South Africa with regard to creation, privatisation, Gear, etc.

South Africans need to wake up and realise that it is time to form a new opposition alliance which will have new black and white leadership, not hangers-on from the past. The NP bandwagon has enough baggage to sink another Titanic. New revelations emerging from the Truth and Reconciliation Commission almost daily have made it increasingly difficult for the NP to rise above its past. In fact the past continues to raise its ugly head, and has had the effect of limiting the NP's appeal to little more than its historical base of white Afrikaners and coloureds.

A new, inclusive political party must be formed and quickly. It is therefore encouraging to see Roelf Meyer make the break with the historically burdened NP. However the United Democratic Movement (UDM) has no clear vision for solving South Africa's many crises.

We need to create a broad party which appeals across regions and across ethnic groups if we are ever to challenge the ANC alliance's current position of overwhelming dominance as the only party with support spread throughout the various regions of South Africa.

The bottom line

The bottom line is that in order for South Africa to become a truly healthy democracy, we are in desperate need of a viable alternative political party to the ANC that will eventually have a sufficient powerbase to form its own government, or at a minimum exert sufficient pressure on the ANC to inject more of a sense of urgency into its elite.

Few would argue that re-electing the same governing party in more than two or three successive elections is healthy for a true democracy — regardless of whether or not they support the ruling party.

South Africa's own history has shown that graft and corruption can set in after retaining the same governing party for more than a few elections. To keep our government on its toes, it is critical that it face the constant threat of losing power if it does not deliver the goods, i.e. deliver on its multitude of election promises.

What is clear in South Africa today is that no such threat (however small) to our government exists, since we have no nationally cohesive cross-cultural opposition party.

It would appear that the NP is spending so much time and effort on refuting the many allegations concerning its past, that

South Africans have heard little from it in the form of new policies and suggestions to improve the lifestyles of all South Africans.

The ANC has been allowed to hide its own inadequacies behind the constant revelations of the Truth and Reconciliation Commission concerning the NP. It is able to point out what a beast the NP was, and that anything is better than the NP. The continuing weakness of the NP just helps to make the ANC even more complacent, confident that it will remain in power for as long as it likes, so long as it can carry its broad spectrum of supporters along with it.

All patriotic South Africans should be concerned about the lack of a viable opposition party which could one day threaten the ANC's dominance. It is not healthy for South Africa to have weak opposition parties with no real teeth. It is high time that we all woke up and pitched in for the good of the country, whether we support the ANC or not.

CHAPTER SIX

The Power of the Markets — Attracting Investment and Foreign Exchange

M ORE POWERFUL THAN MULTINATIONAL organisations such as the World Bank, the IMF and United Nations are today's global financial markets, which serve as both a fair judge and jury on the economic path adopted by all countries.

For example, take the prospect of a possible downgrading of South African government bonds (gilts) by influential bond rating agencies such as Standard & Poors or Moody's, because they believe South Africa is slow in undertaking needed economic reforms. This would cause our government to have to pay higher rates of interest on any foreign borrowings, which would throw its budgeted interest payments out of kilter, creating the need to seek more revenue in order to meet the sudden higher interest payments. A ripple effect would also be felt in the stock markets where portfolio investors in South African equities might decide to take their money and run, thereby leading to a large outflow of capital. This scenario occurred in 1998.

A single large downgrading could in fact force our economic planners to rethink a large part of their strategy, leading to the overdue implementation of many policies that have been slow to receive the time or attention they deserve. At present (July 1998) Moody's is reviewing its rating of South Africa.

The rand's 30% decline in value between May and July 1998 is a case in point. Almost overnight our economic policy-makers were forced to react to the harsh fact that the international capital markets were growing uneasy about South Africa's lack of economic resolve to reform. At that point the name of the game relating to privatisation had been one of "procrastination" with no clear policies being spelled out.

With the benefit of hindsight, it can be seen that the markets are a wonderful way to wake up any sleeping politicians or business leaders.

Their jobs are on the line when the markets give a big vote of no confidence, and swift action usually follows. Happily, in the case of South Africa, after the 30% depreciation in the value of the rand in dollar terms in 1996 and losses in the stock market, our government took only four months to unveil the first meaningful economic package in two years (Gear) — designed to offer a blueprint for bringing South Africa back to sound economic health, while making the country more attractive to outside investors. Sadly, by July 1998 the markets had given Gear a vote of no confidence. Either we get Gear into high gear or we throw it out and start again.

South Africa requires a free and open market where the fruits of capitalism are available to all. Small monopolies of companies and elite groups of executives who receive favours from power brokers and politicians in high positions are the hallmarks of Africa and the Middle East.

If one meets the President of the Chamber of Commerce of Japan or the US, then one can be said to have met a real power player, perhaps one of the most important and influential people in the land. However, meet a person in the same position in Morocco, Kenya, Tunisia or Zimbabwe and the same is generally not true, since the power lies in the hands of a few government leaders.

Our new masters

In many ways, international capital markets have more power to affect our economy and the future policies we will need to adopt, than anything our own policy-makers may be dreaming up.

We have to understand the way the markets work — what drives them up or down. The world has changed and we must appease our new masters if all our citizens are to enjoy an improved quality of life. Every day the capital markets are deciding which countries of the world are worth investing in and which are ready for the trash heap, or have a long way to go before they, the markets, will reward such countries with a signal to buy.

Today the bond markets of London, New York and Tokyo decide whether South Africa or Argentina is the country to invest in.

We cannot afford to thumb our noses at these powerful market forces. We should have learned our lesson in the 1980s from the reaction to P. W. Botha's Rubicon speech, which sent the rand tumbling, losing at least 40% of its value in the six months subsequent to that speech. By the end of July 1998, the rand was at its most undervalued (based on purchasing power parity) since the Rubicon speech.

The Need to Recruit the Most Qualified Team

The criteria for high public office should not be based purely on friendship, or the length of prison sentences served. The best, most highly qualified applicants should get the job, otherwise what we have is some form or another of job discrimination.

In a global economy, government cannot escape the whims and power of the international financial markets. To taunt these markets is disaster. The markets can be unforgiving, and they generally have an uncompromising attitude towards governments they view with suspicion. Government can certainly learn from the free market how best to run an efficient public sector. To survive, businesses must adapt to the needs of their customers, understand their customers clearly, and run their operations with as little wastage of resources as possible (human and otherwise). Corruption and exploitation in a business leads to mismanagement and finally, ruin.

As in the case of a business which is certain to fail miserably if it continually spends more than it earns, so too a government which continually runs up larger and larger deficits will ultimately drive a country to bankruptcy — or more euphemistically, force the country to default on its loans.

Investing in Our Future

The size of our government spending is way out of proportion to our economic size. At present public sector spending accounts for a record 20% of our Gross Domestic Product (GDP) — in other words, one out of every five rands spent goes towards the public sector. Staff costs in the public sector soared by 19.2% in 1996/97, grew by a further 9.1% in 1997/98 and are expected to exceed 8.8% growth in 1998/99 (budget year March to the end of February).

Despite a government pledge to cut the public service by 100 000 jobs a year (according to Gear), the number of public servants employed by national departments in fact rose by 0.4% between March 1996 and March 1997.

Back in 1946 both Germany and Japan lay in ruins. Their leaders were forced to make hard choices. Our governments have spent themselves into massive debt, while at the same time over-taxing the South African population. We now find ourselves in the dubious position where there is precious little room to raise taxes further in order to reduce the deficit and cut the debt burden, without creating an ever greater disincentive to wealth creation among our nation's new entrepreneurs. In fact, tax levels are so high that any considerable increase will most likely drive future wealth creators from South Africa. (While the US has 1 in 4 people becoming entrepreneurs, South Africa's dismal performance is just 1 in 30.)

Since government cannot raise taxes any further without seriously hampering South Africa's chances of higher economic growth, it must streamline its spending as a matter of urgency. For example, South Africa currently has the highest wage bill as a percentage of the GDP of some 13 developing countries surveyed by the South African Foundation. The government wage bill is approximately 11.5% of the GDP; it has almost doubled over the past decade, whereas this ratio fell during the same period in 10 of the 13 countries surveyed.)

It is clear that there are still far too many individuals in government who are draining the nation's resources with little productivity to show in return. Government should cut its net employment by some 300 000 by the year 2000. At least 1.5 million workers are employed by government. This is excessively high as a percentage of the total workers employed in the formal sector. Most observers believe this may well be an under-representation of the true numbers. As previously mentioned, some 54 000 salaries are being paid out to employees who do not have work — those people for whom there were no posts when the 11 government services consolidated in 1994.

Overall government spending in developing countries averages around 26% of the GDP, whereas in South Africa it remains above 31%.

Back in 1950, for each employee in general government there were 13 employees in the private sector and in parastatals. By 1994 there were little more than four workers outside of general government for every one such worker in government. This ratio is excessively high and reflects the socialistic tendencies of government over the past four decades).

During the late apartheid years, the Nats realised they could no longer increase tax rates substantially and began to borrow funds to cover their growing budget deficits. And so we find ourselves today saddled not only with tremendous debt but also with high taxes. How then does government fund new public works programmes, the Reconstruction and Development Programme, and further shortfalls in the budget?

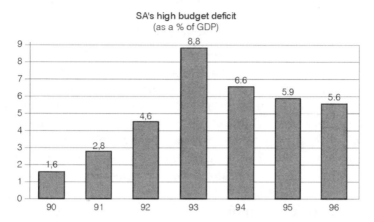

Figure 20   *South Africa's high budget deficit (as percentage of GDP)*

The Need to Foster New Investment

There can only be one answer: our economy must grow sufficiently to dramatically increase the number of employed workers in our country who earn salaries and pay taxes. However, to spur this job creation, we need to attract and encourage new investments.

We must request our leaders to research and implement policies to encourage and foster long-term, labour-intensive, domestic and foreign investment. Incentive policies have been implemented in numerous countries to encourage research and development as well as new investments in both people and equipment. Is our government even studying such policies? If so, why have they failed to implement any of them?

The majority of economists believe that to even begin cutting into our high unemployment numbers, South Africa requires a sustained growth rate of 5–6% per annum for the next ten years. If South East Asia could average 8% growth for a decade, why is it so far-fetched to believe that, given the right economic policies and investment incentives, we might not average 6% for a similar period of time?

Unfortunately, our leaders must have the foresight to be bold enough to permit the right conditions to exist in our country before we will ever be able to sustain average growth rates of 6% for the next decade. At this point achieving such growth rates remains but a distant dream. Can we not learn from such countries as the Czech Republic, Japan, Chile, Singapore, Malaysia, Taiwan and Hong Kong?

We need to ask our leaders why they have been slow to adopt any (if not all) of the economic policies and lessons of the world's fastest growing economies over the past three decades. Privatisation is a case in point, as is the implementation of detailed trade and investment incentives. Both measures would help make South Africa a far more attractive location for foreign investors. We are in the fortunate position of having many empirical examples of other countries that have successfully met highly complex economic challenges. In South Africa we need some bold new thinking.

We need to learn from the experience of others — which policies succeeded and which policies failed, and for what reasons?

The Need to Get Serious

Statements by Sam Shilowa, secretary general of Cosatu, such as "You know, if this country was a socialist republic or a communist republic I would be happy," will continue to scare off investors.

The current foreign investment hype reported in our newspapers and by such groups as the much-quoted US Investor Responsibility Research Center of Washington DC should be taken with a pinch of salt. Much of this investment will do little to generate either jobs or exports. The foreigners investing in South Africa do not generally establish new plants and factories employing large numbers of people; in many cases they establish small sales, distribution and marketing operations in such plush suburbs as Sandton, Berea, Claremont or Rosebank with minimal staff. Alternatively the foreign funds flowing into South Africa are short-term portfolio investments on the Johannesburg Stock Exchange; or hot money currently going into our bond market to finance government's debt at a tremendously high interest rate (the recent range was 14–16%). Such high interest rates are double edged. They lure hot speculative money, while destroying any chance for significant economic growth.

The highly respected Economist Intelligence Unit, which had been rather sympathetic towards the ANC's handling of the economy, surprised many when it came out with this blistering attack in November 1996: "Weak leadership on the part of President Mandela recently, ever-changing policy directions on privatisation and labour, evidence that a number of senior ANC politicians are involved in corruption and an explosion in violent crime, has led to investors' confidence being shattered."

The report continues: "Will the government stick to its policy of economic growth or will the themes of 1996 remain, leading to a further loss of business confidence and an economy that barely grows?"

What the Unit failed to mention is that the current policies of government are woefully inadequate for addressing the creation of 425 000 new jobs per year or generating an economic (GDP) growth rate of 6% per annum. These remain but a pipe-dream. In a damning sentence the report states: "There remain as many business leaders who believe that South Africa will fail as those who believe it will succeed. Certainly no new Asian Tiger will reside south of the Limpopo for a good deal of time." A vote of no confidence in its truest form.

The need for 6% economic growth

Although attracting foreign investment into South Africa remains one of the key ingredients for South Africa's future economic growth and a key component in the absorption of some of the 6 million unemployed workers into the economy, precious little is being done to formulate an approach that makes South Africa a competitive investment location for international investors. Although government has come out with a macroeconomic policy statement (Gear), South African business interests and labour appear somewhat reluctant to propose any sweeping changes that will make South Africa a more competitive investment location for long-term foreign capital.

Gear's goal of achieving 6% economic growth by the year 2000 defers the problem of economic growth. South Africa needs a 6% growth in GDP today. Indeed, we needed it last year and the year before. The longer we wait, the deeper the hole we are digging for ourselves, and the more unemployment will grow.

If we muddle along with 2% and 3% GDP growth for another few years, a GDP growth rate of 6% per annum in 2000 will be insufficient even to cut into our unemployment problems, and will barely absorb the number of new entrants into our labour market. By the year 2000, South Africa will most likely need to generate at least 500 000 new jobs per year to begin cutting into the unemployment problem in any meaningful way. It is expected that by the year 2000, the number of unemployed people will have grown by 1.5–2 million if our economy just muddles along at 2–3%. This is the stark reality facing South Africa.

Government must aim for growth immediately and not put a limit on the size of it. If other countries can generate 8–10% GDP growth for up to a decade or longer, why should we not have a similar target? Why is government selling us short as a nation? Is it perhaps due to their more socialistically inclined alliance partners, who wish to redistribute as much growth as possible in the form of policies that will never permit our country to achieve a growth rate of more than 4% per annum?

Our President, whom we all revere as a true hero, a living legend, and a man of principle, has unfortunately been decidedly absent from much of the economic policy debate.

President Mandela is unquestionably the world's leading statesman as the end of the 20th century draws closer. However, the respect he generates may have a strange negative consequence — foreign leaders are afraid to rake him over the coals concerning our country's dismal economic performance, while economic policy-makers within South Africa are afraid to criticise his handling of the country.

The truth according to *The Economist*, is that by many economic standards the ANC's tenure has been marred by indecision and little improvement in the average South African's lifestyle. President Mandela's public relations presence for South Africa is terrific, but we as a country need more of his leadership to generate the sorts of jobs and opportunities that were promised. It is high time that he, along with Deputy President Mbeki, grab control of the country and begin to steer our ship in the direction of high economic growth.

If the President's current lieutenants and copilots do not perform adequately, he alone has the authority to replace them. At the end of the day his own enduring legacy is on the line. As the captain of our ship he must take ultimate responsibility for the lack of economic progress.

It is all too easy for our President to surround himself with yes-men who reinforce the feeling that he can do no wrong. We must stand up and demand even more from such a venerated figure.

When policies are wrong and inferior, Mr Mandela's yes-men are doing him and the entire nation no favours. To label legitimate criticism as racist is senseless. Criticism comes with the territory. As Harry Truman once said, "If it's too hot get out of the kitchen."

Getting the Right Foreign Investment

The current levels of passive foreign investment (investment in gilts and equities) exceed direct investment as the main source of foreign funds. In fact this has been the case since 1976. However, indirect investment by its very nature is volatile and is affected by the mood of the markets. More importantly, such investment does not create a direct impact on the generation of jobs nor the transfer of technology. In June 1998 this hot money left South Africa in substantial amounts, dramatically depleting our foreign currency reserves and leaving our currency in tatters. Passive portfolio investment is fickle at the best of times.

The Need for New Ideas: Create a Ministry of Foreign Investment

South Africa clearly needs a government heavily loaded with private sector expertise, preferably with international experience. Why is it that South Africa remains among a small minority of countries with only two Ministries devoted to fostering foreign investment and economic development? Besides the typical Minister of Finance and a Minister of Trade and Industry, the vast majority of successful countries have established specific Ministries devoted to attracting Foreign Direct Investment (FDI), largely staffed with individuals who have a strong background in the private sector and training in international finance and tax issues.

Is it any surprise that amongst this list are many of the fastest growing economies of the world, including Barbados, China, the Czech Republic, Costa Rica, India, Ireland, Morocco, New Zealand, Sri Lanka and Argentina?

These countries and numerous others have shown that their commitment to attracting foreign direct investment goes beyond speeches and ad hoc trade missions. How can South Africa possibly compete against countries which have not only shown their seriousness in attracting FDI by making Cabinet-level appointments, but in addition have put their money where their mouths are by developing comprehensive investment policies to stimulate both foreign and domestic fixed investment? These programmes go far beyond a few tax gimmicks and include such labour-intensive policies as employment subsidies (employment tax credits), training allowances, research and development credits and grants, export trade incentives, investment tax credits and import duty-free exemptions.

Is it not time that our leaders finally woke up to the fact that South Africa has a lot to learn? The stinging vote of no confidence we received both in 1996 and again in 1998, as 30% of our country's net worth in dollar terms disappeared, should be reason enough to follow the successful examples set by those countries generating enormous amounts of employment, foreign exchange earnings, and export growth — all as a result of large-scale FDI.

Promotion

To assist prospective investors, the Department of Trade and Industry has established the Industrial Development and Investment Centre to identify and eliminate impediments to industrial growth, promote investment in South Africa and provide a one-stop-shop service to prospective investors in the industrial sector. Although this is to be applauded, there remain disturbing tales of foreign investors unable to get work permits and numerous bureaucratic delays in this regard.

Since many potential foreign investors by necessity use their local embassy or consulate as their first port of call concerning information on investing in South Africa, it is also imperative that trained trade and investment personnel staff South Africa's embassies and consulates abroad. These foreign missions should have the necessary full range of information and technology needed to assist potential foreign investors when they receive inquiries.

Rather than being solely reactive to inquiries, these skilled "trade and investment ambassadors" should promote South Africa's investment potential. Unfortunately, at present, far too often these departments within embassies and consulates remain hidden from public view and the Consul General or Ambassador does not play a proactive role in addressing and promoting this important function of his or her mission. If anything, this function should be at the top of the list of priorities.

Certainly this would go some way to justifying the enormous expenses we incur in staffing our foreign missions all over the world. It is crucial that they be staffed by competent personnel with experience in dealing with senior private-sector executives. They are often the first point of contact, and this first impression may ultimately result in the executive undertaking a journey to South Africa to further inspect and research the possibility of establishing a presence in the country.

Sadly, South Africa ignores this wisdom. A case in point is the US, where South Africa has no trade consul or representative for the entire western region (approximately ten states, including California, which alone is the tenth largest economy in the world) — although we *do* staff an entire consulate in Los Angeles with political and other functionaries.

Time to put our money where our mouth is

By establishing a separate ministry focused on attracting FDI and stimulating international trade, South Africa will finally be sending an important message to the international business community. Rather than relying on ambassadors and consuls general who do not have the requisite private sector background to stimulate and attract the interest of foreign business leaders, many countries have established a separate ministry, backed up by an energetic team of professionals with international private sector experience. (See **Table 2** below).

Besides having a Ministry of Finance and a Ministry of Trade and Industry, the following countries also have the following Ministries dedicated to attracting Foreign Direct Investment (FDI):

Table 2 *Ministries dedicated to attracting foreign direct investment (FDI)*

Australia	Minister of Development, Minister for Consumer Affairs, Minister for Small Business
Barbados	Ministry of International Business

Canada	Ministry of International Trade
China	Ministry of Foreign Trade and Economic Cooperation (Foreign investment now accounts for 25% of China's exports.)
Colombia	Ministry of Foreign Trade
Costa Rica	Ministry of Foreign Trade
Czech Republic	Minister of Economic Competition, Minister of Economy
Egypt	Ministry of Economic Affairs, Ministry of Economy and International Cooperation, Ministry of Internal Trade
France	Ministry for Small and Medium Business
India	Minister for Commerce
Indonesia	Ministry of Investment, Ministry for the Economy
Italy	Ministry of Foreign Trade
Japan	MITI — Ministry of International Trade and Industry
Korea	Ministry of International Trade and Industry
Malaysia	Ministry of International Trade and Industry, Ministry of Entrepreneurial Development, Ministry of Domestic Trade and Consumer Affairs
Morocco	Ministry of Foreign Investment, Ministry of Foreign Trade (Manufacturing GDP grew by an average of 4.2% in 1980–92.)
New Zealand	Minister of Commerce, Ministry of Consumer Affairs
Philippines	Minister for Economic Affairs in the Office of the President
Poland	Ministry of Foreign Economic Relations
Russia	Ministry of Foreign Economic Relations
Singapore	Ministry of National Development
Sri Lanka	Ministry of External Trade, Ministry of Industrial Development
Sweden	Ministry of Foreign Trade, Ministry of International Development
Taiwan	Minister of Economic Affairs
Thailand	Ministry of Commerce
Tunisia	Ministry of Foreign Investment, Ministry of

	Economic Development (Manufacturing GDP grew on average by 6.3% in 1980–92.)
UK	Three Ministers of Trade and Industry, besides a President of the Board of Trade
USA	Secretary of Commerce, US Trade Representative
Vietnam	Ministry of Planning and Investment, Ministry of Economic Affairs, Ministry of Commerce

This is an impressive list of countries which have successfully understood how foreign investment decisions are made in the world's industrialised nations. Such a cabinet level ministry should have a mandate that includes the following:

- develop extensive foreign media contacts to ensure an accurate portrayal of South Africa as an attractive investment destination (The only coverage South Africa receives on a continual basis relates to crime, violence and the flushing out of old wounds by the Truth and Reconciliation Commission.);
- interact and negotiate in the boardrooms of leading multinationals, seeking to attract these firms to invest;
- develop and pass specific pieces of legislation designed to attract FDI, as well as stimulate domestic investment;
- organise regular international symposiums and conferences;
- appear frequently in public, in the world's financial capitals;
- regularly take advantage of the contacts offered by their own nationals who are residing or working abroad;
- develop co-ordinated marketing material which can be distributed to influential business leaders (Material includes detailed case studies of existing foreign investors who have been successful.);
- organise regular foreign investment missions abroad which are accompanied by leading foreign investors who are eager to tell their story as to why they chose to invest in South Africa;
- appoint individuals with private sector experience to head divisions in overseas embassies and consulates to proactively foster FDI.

The increasing trend by governments is to appoint Cabinet Ministers with strong private sector backgrounds and links. A recent example of this trend can be seen in the UK, where Tony

Blair appointed Lords Sainsbury and Simon as junior ministers in the Department of Trade and Industry.

In the majority of successful countries today, the Minister of Finance is tasked with focusing largely on budgetary issues such as government spending priorities, while the Minister of Trade and Industry deals almost exclusively with trade-related issues such as negotiations regarding the World Trade Organisation, fostering bilateral trade agreements, and streamlining customs and import duties. In South Africa this is also true, but these ministries are still expected to focus on attracting FDI. Compared to the effort and energy devoted to FDI by many other countries, South Africa's efforts are poor and *ad hoc* at best. It is unrealistic to expect to successfully compete for FDI given our Cabinet's current structure.

Table 3 *South African growth, world comparison*

	Period	Investment (% of GDP)	GDP growth (% per annum)
Thailand	1980–90	27.9	8.0
Malaysia	1980–90	30.8	6.0
Indonesia	1980–90	30.3	5.6
South Africa	1980–90	7.7	1.5
Chile	1986–91	22.7	6.4
South Africa	1990–93	20.7	–0.4

In comparison with other emerging economies over the last decade, South Africa grew more slowly and invested less.

According to a recent IMF paper, for South Africa to even sustain a GDP growth rate of 3.5%, requires raising the ratio of investment to GDP from its present level of under 20% to under 27%. For a sustainable 6% growth rate as envisaged by the government's own Gear plan, the ratio would have to be closer to 35% of the GDP.

With the complete relaxation of exchange controls in sight and the expected outflow of pent-up capital from South Africa (mostly among institutions and companies), the need to attract FDI is now more critical than before. Many of South Africa's largest companies are eager to expand and diversify abroad. When they reduce their investment plans within South Africa, FDI will need to pick up the slack and play an increasingly important role.

Accounting for FDI in South Africa

While FDI floods into Latin American and Asian developing nations, South Africa received insufficient foreign capital inflows in 1996 to even cover our current account deficit. Such recent events as the rand's mid-1998 crash show just how vulnerable our capital account (on the balance of payments) is to a sudden change in sentiment. Those in South Africa who are celebrating because they thought the rand had improved somewhat during 1997, are no different to the patient who celebrates because only one of his legs has been amputated. Over time the rand is headed only one way — down — while privatisation policies remain muddled (selling off 30% of Telkom is not full-blooded privatisation), and the goal posts for eliminating exchange controls continue to move.

Miserable FDI performance

According to the September 1996 Reserve Bank Quarterly Bulletin, during the first six months of 1996 a total of R7.32 bn long-term capital movements entered South Africa, of which R7.1 bn comprised portfolio flows into the capital and equity markets. Thus just R220 m (US$50 m) of net FDI was recorded. Compare this with Brazil, where $15.8 bn was received in the first six months of 1996, of which $12.4 bn was FDI. South Africa's FDI was barely positive during this period. Mexico, which suffered its worst ever currency crisis in late 1994, still attracted $7 bn of FDI in 1995.

Without a significant inflow of FDI to restock our miserably low foreign exchange reserves (which are lower even than Botswana's), South Africa will not be able to sustain its current trade position (especially given South Africa's propensity to import) without another severe devaluation of the rand. FDI is critical, therefore, both for employment creation and for our economy in general.

Relying on devaluation alone to boost exports is insufficient in the South African context. The levels of exports remain disappointing when one considers that South African goods are now some 60% cheaper to world buyers compared to 1996. South Africa's exporters have not raised their export levels to compensate for the rand's devaluation over the past three years.

Gear and the capital-intensive nature of business in South Africa

The clear shift towards capital-intensive plants in South Africa is sufficient to dispel the optimism evident in the Gear plan, which projects huge employment creation in South Africa over the next few years. With unit labour costs up by an annual average of almost 14% between 1985 and 1995, and expected increases of no less than 8–10% between 1995 and 2000, South Africa remains an expensive labour market given our low productivity levels. The capital stock per worker rose from an adjusted R90 000 in 1970 (using 1995 prices), to approximately R170 000 in 1995.

According to many South African economists Gear is not convincing in presenting evidence that a growth rate of 6% can be maintained or that 400 000 new jobs per year can be sustained for any length of time. According to the late Ronnie Bethlehem, "sudden growth literally comes out of nowhere in the last 18 months of the Gear plan." Since the world is an uncertain place, any growth will depend on global circumstances in four years' time. How realistic can Gear really be in creating jobs that far into the future? Gear clearly needs to be reworked and rethought, given our present circumstances of exhorbitant interest rates and a depressed currency.

Without significant doses of FDI injected into new production capacity, it is unlikely that any major job creation will result even in the event of achieving a GDP growth of 4.5% by the turn of the century.

Gear provides very little fiscal stimulus to attract FDI, besides meagre tax holidays which few companies have leapt at. Lower interest rates are among the leading reasons indicated for sustaining a growth of 400 000 new jobs per year. Clearly a low cost of credit is not in the offing in the near future. Gear represents an employment growth rate of 2.9% or 1.35 million jobs over five years (up to the year 2000). Given the labour force growth rate of 2.5% a year, it is clear that such a strategy will have little impact on cutting unemployment.

Furthermore, Gear envisages that 25% of the new jobs will be created through accelerated infrastructural development and the maintenance of public works programmes. These programmes are generally short term and will not provide long-term employment.

South Africa's disincentives to foreign investors

Many countries, such as Malaysia, Dubai, Chile, Hungary, Ireland, the Czech Republic, Brazil and Singapore, offer numerous attractive investment incentives to lure FDI. This has led to fierce competition.

Foreign investors are therefore not waiting for South Africa to get its act together, but are rather going elsewhere, to countries offering more attractive and comprehensive incentive packages.

South Africa currently ranks poorly in comparison studies with other countries' investment-friendly tax systems. In fact, South Africa's high effective corporate tax rate ranks it by many accounts as an unfriendly tax climate for foreign investors.

If South Africa ignores the international rules of the game it will remain at a competitive disadvantage in attracting foreign investment. Foreign investment is vital not only because it contributes much-needed capital, but because of the quality of such capital, since imported capital for the purposes of long-term investment is in most cases technologically advanced and is coupled with international know-how and skills that are lacking in South Africa.

Tax incentives

Even our so-called tax holidays have not been well conceived. These incentives do not take into account international tax rules and are, therefore, in many cases not as attractive as they may appear on paper from a South African perspective. Multinationals based in countries operating foreign tax credit systems are unable to fully benefit from our tax holidays, since their home countries still require them to pay a certain rate of tax on worldwide profits. The point is that the most well-intentioned incentives will be totally neutralised in the foreign investor's home country if they are not carefully thought out. If nothing else, South Africa will forgo tax revenue only for it to be passed on to the home country.

Other concerns foreigners have relate to the South African tax system, which penalises companies wishing to distribute dividends because of its Secondary Tax on Companies (STC), as well as its relatively high withholding taxes.

The STC is another example of the disincentives our country offers to foreigners. The STC is not recognised by many industrialised countries, thereby limiting the usefulness of our tax treaties with these countries. Most countries' tax treaties with

South Africa have no provision for the STC, a tax they do not understand. Foreign companies would rather take their business somewhere else where they will incur a far lower tax burden. The current Gear tax incentives are also too onerous and impractical, resulting in few takers. The incentive period falls far short of the long-term incentives on offer elsewhere around the world.

Tourism is Not a Panacea for Foreign Exchange and Jobs

Although tourism has been counted on to build up the country's foreign exchange, the high crime rate, "slack service and high prices in [our] hotels, coupled with a hopelessly inadequate tourism [promotional] budget are factors threatening to bring the country's tourism honeymoon to an abrupt end" (*Finance Week*, 22 November, 1996). Two recent mentions of South Africa as a tourist destination, one in the Los Angeles Times newspaper and the second in America's leading travel magazine *Condé Nast Traveller* indicated that Johannesburg has become the "murder capital of the world". Amongst other notable recommendations in *Condé Nast*, tourists were advised to contact the newly established tourism police taskforce in Gauteng for protection. Tourism is a very fickle business, especially when it relies on foreigners whose perceptions of one's country can change in an instant, following a news broadcast.

In the long term there is little question of South Africa's potential of becoming a popular tourist destination for the international traveller, since at present the sector only accounts for 4% of the country's GDP against a world average of 10%. Tremendous capacity exists for growth, and tourism can be expected to employ many more than just one out of 70 workers in South Africa: the world average is one out of ten workers. However, costs and crime must be kept under control, if our country is ever to attain the world averages. South Africa is a long haul destination and travellers require good value for money. Close to 1 million new tourism-related jobs can be created within a decade.

Time for a New Approach

South Africa clearly requires a new attitude if it is to attract large-scale FDI. It should concern us that many of Germany's largest companies, which have always been favourably disposed towards

South Africa, recently indicated their disinclination to invest in South Africa in the near future. These companies — including BASF, Mannesmann, Krupp, Bayer, Siemens and Lufthansa — already have operations in South Africa, but are unwilling to make additional commitments until they see a stronger economy and a sincere commitment on the part of South African business and government to open up the country to free and fair competition. If our best friends are holding back, most potential first-time investors in South Africa will continue to err on the side of non-investment until they feel more secure about the country's economic future.

Given the high growth rates in such economies as Brazil, Ireland, the Czech Republic and China, there is little urgency in the boardrooms of the world's leading companies to risk investing in South Africa where crime, an unstable currency and tough labour unions stand at the welcoming gate.

Facing Up to Reality

Like it or not we are not at the centre of the universe — the continent to which we are attached affects perceptions of us. Most foreigners remain uninformed about the differences between South Africa and the rest of the continent, and just lump us together with the rest of Africa, with its unfortunate history of miserable economic and political performance over the past three decades. We need to realise that we are a long way from the world's leading industrialised markets, located as we are at the very bottom of Africa.

We will have to be very aggressive if we are serious about attracting the necessary large-scale direct long-term foreign investment. Just copying other countries' investment or tax incentives will no longer do. Perceptions are important in attracting this sort of long-term capital, and the lack of progress made on the privatisation and exchange control front is disturbing to foreign executives who might otherwise have a far more positive impression of South Africa.

Our Labour Relations Act also does little in the way of encouraging foreign investment, weighted as it is in favour of the large trade union groups. A co-ordinated strategy is what is needed. This cannot be done in isolation.

Tax and investment incentives, labour policies, scrapping of exchange control, boosting exports, easy access to work and residence permits for foreign investors, clamping down on the out-of-control crime wave sweeping the country, and streamlining bureaucracy — these must all be tackled if South Africa is to ever enjoy the level of long-term direct foreign investment so urgently required to generate jobs and foreign exchange reserves.

A New Strategy Required

The government's key strategy for improving the lot of South Africans, the Reconstruction and Development Programme (RDP), quickly became a bureaucratic black hole into which all the country's dirty laundry was thrown — from trade policy to housing, water and electricity needs.

As a result, fewer than 5 000 houses were built by July 1995, although 250 000 had been promised by that date. Within government there is a critical need for greater co-ordination of fiscal and economic policies. In addition, co-ordination is severely lacking amongst departments regarding the implementation of new policies. Funds allocated to the old RDP Ministry were allocated far too soon to be utilised. Our country could have benefited from allocating these funds elsewhere in the interim, such as to paying off our debts. The funds were not utilised for more than a year in some cases.

The RDP was meant to be the ANC's New Deal — it was to deliver 1 million homes, electricity to 2.5 million, and piped water to 1 million in five years.

The overzealous so-called RDP Ministry was shown to be an unwieldy bureaucracy; it has since lost its funding and been abolished and subsumed within the Deputy President's Office. The planned increase of R2.5 bn per year that was to be awarded to the RDP appears to have disappeared from the fiscal plans, thank goodness.

Losing Out

Our uncompetitive policies on foreign investment have recently driven away at least two potentially huge investors. Taiwan's Chinese Petroleum Company was proposing to build a R10 bn petrochemical operation in South Africa, but ultimately decided to locate it in Thailand. The Korean conglomerate Daewoo and Anglo American had signed a R600 m joint venture to manufacture television tubes, but our government rejected Daewoo's insistence on 60% tariff protection in the initial years, so Daewoo took its capital to Vietnam's free trade zones, where it is now building a second plant for this purpose.

According to Anglo American, government wanted the joint venture to disclose what additional plans it had for investment, a request impossible to comply with. It is useful to recall that in every country Daewoo has entered, it has always followed up its initial investment with a second major investment within a year. Perhaps even more importantly, many smaller Asian companies follow the lead set by their regional conglomerates. In other words, the fact that Daewoo has a plant in Vietnam will influence other Asian companies when the time comes for new investment and they need to decide where to locate their plants.

Current Foreign Investment Performance

Since July 1991, when the 1986 ban on new US investment was lifted by President Bush, the number of US companies with non-equity links in South Africa has jumped from 184 to 448. However, this is not the sort of investment that South Africa really needs to create jobs. Most of these companies are still hedging their bets, rather than capitalising a South African subsidiary. No serious investment is made when non-equity links exist. Even the manufacturing investment which has taken place has been largely capital intensive, creating few new long-term jobs.

The real test is how many new companies from the US come to invest in South Africa, by which I mean those which have not had a previous presence in South Africa, and which do not have the advantage of a possible buyback agreement sitting in their lawyers' offices following their original disinvestment.

The biggest beneficiaries over the past six to seven years of new investment in South Africa have been the local South African management teams which had previously bought out the US companies. These local managers' investments have now been reacquired by the same US companies they previously bought out, but at a substantial premium. Goodyear, Ford and IBM are but a few examples of this. As indicated previously, the vast majority of long-term foreign investments are passive portfolio flows.

Size of the Local Market

Although South Africa has a large population of some 42 million, in some respects the domestic market remains small for many would-be foreign investors interested in developing their manufacturing operations. Although Australia has a population of just 15 million, its GDP is more than five times South Africa's. As a result, Australia's per capita GDP is 14 times greater than South Africa's, providing would-be foreign investors with a greater domestic market on which to base a manufacturing operation.

Concerns of Foreign Investors

Foreign investors view with suspicion the tightly controlled South African market with its web of interlocking shareholdings and directorships. The takeover-proof nature of South Africa's major corporations concerns foreigners, who believe that South African management has less accountability to owners of companies than is the case in more industrialised nations. According to Sir Alan Walters (Margaret Thatcher's former private economic adviser) and George Guise, "[South Africa's] pyramidal or interlocking shareholdings lock out external shareholders from any influence over management and protect their management from any true accountability to shareholders" (*Forbes Magazine*, 1996).

"Few managements in South Africa fear a takeover bid," according to Walters and Guise. They conclude: "The main task of a reforming government must be to insist on the disentanglement of the crossholdings of the conglomerates and the opening up of South Africa to foreign as well as domestic corporate raiders." This, they say, will help bring South African industry in line with the more efficient capitalist economies, and also awaken the sleeping assets buried within the conglomerate structures.

Constraints on Boosting Foreign Investment in South Africa

South Africa's case is complicated by the fact that the trade unions' relationship with the ANC means that the latter is continually striving for the betterment of its union friends. Continuing along this path will effectively price South Africa out of the manufacturing market altogether, if it has not already done so. Even at existing wage rates, South Africa cannot compete with the low wages found in South East Asia and China.

The unfortunate lack of interest in foreign investment in South Africa from the US and other parts of the world will continue to limit the job creation and economic growth prospects of our country. In order to attract long-term direct "bricks-and-mortar" foreign investment, South Africa must begin to compete more effectively for foreign investment dollars which continue to flow to such countries as China, Hungary, Chile, Ireland, Taiwan, Singapore, Thailand and Malaysia. These countries all have attractive incentive-style legislation that draws foreign investment that might otherwise go elsewhere.

Welcoming Foreign Investment

The hard truth is that South Africa is not at the top of foreign investors' shopping lists for places to build new labour-intensive factories and projects. To attract such foreign companies, the country must meet world market standards which are more demanding than they were 30 years ago. Today that means providing attractive features such as guaranteed low tax holidays, relocation allowances, training incentives and much more.

The vast majority of foreign companies would not consider South Africa unless such tax incentives, training subsidies and other fiscal benefits were included in their package of attractions.

The multiplier effect

The more foreign companies establish plants and factories in South Africa, the more workers gain employment, and the greater the multiplier effect will be as new employees begin to play an active role in the country's economy. Sizeable numbers of new workers will increase domestic demand for goods and services, and taxes on their wages will significantly add to government revenues. Each new job adds vibrancy to the economy.

Cost to government

Government is not likely to enjoy revenues from these companies if it does not offer initial fiscal benefits. The government enjoys a net benefit after a very short period of time, when it begins to receive increased tax payments from these foreign companies both directly (as certain tax benefits recede) and, more importantly, indirectly, through additional workers and supplies purchased from local companies, which in turn expand.

Threat of our neighbours

If South Africa does not begin to offer such incentives, it may well find its own companies hopping across the border to Maputo or Walvis Bay to begin manufacturing there, drawn by a wide range of tax and other fiscal benefits, and free of the ever more demanding South African labour unions. As stated previously, for a foreign investor to set up in South Africa primarily for export purposes, its inputs will need to be as competitive as any other world player in its field. The cost of its inputs and raw materials must be no higher than anywhere else. Duty-free imports of raw materials and other inputs necessary for the production of finished goods destined for export are therefore critical if we are to encourage foreign investors to use South Africa as an export base, as is the case of most countries that are successful in attracting foreign direct investment (FDI).

The Result of Free Trade

Although government may fear the loss of import tariff revenues, such revenues are more than compensated for by the overall increase in economic activity generated by large-scale foreign investment. It is worth noting that the government has effectively been paying out billions of rands annually to the largest South African companies, as part of two export promotion programmes. If it could afford to do so for so many years, why not give away the same amount in tariff reductions in the form of an Export Processing Zone (see Chapter 8)?

Benefits of the High Road (EPZs) for the Local Industrialist and Trade Unionist

The South African industrialist and trade unionist will ultimately be the major beneficiaries of a government policy which actively encourages foreign investment in South Africa. The unionist will benefit from an increased labour pool from which to source his growing membership lists and powerbase. The industrialist will enjoy the transfer of new technology brought to South Africa by foreign investors. Through joint ventures with foreign-owned manufacturers, local industrialists will benefit from foreign expertise and technologies not yet implemented in South Africa. By becoming more productive and export-driven, industry will ultimately improve its margins and its ability to compete.

Competing on the World Stage

It is clear that a large proportion of South Africa's exporters find it difficult to compete with international rivals due to higher input costs, as a result of duties and surcharges on imports and the emphasis that is placed on the use of local inputs. It is clear that South Africa's trade policy should be geared to eliminating these obstacles for exporters and thus enabling them to obtain access to high quality inputs at world prices (i.e. duty free). This should not be done at the expense of economically viable producers who supply the local market. The export of merchandise should be liberalised through the total eradication of import duties. The bureaucratic import duty rebate system should be dramatically simplified, allowing importers to receive inputs which go into the manufacture of exported duty free products.

Conclusion: Export-driven Industrialisation

South Africa needs to generate substantially more foreign exchange by developing an export-driven culture. The best of both worlds would be to couple such export-led industrialisation with labour-intensive manufacturing in industries where large, untapped export markets exist. By so doing we could begin to soak up unemployment while also generating foreign exchange earnings, and ensuring a healthier balance of payments and a stronger and more stable rand.

In the meantime our country's policies are to reward capital investment with various tax breaks to the detriment of hiring additional labour. Why are we encouraging factories to invest in more and more capital-intensive goods, rather than encouraging investment in human resources?

Tax allowances for land and buildings, wear and tear allowances for plant and equipment, in addition to accelerated depreciation allowances, all combine to make it increasingly attractive and tax efficient for our companies to discard workers in favour of new machinery. The new labour levy of 1% of payroll only adds to the capital-intensive bias.

We need to invest in our people with training and education. Government's policies should reflect this. Incentives can be easily created so that an investment in labour proves far more rewarding than spending small fortunes on assets that have a limited life and may become obsolete a few years down the road. Numerous countries have implemented labour-intensive incentives which have helped stimulate companies to hire more workers rather than to build a machine to replace workers. For instance, tax credits should be considered for companies who hire additional workers.

We can no longer be complacent. In order to create an export-led recovery, wages in South Africa should only be allowed to rise dramatically when this is in concert with increases in productivity. It would certainly help if our labour rates were more competitive with those of other countries with similar economic and productivity standings.

To encourage firms to export they require competitively priced raw materials, machines and other inputs, many of which must be imported. This calls for an essentially low or zero trade protection policy — not that different to the successful free trade zones and export processing zones found in many of the world's fastest growing economies. Government has only belatedly and half-heartedly discussed the establishment of industrial development zones. This is some three years after my involvement in the creation of Namibia's export processing zone, at which time I begged the South African government to consider the concept seriously. Alas, it appears that government is not interested in creating full-on free trade zones.

We must spread the ownership of wealth throughout our country, in order to ensure that as many members of our society as possible benefit from this necessary change and the related economic growth. Talk is cheap, though. We need to get on with privatising many of our state-run enterprises. Employee stock ownership plans should be more widely instituted in the private sector, and profit-sharing schemes could provide the necessary incentives to encourage greater productivity. We cannot rely on the IMF and World Bank to solve our problems. In fact, their advice and assistance remains somewhat textbook-oriented and has not solved many other African countries' problems. Textbook answers are no longer good enough for South Africa. We need to understand what made countries such as Malaysia grow by an average of 8% annually over the past eight years. How is it that such a country (whose economy was also at one time mostly based on mineral resources), transformed itself into one of the world's most successful and competitive power houses, largely based on labour-intensive, export-driven manufacturing, which actively seeks out and campaigns for direct foreign investment?

Numerous developing countries have grown their export-led industrialisation programmes by providing incentives to foreign manufacturers based almost exclusively on the level of exports they subsequently generate. The beneficiaries of such incentive programmes are not only foreign investors who are almost solely interested in manufacturing for export purposes, but the countries themselves, which benefit from job creation, a healthy trade balance, more revenue raised from taxes paid by additional workers, and greater taxes paid by local suppliers who service foreign manufacturers. Such foreign investors are not interested in threatening local market players, since local markets are normally too small and undeveloped for them.

South Africa's policy-makers must realise that our domestic market capacity remains little more than a blip on a foreign investor's radar screen. To keep South Africa's economic size in perspective, its economy is no bigger than that of the city of Los Angeles. Any of numerous potential US manufacturers in South Africa — such as Reebok, which might plan to manufacture millions of its sport shoes here — would view the local market as less important than the tax, trade and customs duty agreements it might benefit from if it used a South African factory as a suitable base for the distribution of its products to numerous larger markets around the globe. At an average price of R350 per takkie, it is questionable whether Reebok or LA Gear would expect to sell more than 5% of such a factory's output to South Africans.

CHAPTER SEVEN

Export Processing Options

Wₜ WALVIS BAY NOW DEVELOPING into a growing and successful Export Processing Zone (EPZ), South Africa would do well to seriously consider enabling legislation to permit various planned regional EPZ projects. Failure to do so at national level will tempt South African industries to invest across their borders in neighbouring EPZ (and free trade zone) projects. Namibia's EPZ, in just its first two years of operation, has already attracted more than 50 companies from around the world (representing R600 m of new projects), and is at present targeting South African exporters. Advantages for South African exporters wishing to relocate include wages that average only half and in some cases a third of those paid in South Africa for identical work; the absence of corporate income taxes, import and customs duties; as well as free trade access to both the European Union and South Africa. The main criterion for being granted EPZ status is that at least 70% of the company's production should be export oriented.

The EPZ concept may be one of the most effective ways of attracting international investors to South Africa, creating job opportunities for great numbers of the unemployed, building a secondary industrial base from which to foster further economic growth, and at the same time strengthening our trade balance. The transfer of foreign know-how and better management skills, improved technology, expanded exports and foreign exchange earnings, and increased productivity will result from the successful implementation of an EPZ structure in various parts of South Africa.

Definition

EPZs are special industrial estates which have as their purpose the production of exports that are physically and administratively located outside the host country's tariff and currency barriers. In order to challenge global competition successfully, EPZ manufacturers must be free to acquire their inputs at the lowest possible world prices (i.e. duty free) and without foreign exchange constraints.

Local Involvement

Past experience with EPZs shows that their presence fosters the growth of local input suppliers, especially if backward integration between export-oriented producers and local suppliers is officially encouraged through appropriate incentives. The long-term result has often been the transformation of entire sectors or even a whole country (Mauritius, Hong Kong) into the equivalent of a giant export-driven EPZ. This is because as the efficiency of the export sector increases, the balance of payments constraints become less rigid, creating room for liberalising tariff protection and promoting a duty-free culture.

Opposition

Historically, opposition to the formation of EPZs stems from those with vested interests in tariff-protected industries, including factory owners, organised labour, administrative bureaucrats and status quo politicians. These groups all inherently know that major adjustments are required by their home-grown factories before they will be able to compete in the open market. The owners fear losing their capital investments in increasingly idle plants, unionised labour fears having to rely on productivity improvements for raises, the bureaucrats administering a host of complex tariffs and duties fear losing their jobs, and the politicians loathe losing the proceeds from high tariffs and duties. The real beneficiaries of a new export and import dispensation will be consumers and the jobless — the majority of South Africans.

In the case of South Africa, EPZ opponents cite pilferage and smuggling as reasons why EPZs are impractical, and object to the preferences extended to those operating within the EPZ as unfair. Pilferage and stealing have been controlled even in developing societies where EPZs have been introduced — the Dominican Republic, Sri Lanka, Malaysia and China.

The desire for smuggling goods across the border is removed when there is no financial benefit. The lower our import duties become, the less smuggling there will be. Entire countries which now operate as free trade zones, such as Hong Kong, Mauritius and Singapore, experience little or no smuggling of legitimate manufactured goods, since there are no savings offered by smuggling duty-free goods into these countries. By contrast, at present, South Africa has one of the highest rates of cross-border smuggling anywhere in the world — as a direct result of some of our draconian import duties, designed to protect entrenched interests in South Africa.

Existence of EPZs

The truth is that EPZs in a more convoluted form have already existed in South Africa for a select few, and have provided and continue to provide support for the very same businessmen who are now against the idea. Particular industries and products, including motor vehicles, television sets, and textiles and clothing, have been able to enjoy an EPZ environment through the state's rebate system, which effectively allowed these companies to pay little or no import duties on their inputs. The only requirement was that a certain amount of local content was necessary (40% on average). In the case of the textiles and clothing industry, the requirement was that exports account for only 2.5% of total turnover in order for a business to benefit from the rebates on import duties.

Although import duties on built-up cars have been reduced from 115% in 1993 to 61% in 1996, and are expected to eventually be phased down to just below 30%, the ultimate goal still affords significant protection to our local car manufacturers, many of whom could not compete on the world market. In addition, import duties for automotive products can be offset by export credits on a rand-for-rand basis — creating a special dispensation for the automotive industry similar to an EPZ, although more cumbersome and bureaucratic. The offset means that the more these manufacturers export, the more effective they will be in reducing the current import tariff to zero. This scheme is referred to as the Motor Industry Development Programme, and caters of course to this special interest group, and not to a broad range of foreign or local private sector investors, or to the South African population.

Other common arguments are that the playing field for those companies not operating within an EPZ would not be level, despite the fact that it has been an uneven playing field for all those industries not afforded the same benefits as vehicle and TV manufacturers.

EPZs are worthy of creation in South African regions that are currently underdeveloped, and offer a far better chance to attract long-term foreign investment into the country than any other idea currently being proposed by the unions, the South African Chamber of Business or government. Sadly the 1998 jobs summit never had any intention of featuring such realistic job creation proposals.

Expansion of epzs Continues

There can be no doubt about the positive effects that the introduction of free zone manufacturing designed for export has had on developing countries. It has laid the basis for much of the success enjoyed by numerous Asian and Latin American economies. Its benefits to industrialised societies are less frequently noted.

Today consumers worldwide take for granted freely available inexpensive items, from clothing to toaster ovens, that are remarkably well made in low-tax EPZs.

The motivation for EPZ legislation in host countries includes much-needed employment and the desire to earn foreign exchange. EPZs are the stepping stones to an export-driven industrialisation process through which host countries hope to attain a better standard of living for their citizens, who increasingly have the right to vote.

South Africa, with 6 million unemployed voters, is desperate for long-term capital and job creation. According to our Minister of Finance: "South Africa must move to manufacturing if it is to prosper." While this is true, labour productivity in South Africa has continued to hide behind the protective barrier of import substitution tariffs, and not surprisingly is viewed as relatively unproductive, expensive and not up to world standards. Exposing unproductive labour to open competition may well be the best way to unlock the potential productivity gains that exist among South Africa's workers who at present may see little reason to improve efficiency.

The choice will be between gradually expanding exposure as a function of World Trade Organisation-mandated tariff reductions, or more immediate exposure through an expanding industrial segment of EPZs located as a function of economic need.

On account of the disproportionate size of our economy relative to the rest of Southern Africa, the South African decision will influence an unusually great number of lives. A discussion document in the form of a draft EPZ Act has been circulating in Pretoria since November 1993, and while there is strong interest in EPZs at regional level, central government inaction on this issue is not likely to lead to EPZ legislation in the near future.

Unknowingly, government's recently introduced tax incentives have moved the country one step closer to adopting an incentive-style EPZ.

EPZ-style incentives

- Imports into the EPZ are duty free and free from customs duties so long as the goods remain inside the EPZ area — this includes plant, machinery and raw materials.
- There is exemption from export levies where these are applicable.
- Zero or very low company tax rates apply; other tax benefits, such as training allowances and relocation grants, are made available where deemed proper.
- Exemption from VAT is permitted.
- There is unrestricted transfer of dividends, royalties and interest.
- The maintenance of foreign currency accounts with registered banks is permitted.
- Depreciation and wear and tear benefits normally apply.
- There are corporate tax incentives (credits) for new workers hired.

Success Stories of EPZs

Over the past decade, an increasing number of less-developed countries have embarked on incentive programmes in order to encourage foreign investors to manufacture and assemble products in their countries. Currently in excess of 220 EPZs are in operation throughout the developing world, more than 100 are under construction, and at least another 50 are in the planning stage.

Total employment in such zones currently exceeds 2 million workers. Exports from zones in developing countries are currently estimated to total between $18 bn and $20 bn.

Recent examples of significant EPZ growth can be found in Costa Rica, where employment grew fivefold between 1986 and 1990, while in the Dominican Republic it tripled, and in Jamaica it doubled. Five of the eight EPZs that employ 30 000 or more

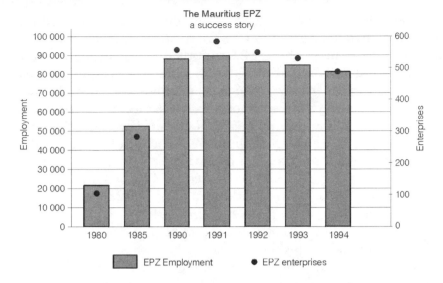

Figure 21 *The Mauritius Export Processing Zone: a success story*

workers are in Asia, while the others are in Mauritius, the Dominican Republic and Mexico.

If one compares the foreign exchange earned by successful EPZs through their growth in exports, the most impressive EPZ growth worldwide occurred in Mauritius, where EPZ exports grew sixfold

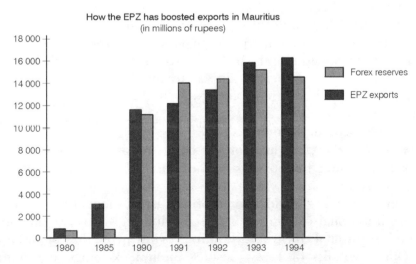

Figure 22 *How the EPZ has boosted exports in Mauritius (in millions of rupees)*

between 1983 and 1989, to US$600 m; the Dominican Republic, where EPZ exports trebled to US$710 m between 1986 and 1989; and the Philippines, where EPZ exports doubled over the same period. Average economic growth of 6% has been recorded by the Mauritius EPZ sector over the past decade. Currently 91 000 workers are employed in some 564 EPZ factories in Mauritius.

In the case of Taiwan's three EPZs, between 1966 and 1980 the foreign exchange earnings of the EPZs accounted for nearly 70% of Taiwan's total foreign exchange earnings. During that 14-year period, these three EPZs also accounted for 48% of Taiwan's trade surpluses, resulting in a net trade surplus of US$2.6 bn.

If a foreign investor wants to set up in South Africa primarily for export purposes, his inputs will need to be as competitive as any other world player in his field. As such, the cost of inputs and raw materials must be no higher than elsewhere. Duty-free importation of raw materials and other inputs necessary for the production of finished goods destined for export is therefore critical if we are to encourage foreign investors to use South Africa as an export base.

Role of an EPZ

The usual objectives of EPZs are to earn foreign exchange and to create employment through exports of manufactured goods. An EPZ can achieve this by attracting local and foreign investors who bring with them a package of management, technology and marketing skills, along with international connections.

From the government's point of view, EPZs serve to increase industrial development and to attract new manufacturing companies. One of the key aims is usually to replace an import substitution policy. Important goals to be achieved by EPZs include:

- increased employment;
- increased exports and foreign currency earnings; and
- further investments outside the zone — by suppliers of zone operators.

Throughout the world a common feature of successful EPZs has been a national commitment to removing legislative, regulatory and institutional constraints holding back the free flow of trade.

Other benefits of EPZs, besides foreign exchange earnings, employment and spillover effects, include the training, skills and know-how acquired by locally owned firms, the advantage of foreign investors and buyers using the local economy as a source for inputs, and the upgrading of the capabilities of local suppliers and officials in response to exacting foreign demands.

Peter Drucker coined the term "production sharing" to explain world economic integration of the production process by stages. According to the management guru and author, "Production sharing offers developing countries their only real opportunity to provide the jobs and skills their people need."

By opting for a development policy oriented towards exports, while offering companies from industrialised countries a reduction in their costs of production, EPZs are among the best mechanisms to achieve this goal.

Ingredients for Success

One of the key ingredients for the success of an EPZ is to have as many favourable multilateral and bilateral trade and tax agreements as possible — which have the effect of providing operators in the EPZ with the benefit of lower import and customs duties into the destination country for their exported goods. Trade and tax agreements can generally be more favourably concluded *before* the establishment of low tax jurisdictions, rather than afterwards. For instance, Cyprus, as a non-aligned state during the super-power struggle, and with a mostly agrarian economy, was able to negotiate an extensive range of unusually favourable bilateral trade and tax agreements which it would not be able to duplicate now that its economy is more developed, and it has become an important international offshore financial centre.

Employment within EPZs will be stimulated through the processing of goods for re-export to third countries. The establishment of light manufacturing factories as well as warehouses to package and store products are required. At the port facility (often called a free port) the breaking of bulk and the manning of a well-developed cargo handling facility will require labour. These free ports play an important role as transhipment centres and have been introduced in Singapore, Hong Kong, the US, Mauritius and a number of other successful countries. The free port in essence does not impose any duties or taxes on goods that are stored, repackaged or assembled in the designated areas of the port. Cape Town, Port Elizabeth, Durban, East London and Richard's Bay are perfect locations for such free ports.

If South Africa truly wishes to become the African manufacturing base of choice for foreign companies wishing to export to the rest of the subcontinent, why do we fail to heed the lessons of others? It is truly astounding. It would indeed be a tragedy for South Africa if we were to allow Walvis Bay and Maputo to take the lead as free ports and EPZs, and firmly establish themselves as transhipment and export bases for the African continent.

It is important to remember that an EPZ on its own has limited attractiveness. A well-developed financial services infrastructure, including high-calibre international banks, is necessary to multiply the usefulness and advantages which an EPZ would be able to offer.

In many cases foreign investors will be far more willing to establish a plant in an EPZ if given the benefit of using a foreign currency account in the host country. This limits their currency exposure.

Licence-based or Territory-based?

Increasingly EPZs are becoming licence-based. For example, both Namibia and Mauritius effectively operate EPZs that are non-territorial, but rather licenced. Experience shows that licensed EPZs offer a greater opportunity for local participation, because local suppliers need not deal with the geographic constraints of an EPZ behind an access-controlled barrier or in a remote corner of a country.

Companies generally qualify for an EPZ licence by meeting a certain level of exports (e.g. 70% or more of their sales). Mauritius has actually abolished the 70% requirement and allows EPZ operators to sell as much as they like to the local market, provided they pay duties and taxes equivalent to domestic importers.

Case Studies of EPZs

In stark contrast, Jamaica, which continues to operate three fenced-in EPZs, excludes almost any local participation, because of the non-availability of foreign exchange to local people and a myriad of customs regulations that preclude many businesses in Jamaica from becoming suppliers to the EPZ. *Recent studies indicate that while EPZ employment in Taiwan (1990: 75 000), Malaysia (105 000), and Mauritius (90 000) has grown dramatically throughout the past decade, in Jamaica the corresponding figure of 14 000 has barely changed since 1985.*

Employment in the Mauritius EPZ as a percentage of total employment in the country grew from 12% in 1983 to more than 40% in 1992.

In terms of the number of firms operating in these respective EPZs, figures for the Dominican Republic more than doubled between 1986 and 1990 to 313 firms. In Mauritius the number grew from 100 firms in 1980 to more than 560 firms in 1998. This compares with an increase of just 24 firms in Jamaica between 1980 and 1990.

Results of Licence-based EPZs

Where an EPZ is not geographically restricted, more linkages with the local economy are fostered. *All cases of successful EPZs indicate that licence-based EPZs result in a more mutually beneficial coexistence and more linkages between domestic suppliers and EPZ operators.*

Integration with the Local Economy

It is generally agreed that the multiplier effect of EPZ operators on the macroeconomy will far outweigh any tax revenue lost due to a lower EPZ tax rate. This multiplier effect helps stimulate the local economy and provides a new and larger revenue source for the government's tax coffers.

This generally occurs in two forms:

- As new operators set up in a country's EPZ they will require local workers. This growth in employment opportunities leads to new income tax takings on the wages of the workers, and government enjoys a new source of revenue. The workers are also likely to stimulate the economy by having greater purchasing power.
- The more enterprises that are attracted to the EPZ, the greater the probability of increased backward linkages between these enterprises and local suppliers. *In the case of Taiwan and Mauritius, for every EPZ enterprise there exist four to five local suppliers, which has helped boost local employment by creating a greater demand for goods and supplies in those countries.* As these local businesses grow they will pay increased taxes, and hire additional staff who themselves will be liable for income tax and whose new source of income increases the

level of domestic purchasing power and local demand for goods — stimulating the economy and generating economic growth.

Multiplier Effect of EPZs

As such, the tax revenue generated directly from the EPZ enterprises themselves is the least important factor in the multiplier effect. As in the case of the most successful countries with EPZs, the more EPZ operators are drawn to the country in question, the larger the multiplier effect.

By instituting tax incentives as part of the Gear programme, government has indicated its understanding of the principle of the multiplier effect created by new employment opportunities. The question is why does government then remain so vehemently opposed to an export processing incentive programme that will have the effect of stimulating dramatic amounts of new foreign investment, increased usage of South African port facilities, and by implication many new jobs and badly needed foreign exchange? Successful export processing in South Africa would lead to a dramatic turnaround in the country's unhealthy trade deficit. The only sword in the government's armoury to fight this current account deficit is a weak rand and high interest rates (to keep passive foreign investment coming in). These are not adequate solutions.

EPZs, by boosting long-term foreign investment and simultaneously creating hundreds of thousands of new jobs, are the best solution for South Africa's ills. EPZs kill two birds with one stone. They solve the problem of our lack of foreign currency and reduce unemployment. Who can argue with that? Government's recent Industrial Development Zone (IDZ) schemes are a half-hearted approach and at present not properly regulated or marketed. They are a convenient way of side-stepping the EPZ issue and remain a toothless inducement to any foreign manufacturer considering South Africa as a base to manufacture.

Local Investment

In order for the local population to derive the maximum benefit from EPZs, the EPZ plan must lend itself to a high proportion of local involvement. Mauritius has over the years gone so far as to mandate that Mauritian banks set aside a percentage of their lending monies for local investors wishing to begin an EPZ operation, either independently or in the form of a joint venture.

Reasons for EPZ Success

The success of the majority of EPZs is in large part attributable to the active participation of local companies and investors. For example, 65% of the capital invested in the Mauritian EPZ is local. The importance of this equity linkage can be gauged from the fact that, today, approximately one third of all EPZ enterprises throughout the world are joint ventures between domestic and foreign enterprises.

Local subcontracting is an important instrument in the transfer of technology and know-how to local companies.

Effects

The effects are to introduce much higher standards of quality and performance into local industry. By requiring higher standards from their subcontractors (and assisting them in this difficult learning process by seconding highly qualified personnel, for instance), foreign EPZ firms can help to raise their partners' technological level. This increase in local technological capacity can gradually percolate into the normal economy through the linkages of subcontractors with other domestic suppliers and customers. As such, the success of the EPZ as an instrument of development in the long run negates the enclave principles that formed the *raison d'être* for such zones in the first place.

In the case of the Masan EPZ in South Korea, initially linkages between the local economy and the EPZ were negligible. In 1971 a small proportion of either export value or total raw materials used in the EPZ was accounted for by domestic raw materials (2–3%). However, by 1985 the proportions had increased to 23% and 33% respectively — successfully stimulating the local economy.

Clearly, local involvement in the EPZ is vital and needs to be fostered. This involvement does not refer purely to labour and jobs, but also to domestic investment and shareholding in EPZ enterprises. Again, the successful EPZs all encourage local involvement and joint ventures with foreign enterprises.

Interestingly, one of the few weaknesses of the Mauritian EPZ is that although 80% of the EPZ is related to garment producing, all its wool is imported. Nevertheless, the Mauritian EPZ's advantages, which include reasonably priced labour and excellent trade agreements, far outweigh this disadvantage.

It is important for companies wishing to establish a presence in an EPZ to study the potential export markets. Manufacturers must have a certificate of origin from the country within which the EPZ is situated in order to then qualify for reduced import duties and higher quotas when the product is finally exported to its destination.

Therefore, if a manufacturer's own country does not qualify for many duty-free preferences offered by trade agreements such as the Lome Convention of the European Union (EU) (targeted at poorer countries), it makes a lot of sense for such exporters to manufacture in the EPZs of less-developed countries.

It is critical that South Africa's pending trade deal with the EU help to set the stage for South African exports to receive favourable duty-free entry into the EU. This would make South Africa a popular manufacturing location for exporters to the EU, especially given our added benefits of fast, efficient shipping and air connections and our generally good infrastructure.

Tax Rates and Allied Incentive Schemes

The eradication of exchange controls and the possibility of transacting in any freely convertible currency are major plus factors that an EPZ can offer. In this manner, a country may be able to begin to liberalise its trade and finance policies, much in the way that China has done over the past decade, with the benefit of its experience in Guangdong and in other so-called special economic zones. Even Cuba has recently adopted a free trade zone regime to attract foreign manufacturers.

By permitting Offshore Banking Units (OBUs) to offer freely exchangeable foreign currency to EPZ operators (such as in Subic Bay, the Philippines), the entire EPZ package becomes that much more attractive to foreign manufacturers.

Many successful EPZs tax expatriate managers sent to manage production at the EPZ local plants at only 50% of the host country's regular individual tax rate. Madeira and Singapore offer staff training subsidies of up to 100% of eligible costs.

International Tax Issues

Often large international corporations wishing to reduce their global tax rate attempt to concentrate as much of their profits as they can in low tax jurisdictions in order to incur a lower global tax charge. As international tax rules have developed, it has become crucial for many such multinationals to show an actual presence in the low tax jurisdiction, and this makes it imperative that a majority of these multinationals invest in the jurisdiction.

All the most successful countries offering EPZs employ tax incentives that relate to net profit figures, not to turnover or sales figures. For example, Mauritius offers a 15% corporate income tax rate in its EPZ. In the case of Vietnam legislation specifically excludes any turnover tax, and instead grants a 10% tax rate on profits in the case of production enterprises and a 15% tax rate on profits for service enterprises.

Both Singapore's and Malaysia's tax and investment incentives for export-oriented operations relate to income tax rates of 5% and 10% respectively, while Thailand's three investment promotion zones all offer a 10% corporate income tax on net profit. The two most successful EPZs in the Caribbean region, Jamaica and the Dominican Republic, both base their tax incentives on profits and not on revenue. Togo recently instituted an EPZ programme which offers a corporate tax holiday for ten years followed by a 15% flat tax rate. Namibia offers a zero tax rate for licensed EPZ operators.

Tax incentives

Although the tax incentives offered are attractive, tax incentives offered to foreign investors are unlikely to be a significant motivation in themselves. What often proves equally attractive is the possibility of obtaining some form of local financing at moderate interest rates. *The importance of this issue can be judged from the fact that approximately half of all investment in such zones is currently financed through loans rather than through equity. As such, by attracting both international and domestic financial institutions to assist new EPZ operators or licensees in transacting in any currency* free of exchange controls, the chance of success of the EPZ is greatly increased.

Administration of the EPZ

Looking back at the failures of certain EPZs, it appears that the main shortcomings were often of an administrative nature, and were frequently related to the lack of authority and responsibility of the zone's administration. For example, as a "one-stop-shop" many zone authorities (administrators) not only have the right to register companies, but are also empowered to allocate work permits. As such the authority must have the requisite political and administrative authority.

In addition, local participation was often restricted in those EPZs which failed.

It is clear that a "one-stop-shop" is imperative for the EPZ to have the best chance of succeeding. This is easier than it sounds. Issues relating to work permits, import/export permits, processing goods through customs and minimum wage levels for EPZ workers all traditionally implicate government ministries which wish to maintain their bloated bureaucratic powers. The EPZ authority clearly needs to have as much power over these issues as possible. The head of the EPZ authority must have significant political clout.

Our Competition

Between 1986 and 1989, Costa Rica, the Ivory Coast, the Dominican Republic, Malaysia, Malta, Mauritius, the Philippines, Mexico, Malta, Thailand and Singapore each succeeded in attracting between 5.1% and 10% of their GDP in the form of foreign investment inflows. South Africa remains at less than 3%. Foreign investment drove these societies to become free trade icons. Their EPZs, free ports and regional headquarters incentives continue into the 1990s. Singapore still offers multinationals a 5% tax rate for setting up regional headquarters there. Training subsidies can still be found throughout Asia. Ireland's fast growing economy (the fastest in Europe 1996–98) is largely based on investment incentives targeting foreign manufacturers. Mauritius, after suffering from high unemployment as recently as 1980, has full employment and must import labour or discourage foreign investment in labour-intensive processes. Mauritius nevertheless continues to offer training subsidies and other investment incentives.

Even our own neighbours are more successful in attracting Foreign Direct Investment (FDI). Lesotho, Botswana, Mozambique and Namibia have all recently instituted FDI regimes that reward export-oriented investment and provide for a wide range of investment incentives and duty exemptions on inputs.

My own involvement in drafting Namibia's EPZ legislation has already led to more than R600 m in approved investments centred on Walvis Bay, with some 5 000 new jobs created. Close to 100 applications to operate in the EPZ have been received; it provides an attractive location for FDI (no taxes, no customs duties and the benefit of free trade agreements). In Namibia EPZ status may be granted anywhere in the country — so long as the operator is predominantly export oriented.

Already EPZ licences have been granted from the south of Namibia (to package and export fruit), to Tsumeb (processing and exporting charcoal), and to Swakopmund (manufacturing teddy bears). The incentives are of unlimited duration and apply equally to Namibian and foreign-owned companies. Botswana offers attractive labour and wage subsidies — paying the majority of the first-year labour costs of a new manufacturer.

Cutting budget deficits, scrapping exchange controls and pushing privatisation forward are all desirable; however, these measures only have an indirect effect on job creation. If anything, privatisation will initially throw more people out of work. Exchange control relaxation will encourage foreign investment and capital which may well stimulate the economy, but one's assessment of this situation would be based on sentiment alone, as in essence exchange controls no longer affect foreign companies who wish to put down firm roots in South Africa. EPZs are the most effective way forward.

Additional pillars must be created if 400 000 new jobs per year are to be generated and a 6% growth rate achieved. EPZs are one of the most effective and proven ways to simultaneously attract long-term foreign investment, produce local jobs and boost exports, thereby generating foreign exchange and a much more favourable trade balance. Empirical evidence can be found in numerous parts of the world. This is not a game of smoke and mirrors.

Until South Africa is able to attract foreign capital competitively, the rand will continue to fall and the brain drain will continue. No country can afford to lose its best and brightest without suffering severe consequences.

EPZs and Labour Issues

Generally, the smaller the percentage of unionised workers inside the EPZ the better, as unions tend to scare off foreign investors. The Dominican Republic has gone as far as to declare it illegal for union representatives to enter its EPZs. Namibia, on the other hand, has found an acceptable balance between the unions and EPZ operators.

It is interesting to note that successful EPZs recognise that the cost of labour is only one of many considerations in the investor's decision to locate in their zone. In most zones an American investor will experience wages that are roughly 10% of his previous labour costs. "It makes little difference to him if they are 5% or 15% as there is a significant saving," according to Robert Haywood of the World Export Processing Zone Association.

Regardless of the wage rate, most EPZs offer inherently lower-priced labour than the industrialised countries. Given South Africa's huge unemployment problem, the outside world expects South Africa to offer a reasonably priced wage rate that remains competitive with other developing countries in similar circumstances.

There is no reason why unions should not be able to operate inside South African EPZs. EPZ operations are not designed to be sweatshops, and should have nothing to hide. Workers in EPZs in Singapore, Mauritius and Namibia enjoy enviable protection.

EPZs and Offshore Banking

A vital component in fostering foreign investment in an EPZ is a strong, experienced international banking infrastructure directly involved in the services of the EPZ.

Hence it is important that internationally respected banks be given strong incentives to establish offshore banking services (letters of credit, loans and deposits in hard foreign currency denominated accounts) for the benefit of operators in the EPZ who may wish to reduce their exposure to the rand as much as possible. The only times the foreign EPZ operator might need to convert his dollars, deutschmarks, pounds or yen to rands is on payday to pay his workers, and when paying local suppliers for goods ordered. This limits his exposure to any rand weakness which might severely undercut his foreign expectations, valued in a stronger currency.

Reasons for the absence of exchange control restrictions on EPZ enterprises

Successful EPZs such as those in Taiwan, China, Costa Rica, Brazil, Uruguay, Thailand, Vietnam, Mauritius, the Dominican Republic and Singapore allow EPZ operators the freedom to hold foreign exchange accounts, along with the total freedom to repatriate profits, dividends, and capital whenever they wish.

Many potential EPZ operators who might be drawn to an EPZ may have existing exchange control restrictions in their home country. Their home country's currency may also be volatile. An EPZ which offers international banking facilities and the option of transacting in US dollars, pounds, yen or deutschmarks, would prove a major attraction to such companies. Such an offshore manufacturing operation would drastically reduce a company's currency risk.

Hong Kong has gone as far as pegging its own currency to the fortunes of the US dollar. As a result, US operators in Hong Kong have no currency/exchange rate risk whatsoever.

Attracting large banks

Despite its small size Mauritius has been able to attract eight foreign-owned offshore banks to operate offshore services. The existence of 565 EPZ operators was more than sufficient for these banks to stake a claim in Mauritius's international banking sector. The leading offshore banks in Mauritius include Barclays, Banque Nationale de Paris, Hong Kong & Shanghai, Crédit Lyonnais and Rothschilds.

Conclusion

The reasons for locating manufacturing operations in certain EPZs are complex and numerous, but the strongest attractions are to be found in certain anomalies: duty-free access by these EPZs to choice markets, including the EU and North America, and the need for manufacturers in currency-restricted countries to convert some of their assets into hard-currency form.

As value is added in an EPZ, which makes it possible for EPZ manufacturers to concentrate profits legitimately in the low-tax EPZ jurisdiction, significant tax savings may be achieved within the EPZs themselves. However, a number of EPZs currently do not offer the international banking services or management services which make it possible.

In many respects Ireland's 10% tax rate for export-oriented manufacturers, as well as the International Financial Services Centre in Dublin, with its own freedoms and low tax rate, have effectively created this combination within the EU. Microsoft, Citibank and numerous other companies have established plants or large operations in Ireland to take advantage of Ireland's attractive fiscal benefits. At present 75% of Irish-manufactured exports result from Foreign Direct Investment (FDI). Some 45% of manufactured employment results from FDI.

It is high time that South Africa got off its high horse and began to open its eyes to the large number of economic success stories the world over. We do not need to reinvent the wheel, but rather to become more open-minded about particular strategies that will enrich our country.

It is a very sad state of affairs when the success enjoyed by the Singapores, Chiles and Hong Kongs of the world are quickly dismissed by South African policy-makers because they believe these countries to be running sweatshops. They have not even visited any of these jurisdictions.

Minimal regulation, responsive government, lower taxation levels, freedom of currency movement and a range of investment incentives – these are just a few of the many common features that have permitted undeveloped countries with no resources to become leading financial centres.

Tragically, more foreign capital flows through the Bahamas, Cayman Islands, Singapore and Hong Kong on most days than South Africa received throughout the course of 1996. With South Africa's 1998 and 1999 growth rates projected to be no more than 1–2% — not even half the required growth rate of 6% according to our government's Gear plan — it is surprising that the status quo of macroeconomic policy continues to meander along.

Time to wake up

South Africa is facing a crisis whether we like it or not — the fact that we developed these problems through mismanagement a decade ago is no longer material. Action must be taken now. Our policy-makers could do a lot worse than to learn a few lessons from the jurisdictions mentioned in this chapter. They are arguably among the world's most successful magnets in attracting investment capital. Given a little ingenuity, common sense and marketing ability, many of these undeveloped countries have become leading beacons for job creation, low unemployment and upwardly mobile per capita incomes.

CHAPTER EIGHT

A South Africa that Works

W HERE IS THE MONEY GOING to come from to fund all the planned public works programmes, millions of new homes, better schools, improved health care services, and infrastructure? We cannot permit our political leaders to be elected until they address these issues. In order to be elected tough questions must be answered honestly.

If we hold our leaders accountable we will have done our duty as citizens of South Africa. You and I will each have done our part in making this land a better place for our descendants, no matter for whom each of us votes.

Economic Growth

Without the benefit of sizeable foreign investment, South Africa will not be exposed to the modern technology and know-how that is frequently transferred through direct foreign investment. Greater access to global markets and increases in exports are direct results of foreign investment, as are the acquisition of new skills and management expertise by those local workers employed by foreign investors. In addition, access to global sources of finance is often enhanced, as international banks tend to follow their clientele to new countries (and not vice versa).

We cannot rely on passive portfolio investment to fund our growing trade deficit with the rest of the world. The faster our economy grows the larger this trade deficit grows — putting strain on our capacity to grow our economy much beyond 3% to 3.5% on a sustained basis. The only way to achieve a higher level of economic growth in South Africa is to have the benefit of foreign direct investment inflows and an export-led industrialisation programme, in order to offset the inherent tendency of South Africans to buy large amounts of imported goods, which accompanies faster economic growth.

Foreign Investment

Since the 1994 elections we have received over R50 bn in the form of portfolio flows into our stock and bond markets. Unfortunately, such investment does little to create jobs in South Africa and is often temporary in nature, as was the case in Mexico recently (January 1995), when most foreigners pulled their capital out of the country, and its currency, the peso, went into free fall. June 1998 saw a similar scenario in South Africa.

Our government has historically performed miserably in attracting bricks-and-mortar foreign investment. A detailed plan must be created. Without significant inflows of direct foreign investment it is unlikely that sufficient jobs will be created to bring down our unemployment levels, as insufficient capacity exists within South Africa's own firms (and nor is our internal demand or purchasing power sufficient) to create 5–6 million new jobs within the next decade. Our growth rate will be constrained by the lack of sufficient long-term foreign exchange reserves that accompany international direct investment.

Fulfilling Our Potential

In order to attract significant levels of foreign direct investment, a large number of reforms must be instituted. These include:
- getting a handle on the excessive crime wave and curbing it sharply;
- improving the competitiveness of our labour market and raising productivity levels relative to other countries;
- developing a tax regime that rewards foreign direct investment and is in line with what our neighbours as well as many other developing countries are offering;
- removing exchange controls completely;
- facilitating fast-track privatisation of state assets;
- ensuring a more stable currency;
- providing simplified customs and import duties;
- reducing import duties (and allowing for duty-free imports in the case of imported inputs used for exports);
- ensuring lower interest rates; and
- developing investment incentives and duty exemptions on a wide range of capital goods and imports to be used as inputs in factories located in South Africa.

Foreign investors wishing to establish a manufacturing presence in South Africa look to our country to offer them a competitive variety of incentives along the lines of what is on offer in numerous other countries. Such a package would include the exemption from customs or import duties on imported inputs, whether they be machines or raw materials used in their factories. In addition, potential foreign investors seek the availability of foreign currency accounts to reduce their need to use rands, thereby lessening their currency risk.

The Case for Freer Trade — A Small Domestic Market

Since the South African domestic market is far too small on its own to attract many large-scale foreign-owned factories which require massive economies of scale to justify new factories, it is likely that foreign multinationals will look to South Africa as a possible export base for their production and distribution needs.

In essence, such investors would require a free trade regime, similar in scope to what is offered by numerous other developing countries successful in attracting such investment.

As in the case of other developing countries, South Africa's domestic market remains relatively small for many foreign manufacturers. For example, an American firm such as Reebok, which produces sports shoes, would not seek to establish a local factory only to service the South African market. In order to generate the economies of scale Reebok is accustomed to, it will only seek to establish a manufacturing plant in South Africa if it is given a range of manufacturing-based export incentives competitive with those available elsewhere.

The vast majority of the millions of "takkies" Reebok would seek to produce would be destined for the export market, since South Africa's domestic "takkie" demand is only a fraction of Reebok's necessary economies of scale. In the event that a foreign manufacturer wishes to sell to the domestic market, local import duties will still need to be paid. Local producers need not be discriminated against, nor should they feel threatened.

Although China, Ireland, Singapore and Chile have larger domestic markets for $150 Reebok/Nike shoes than South Africa, these countries offer low-tax regimes for manufacturers (tax rates of 5–10%) with little or no import duties. South Africa prefers to charge excessive taxes and comparatively high import duties.

Making Labour More Competitive

Our labour market is not a free market where demand and supply meet at a certain price level. Rather, the price of labour is dictated to our corporations. While the largest of South Africa's companies can meet these demands by passing the increases on at the cash register, the majority of small businesses are adversely affected. With an unemployment rate close to 40%, how is it that South Africa's wage rates per unit of output are comparatively higher than those of many of the fastest growing economies of the world, whether in Eastern Europe, Asia or South America?

That is not to say that our workers' rights should not be protected. Sweatshops and the exploitation of workers belong on the garbage heap, together with apartheid. However, our high wage levels serve as a barrier to new investment when entrepreneurs and established multinationals are able to operate their businesses and man their operations in other parts of the world at a fraction of what it would cost in South Africa.

The question needs to be asked: Is it better to have one worker earning R4 000 per month for sweeping the floors of a tobacco factory in South Africa, while five other workers remain unemployed? In this case the excessive salary paid to the cleaner leads to the tobacco factory ultimately relocating to Vietnam, where it can employ a plant manager armed with two university degrees for less than the cost of a factory sweeper in South Africa.

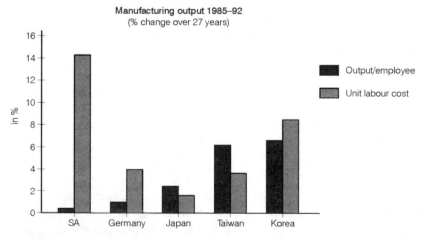

Figure 23 *International comparison of manufacturing output, 1985–92*

Alternatively, the tobacco factory could employ two South African workers each at R1 500 per month and remain in South Africa. What is in the best interests of the majority of our citizens?

Given the current high unemployment rate, crime will continue to escalate as long as there is no realistic chance of finding jobs. Without large-scale foreign investment, it is but a pipe dream to expect South Africa's economy to generate anywhere close to the 6 million jobs needed by 2004.

We in South Africa need to wake up to the realities and get our act together if we ever want to compete successfully for international capital and investment, without which job creation will be almost non-existent. Without a substantial drop in unemployment, South Africa is headed down a slippery slope to a point where the masses will lose faith in the new government and resort to other means.

Low Productivity in South Africa

Between 1985 and 1996 worker productivity in South Africa only increased in one of eight sectors — finance. By contrast, productivity levels fell by as much as 2% in the transport sector and by 1% in construction and mining. To make matters worse all three of these sectors have suffered large-scale job losses.

We can see just how unproductive we are if we compare motor car manufacturing in Australia and South Africa for the year 1992. In order for both countries to manufacture 278 000 vehicles in 1992, Australia (which is not noted for its productivity in motor manufacturing) required 26 000 workers — as against 36 000 in South Africa. This translated into the amount of value added at R216 000 per worker in Australia, compared to just R123 000 per worker in South Africa (South African Motor Industry Task Group figures).

Capital productivity has been declining dramatically since the 1970s. Today South Africa is obtaining far fewer units of output per one unit of equipment: 0.46 in 1960 as compared to 0.32 in 1991.

The Economist magazine recently found that workers in the Mexican textile industry added four times more value to a piece of clothing they produced than their counterparts in South Africa's textile trade.

Sadly, no new supply-side measures are likely to be implemented to make South Africa a more attractive export-oriented location for both domestic and foreign investors, since the Minister of Finance recently conceded that the take-up rate of existing tax incentives was "abysmally low". It should not be surprising that the recently introduced tax holidays for labour-intensive investment have had few willing applicants, given the labour law environment within which companies must operate.

Many of the tax holidays are poorly conceived and remain uncompetitive by international standards — for example, the length of the holiday period is too short (two years), and appears to be an *ad hoc* move on the part of a government with no long-term commitment.

Contrast these few incentives with the investment, tax, training and trade incentives on offer in Brazil, Malaysia, Namibia, Lesotho, Botswana, Singapore and elsewhere.

South Africa is losing in the B-league against its own neighbours when it should be competing in the A-league.

It is no longer useful for our government figures to hide behind such lame excuses as "the jury is still out on the jobless stats" (Trevor Manuel, 23 March 1997, *Sunday Times*). Even the Central Statistical Service's official unemployment rate of 29% which by all accounts is an overly conservative estimate, nevertheless ranks South Africa top in terms of unemployment among countries deemed to be newly developing nations. We cannot afford to be complacent when leading economic forecasters such as DRI McGraw Hill rank South Africa as the second most risky emerging market — only Russia fares worse.

Unemployment and the Unions

While unemployment remains at an unacceptably high level, bricks-and-mortar foreign investment remains as illusive as ever. This is not surprising in the light of South Africa's woeful lack of the competitive incentives which are needed to lure foreign investors.

With an ever-increasing number of unemployed South Africans (estimated at 50% of the black population) and the resulting increase in crime, it is disturbing to note that little is being done by the policy-makers to remove the draconian barriers (taxes, import duties, exchange controls, highly regulated labour markets) which prevent the free flow of foreign investment into the country.

South Africa risks pricing itself out of the international investment market, with extremely high corporate tax rates (43%), a lack of globally competitive investment and tax incentives, extremely complex and high import tariffs which exclude foreign competition and protect inefficient local companies, increasingly militant trade unions coupled with low productivity — and of course an unstable currency due to the uncertainty surrounding the easing of exchange controls and the lack of foreign currency reserves.

Although the government is moving in the right direction by lowering import tariffs, this alone will not solve South Africa's unemployment problems, nor be a sufficient catalyst to attract large amounts of fixed long-term investment. In fact, in the short term, greater unemployment may well result, as inefficient South African producers are unable to compete with cheaper imports. Clearly additional policy measures are needed to generate the employment growth South Africa so desperately needs.

Attracting labour-intensive investment

While the South African government continues to reward capital-intensive projects and provide no incentives for job creation, by contrast, governments in Asia pay for up to 100% of the training costs of firms establishing a presence in their countries. Our neighbours are now offering a wide variety of tax and labour incentives — Namibia, for example, now offers labour training subsidies of 75% of the projected cost of such training. As the unions helped mobilise votes for the ANC in 1994 and are an important coalition partner, they certainly enjoy the confidence of the ANC. Unfortunately for the rest of South Africa, some 1.8 million Cosatu members now appear to control the destiny of all those millions of unemployed South Africans. What kind of free market exists in South Africa when the unions are able to continue striking for ever-higher wages, with some 6 million unemployed willing to work for far less?

These "have-nots" pose a serious threat to the ANC over time, as they amount to some 40% of the electorate and are growing by as many as 400 000 a year. It is dangerous to ignore the economic plight of this growing and restless minority. Half-hearted economic programmes that are not fully implemented can easily lead to ever-increasing socialistic demands by the expanding pool of unemployed.

Hiring the best

If we are to run government along the lines of a well-oiled machine such as a profitable business, who would the electorate as the ultimate shareholders rather have at the controls — a seasoned team of experienced and well-educated experts and private sector executives, or a bunch of unqualified and unseasoned individuals who have little or no experience in the private sector?

When it comes to a life or death situation we all want the most competent doctor. This is exactly what we need right now for the management of our country.

The best economic, investment, health care, crime prevention and education doctors are called for in our time of need. As the majority shareholders of any ruling government we have the choice — we should not make the mistake of believing that the ruling elite are bosses and can dictate to us what is right for us.

That was the mistake of such great US behemoths as General Motors and IBM, which both have revenues similar in size to the South African government.

In 1994, the ruling elite in both these companies was ousted in shareholder revolts. They were guilty of forgetting to whom they owed their positions of leadership.

- We must hold our leaders to account and not blindly follow their lead. We must set reasonable goals and milestones for them to achieve.

- At the same time, if our opposition parties do not adapt to the changes in our new country and become viable as future ruling parties, we must also hold them to account and dispose of them as we did with apartheid. Our hopes of creating a strong and healthy democracy do not lie with numerous nonviable parties.

- South Africa's future prosperity must be enjoyed by all — however, to get from our current position to prosperity for all is a bumpy and difficult road.

- Low growth rates continue to thwart investment from abroad; foreign investors are far more interested in faster-growing markets. Our high tax rates and the domination of the economy by only a few companies also hamper foreign long-term investment in South Africa.

Competing Successfully with Our Neighbours for Foreign Investment

Lesotho, Namibia, Botswana and now Mozambique are all in the process of adopting aggressive free market policies which seek to attract long-term foreign investment. Namibia already has legislation to regulate its Export Processing Zones (EPZs), which includes no corporate income tax, no customs duties and no import or export taxes, in addition to a 75% grant towards staff training costs.

At the same time Botswana is seeking to create a regional financial centre in Gabarone, mirroring the success Dublin has recently had in Europe. (Dublin has become the European administrative centre of choice for many of the world's largest financial institutions, unit trust brokerage houses and multinationals because it provides an attractive fiscal regime for foreign companies wishing to set up operations such as administrative and regional headquarters.)

Botswana is also in the process of developing a free trade zone regime with related tax holidays and incentives. Non-traditional exports (i.e. non-mining) increased by 42% between 1994 and 1995, while textile exports to South Africa grew by about 60%. Manufacturing firms enjoy a 15% tax rate while benefiting from a stable political environment, labour subsidies and a co-operative work force. The motor vehicle manufacturer Hyundai chose Botswana in which to establish its plant rather than South Africa which continues to feel the effects of its high, protective tariff walls and an increasingly volatile workforce. Yet it exports the vast majority of its production to South Africa.

One of South Africa's largest manufacturers, Pepkor, admits that it can no longer manufacture certain products profitably in South Africa. It has subsequently moved certain South African plants to Malawi. Even Swaziland is eyeing new incentive schemes to attract foreign investors.

lesotho and Mauritius

Lesotho has already drawn a sizeable number of Taiwanese and other investors away from South Africa. The ten Taiwanese companies in Lesotho taking advantage of the various fiscal incentives on offer, employ at least 7 000 Basotho — 24 factories alone have created a total of 16 000 jobs in Lesotho recently. Lesotho receives preferential treatment when exporting its products to such countries as the US, Japan and the Scandinavian bloc, in addition to the European Union. Manufacturing entities wishing to set up in Lesotho receive export financial assistance, loan guarantees and exemptions from sales tax on capital equipment and machinery. Add on a low 15% tax rate, lower rental costs and labour costs averaging one-third of those found in South Africa, and it doesn't take a genius to realise why those 16 000 jobs are being created across our border.

When one compares the costs of production in South Africa with those of our neighbours, it becomes evident that we are becoming increasingly uncompetitive. High labour costs, labour unrest and low productivity have already resulted in a number of Taiwanese-owned clothing factories previously located in Cape Town and Kimberley to shift their operations to Lesotho.

The tiny island of Mauritius with no inherent resources and just one million inhabitants has become one of the few economic miracles of Africa. Mauritius has grown its EPZ to the point of capacity, with some 565 different enterprises currently licensed to operate in the EPZ.

With more than 90 000 Mauritians employed in the EPZ, Mauritius is currently riding the wave of robust export earnings which generate strong foreign exchange reserves. Tax rates are generally 15% for EPZ operators, and with near full employment in Mauritius the government is encouraging more capital-intensive, value-added businesses to come to its EPZ, rather than low-skilled, labour-intensive industries. In fact, Mauritius can afford to be so picky that it encourages certain labour-intensive factories to move off the island to other locations such as Madagascar.

But Mauritius is not resting on its laurels. In 1992 the Mauritian government created a free port regime which it has argued is badly needed in the African context, because many African markets are too small for bulk shipments. By using the free port, companies can ship their goods to Mauritius, store them, repackage them and then re-export these goods to specific countries — all duty free.

By 1996 the Mauritian Free Port Authority had issued 330 licences for companies to operate in the free port. Some 90 companies were operational in 1995, with trade totalling $37 m in that year. By the year 2000 the total warehousing space at the free port is expected to encompass some 100 000 square metres.

Shock Therapy

Perhaps some shock therapy, like the movement of South African manufacturers to Walvis Bay (where labour costs are a half to one third of South Africa's) would be a blessing in disguise for South Africa and force significant changes in the country's economic policy. Given the growing number of incentives on offer across South Africa's borders, it is likely that quite a few South African manufacturers that are fed up with the cost of labour, high taxes, import duties on their inputs and the lack of full free trade access to Europe, will be attracted by the availability of foreign currency accounts in Namibia or Botswana, and will choose to relocate a part of their operations there if South Africa does not begin to offer competitive incentives.

Taking the South African clothing sector as an example, where the number of jobs has fallen by some 25 000 over the past five years, the possible increase in the relocation of textile factories to neighbouring countries should be of major concern to us all.

Perhaps South Africa will only truly wake up to the realities of a competitive world when our neighbours have built up successful free trade zones. Sadly, we should not be competing with our neighbours at all, but rather with successful countries in Asia, Eastern Europe, the Middle East and Latin America. By comparison with these regions we are faring poorly, to put it mildly.

High Cost of Inputs

The cost of inputs in South Africa remains incredibly high, because of the numerous customs and import duties, and ever-increasing labour costs that are not being matched by equal productivity gains. In addition, we have a shortage of skilled labour, low levels of domestic competition and a history of ill-directed government intervention. Given these facts, it is quite easy to understand why both foreign investors and South African manufacturers themselves are increasingly eyeing the bait on offer across the border.

We live in a tiny, interconnected world, whether we like it or not. With fierce competition for every investment dollar, each time an investment is made in one country, another country that may have been in the running for the project loses out.

Other developing nations are already eating us for breakfast as we continue to be blind to reality. Nor should we underestimate the potential of the very attractive new fiscal policies being implemented by our poorer neighbours. They are hungrier than we are. South Africa behaves like the overconfident hare discounting anything that the poorer tortoises are able to muster. This would be a mistake. New technologies can create modern facilities anywhere in the world, no matter how out of the way the location may appear to be.

If we foster increased trade with our regional neighbours, there is no reason why we should not be the linchpin of all trade occurring in the region. However, trade is a two-way street, and while we can export more sophisticated manufactured products, our neighbours should be able to sell basic staples and simple manufactured items to us in return.

International Competitiveness

It is the firms, not the nations or governments, which choose the locations for production and investment, import and export. Government must create an enabling environment which will assist South African firms to become more expansionary in terms of investment and export-led growth. This can be done by levelling the playing field and eliminating the obstacles to exports and investment flows. Clearly, exchange control restrictions on South African firms prevent them playing on a level field, since they limit our firms' ability to make strategic investments abroad and expand their international revenue base.

The lesson from Latin America concerning the abolition of exchange control is refreshing. When Argentina, Peru and Chile abolished exchange controls in their entirety, permitting citizens to open bank accounts in any currency they wished, and coupled this with a comprehensive reform package, it resulted in a 20% appreciation in these countries' exchange rates. At the same time, these countries managed to increase exports considerably. A sizeable portion of the capital inflows into Latin America have come from residents who believe in the reforms and have repatriated capital previously held abroad.

Our Reserve Bank and government economic policy-makers must also realise that no country can devalue its way to prosperity in the world we live in today. There are new rules we need to adhere to in order to come out on top.

Lessons from Asia

Despite the current turmoil in the Asian markets, their governments are both lean and very active. While government expenditure as a percentage of the GDP reaches 32% in South Africa, among the Asian "tigers" it is generally around 20%.

South Korea and Taiwan both lacked resource-rich land, but have turned their large rural workforces into profitable factors of production for labour-intensive manufacturing. While in South Korea, government placed an emphasis on the creation of a number of large conglomerates (*chaebol*), Taiwan adopted an approach which encouraged and rewarded small business creation. Rather than relying on increasingly low commodity prices, mineral-rich Malaysia, Indonesia and Thailand actively courted foreign investment to utilise their soil as an export base for manufactured products.

What these countries have in common is the necessity to focus on export-led growth, since domestic markets remained too small to justify import substitution. Between 1960 and 1995, Korea, Taiwan, Hong Kong and Singapore as a group dramatically increased their share of world trade from 2% to 10%. Export-led growth was impressive indeed, with export-to-GDP ratios doubling over the past two decades, attaining 25% in Indonesia, 34% in Korea, 36% in Thailand, 50% in Taiwan, and 74% in Malaysia.

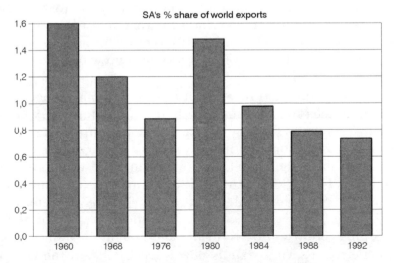

SA's % share of world exports

Figure 24 *South Africa's percentage share of world exports, selected years from 1960–92*

In fact, over the past three decades South Africa's export-to-GDP ratio has hovered around the 30% mark, with little improvement evident.

South Africa in fact generates less than 10% of its GDP from manufactured exports, in comparison with South Korea, which derives 25% of its annual GDP from such exports. Between 1985 and 1996 our exports rose just 42.1% compared to a 94.8% rise in our imports, causing our weak trade balance.

Reducing Poverty, Asian Style

Poverty in South Africa, as defined by an income of less than R800 per month per family, continues to plague our country. Poverty is unevenly distributed; the Eastern Cape is the province with the highest poverty rate. Currently three children in five in South Africa live in poor households. Poverty rates in the Western Cape and Gauteng remain the lowest. Job creation programmes need to be targeted at the most needy provinces first. The attached poverty charts paint a very sad picture. Action plans must be implemented to alleviate poverty in South Africa.

Why South Africa Must Increase its Savings Rate Dramatically

South Africa's totally inadequate gross domestic savings rate of 16.5% of GDP is woefully insufficient and needs to be raised closer to 30%. Most studies indicate that in order for South Africa's economic growth rate (GDP) to move towards a sustained 5% level, the investment-to-GDP ratio must grow by at least 50%, from 17% to around 27%.

Gross Domestic Fixed Investment (GDFI) as a percentage of the GDP is the measure most frequently used to determine whether fixed investment is picking up. Sadly, the accompanying figures (showing an investment rate of just 17%) indicate that South Africa is at about the same level as it was in 1987, when sanctions were in full force. South Africa's level of fixed investment is well below the required level of around 30% (as measured by GDFI/GDP). This is the average investment rate expected of developing countries between 1995 and 2000.

Our personal savings rate is now less than 1% of the GDP — among the lowest in the world. This should not be surprising, since government policies do nothing to encourage savings —

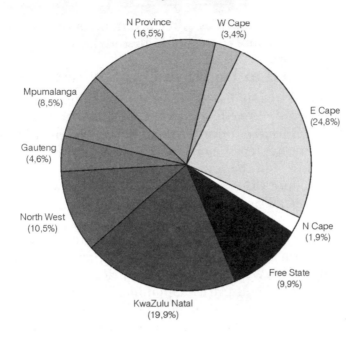

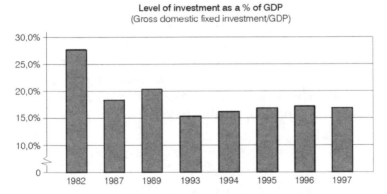

Figure 25   *South African level of investment as a percentage of GDP*
(gross domestic fixed investment/GDP)

personal income tax was increased by 13% in total in the 1997/98
budget and has increased by as much as 72% in the past four
annual budgets. Government is consuming far too great a
proportion of the economy, and personal savings are being eaten
up through higher taxes — R5.6 bn more is being paid in income
tax in 1997/98 after adjusting for inflation.

To encourage savings, government should at least triple the
paltry R2 000 tax exemption on interest. Easy credit coupled with

the highest real interest rates (after taking inflation into account) continue to cripple any chance of higher savings.

Why We Need to Increase Our Savings

Without capital a capitalist society stops breathing. Our economy needs capital, and it needs it now. We must demand new policies of our political leaders in order to stimulate the creation of new capital and the replenishment of our national savings pool, so that we can invest in the future of our country. By increasing our savings, we reduce the cost of investment because we can finance investment out of savings rather than borrowing at exorbitant interest rates.

How can our businessmen invest and compete with companies in the US, Germany and Japan, when our interest rates are four or five times higher than in those countries? We must instil an ethic of savings in South Africa. Spending every cent is no longer the wisest move. Incentives to encourage savings are to be found in numerous countries. We must request our leaders to implement programmes that have been shown to work. As individuals we need to save for our children's school and university costs, among other things. Our government must also be able to project what future costs it must bear, and thus reduce its habitual spending of any rands it can get its hands on. We can no longer live beyond our means. This means reducing the size of our government permanently. The deficit must also be reduced substantially. None of us can afford an irresponsible government.

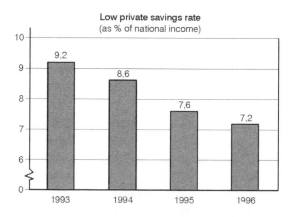

Figure 26   *South Africa's low private savings rate as a percentage of national income*

Our most demanding challenge is economic competition. Government policies must all be redirected to stimulate growth by creating incentives to encourage the private sector to hire new workers, thus creating new employment opportunities.

Comparable Savings Rates

Savings rates in Asia and Latin America over the past three decades have risen tremendously. South Korea's rate has moved up from 5% to 37% in that time and Singapore's from 10% to 45%. Indonesia's rate rose from almost nothing to 37% and Chile recently recorded a savings rate of 27% of its GDP.

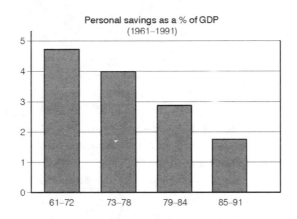

Figure 27 *Personal savings in South Africa as a percentage of GDP, 1961–91*

South Africa's low savings rate does not provide sufficient financing to spur on the large-scale investment required to sustain a high economic growth rate.

When our government borrows it has the effect of reducing our national savings rate. South Africa's continued budget deficits reduce our savings. **At present government eats up more than half of South Africa's national savings to finance the budget deficit.** This means that there is little left of our savings for investment — our productivity goes down, as does our standard of living.

Maintaining a large budget deficit drains savings from the economy. Government is a huge dissaver — we need to strive for a government which adds to the savings rate rather than eating into it.

Higher levels of savings in South Africa would permit the Reserve Bank to lower interest rates as inflationary pressures would subside. Not only would the amount of money in circulation come down but productivity would increase too.

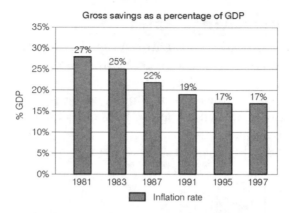

South Africa's savings rate is at a record low of 17%. Even with a higher savings rate of 22%, South Africa will require capital inflows equivalent to at least 2–3% of its GDP to finance the shortfalls in its projected investment requirements, according to the Union Bank of Switzerland.

Over the years the tax brackets were rarely if ever adjusted properly for inflation. "Bracket creep" has also undermined the propensity for saving among individuals.

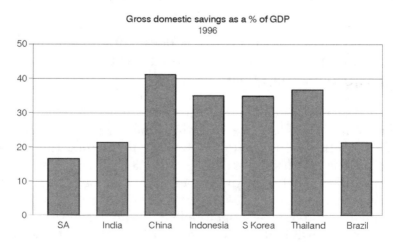

Figure 28   *Gross domestic savings in South Africa as a percentage of GDP (1996)*

It is not a coincidence that countries with the highest level of savings (1965–1995), such as those in Asia, have also experienced the largest growth in their exports. Some studies suggest that a 1% increase in the national savings rate results in a 3% growth in exports. Government would do well to heed this advice and encourage saving. When South Africans do not save enough to meet the demand of the budget deficit and industrial investment, we are forced to borrow from abroad. South Africans' failure to save leads directly to higher interest rates, as fewer rands exist to meet demand.

In both Singapore and Chile a compulsory savings programme tied to the social security system has generated a huge pool of capital. Singapore's savings pool even exceeds the requirements of its economy, and as such is exported.

The media

Having advanced and innovative media remains a source of national advantage. The US is perhaps the best example of this, as it exposes businessmen and their firms to the constant changes around the world in the markets they serve, but also leads to innovations in ways of selling and marketing products and services. US firms are world leaders in marketing technology, and this has contributed to America's unusual strength in consumer packaged goods. The bottom line is that if a nation's firms cannot practice advanced marketing at home, they rarely master it abroad. South Africa's marketing and advertising laws should therefore be brought into line with the best and most progressive international laws so that our firms can compete on an equal footing with global competitors.

The Tax System and Savings

Our tax system needs to differentiate between productive and unproductive uses of resources. South African companies need to be given every incentive to spend money on:
- research and development;
- worker education and training; and
- plant modernisation and expansion.

In many instances tax breaks that encourage individuals to save will save the government more in interest payments than the cost of the incentive itself. For example, in Germany, individuals who have been depositing savings in banks for at least seven years pay no income tax on the interest earned. This not only encourages savings but also permits financial institutions to have a more stable deposit base and a better plan for the future.

Clearly there is no point in encouraging savings to the detriment of the deficit — therefore, any stimulus to savings in South Africa must pay for itself either through lower interest rates, thus saving money for the government on its debt repayments, or through a cut in government expenditure.

South Africans are at their most heavily indebted level ever. We consume too much and save far too little. The rate of investment in our companies remains low — the average age of machinery in South African factories is close to 20 years old.

Unless South Africa as a nation does a far better job of saving, the rand is destined to continue its downward slide and will take our standard of living down with it.

Lessons in Education

In Japan and Korea teaching at all levels is seen as highly prestigious and institutions of learning are staffed with many of the best university graduates. The majority of students now receive education and training with a practical orientation in mind.

Besides the university, there are other respected and quality forms of higher education. Numerous technical universities and vocational schools exist in Germany and Korea. They are respected alternatives — in many cases, depending upon the field, technical universities may be more prestigious than a regular university.

In South Africa there should be a closer link between educational institutions and employers. The German and Swiss apprenticeship system involves millions of young students combining their education with on-the-job training over a period of three years. Many go on to work for the companies who provide such training.

Successful firms play a major role in the education and training of their workers. In Japan, for instance, employees must pass examinations before moving up to another level. Numerous trade associations provide ongoing training in the critical skills needed by an entire industry.

Unemployment

The labour absorption rate in South Africa has been declining at such an alarming rate — in the early 1960s, 81% of annual new additions to the workforce were absorbed by the formal sector. By the early 1990s the rate had fallen to just 8.4%. In the five-year period between 1986 and 1991, when the workforce grew by some 2.4 million people, the net increase in formal employment was a dismal 12 000 jobs (Development Bank of Southern Africa, 1996 annual report).

New entrants to the workforce have been hardest hit — for example, between 1980 and 1994 just one in 30 new entrants to the labour market was able to secure a job in the formal sector. The unskilled worker is hit at least twice as hard as the semi-skilled worker in terms of the unemployment rate, and eight times as hard as the managerial staff.

Unemployment among males already tops the 40% level. Estimates by the South African Foundation indicate that some 2.3 million South Africans in their teens and twenties have no gainful employment, of which 1.5 million have never had a job, and have been unemployed for an average of four years. At least one in five has a matric or higher qualification. This is clearly a recipe for them to turn to crime and other undesirable activities.

All evidence agrees with the notion that South Africa has a major structural (rather than a cyclical) unemployment problem. While our Central Statistical Service figure appears to indicate that unemployment is of the order of 33%, the World Bank has quantified it at 38% based on 1993 data, which in turn suggests it has attained a level of close to 40% in 1998.

Data released by the Reserve Bank in 1993 (*Sunday Times*, 29 August 1993) painted a far more pessimistic picture than previously, suggesting that the unemployment rate was perhaps as high as 46%.

South Africa's manufacturing exports, as a percentage of the developing world's exports, have plummeted in the past four decades, from around 11.5% to 2% while exports of our natural resources have remained constant at about 4% of the developing world's exports.

Falling economic growth rates also lie at the heart of the unemployment problem. Between 1960 and 1974 the economy expanded at an average of 5.5% a year which declined to an average rate of 1.8% between 1975 and 1988, followed by a

negative 1% growth rate between 1989 and 1994. Of course this
has had a profound effect in eroding the per capita income of
South Africans.

To meet South Africa's dramatic skills shortage, urgent
attention must be given to investing in general education as well
as on-the-job training — a better educated and trained workforce
will also go some way to improving labour's productivity, making
South Africa more attractive as a manufacturing base for exports.

Exports

Labour-intensive manufacturing is the best way of linking the
creation of jobs to exports which generate badly needed foreign
exchange for the country.

Manufactured exports from South Africa remain at only one third
of the level of Malaysia's in terms of percentage of total exports —
and less than half that of South Korea, using the same measure.

We need to increase our share of world exports urgently. Over
the past four decades our share of world exports has slipped from
0.6% in 1955 to less than half this figure (0.25%) in the early
1990s.

Boosting exports is the solution!

As import tariffs are removed, the propensity to import is
expected to grow substantially. In addition, because of the
necessary capital repayment (foreign debt) commitments in the
foreseeable future, in order to keep our balance of payments in
line we must generate a positive balance on our current account.
Hence, we need to focus on boosting our exports, while also
creating employment with methods other than devaluing the
rand (which will only boost inflation and drive up the cost of
capital, thereby shutting off capital expenditure and starting
another round of wage demands).

**The method adopted must enable South African interest rates
to avoid upward pressure because of imported inflation. A
stable rand inspires confidence and will encourage long-term
investment, particularly foreign investment, with the security
that imminent devaluation will not wipe out the value of the
dividends expected.**

South Africa cannot afford dramatic 30% devaluations of the
rand every now and then. It turns off foreign investor interest,
and generates panic.

Need for export growth

In order to become more competitive worldwide and create employment opportunities, the country's exports must be expanded more rapidly. Between 1971 and 1988 exports continually hovered around a low 10% of the GDP, although they have increased to 16% of the GDP more recently (1994). By comparison, Sweden, Denmark, and Germany average 27%, 45% and 26% respectively as a percentage of their GDP.

South Africa should have its embassies and consulates staffed with private sector individuals who can promote South African exports and help exporters in their markets.

In South Africa we still prevent our firms from expanding abroad as freely as their international competitors. How are South African firms to become leading exporters when just establishing a foreign operation remains problematic, despite the gradual easing of exchange control?

Developing a free trade area throughout Southern Africa (i.e. having no barriers to trade between Southern African Development Community countries) must be a two-way process, but it is not a panacea to substitute for significantly boosting our employment levels. Inevitably South Africa should be able to export more sophisticated manufactured goods while buying food and basic manufactured items from its neighbours. If South Africa can be seen to be the most viable export-oriented manufacturing base for the entire region, this will boost our chances of generating substantial new job creation. However, this will require effort and sacrifice: South Africa's agricultural sector still enjoys the benefits of protectionist walls which shelter large landowners but hurt workers in the cities.

Although much is made of expanding our exports to neighbouring southern African markets, this market's share of the global economy has shrunk over the past two decades, with trade down from just 0.76% to a current low of 0.58%. South African exporters would arguably be better off focusing on the other 99.4% of the world market. Global rather than regional trade is the key to South Africa's economic growth. South Africa already has a huge share of its neighbouring markets — Malawi, Zambia and Zimbabwe import between 33% and 40% of their needs from South Africa. To increase this share considerably appears to be unrealistic. Our focus should arguably be on boosting exports to the richest, fastest growing areas of the world.

Reserve Bank

A more open system of communication between the Minister of Finance and the Governor of the Reserve Bank should also be encouraged — in line with our major trading partners, including the US, UK and Germany, where regular formal meetings occur between these two parties. Not only would it make these two officials a little more accountable, but perhaps more importantly it will help to lift the veil of secrecy that shrouds South Africa's financial and macroeconomic decision-making policy. Such a move would engender greater confidence among foreign investors, who would view such a move as progressive. Our above-mentioned trading partners (the UK and the US) publicly disclose the minutes of the meetings held between their top two economic decision-makers a few weeks after each meeting. South Africa should do likewise.

From 1996 through to mid-1997, the Reserve Bank's exposure of some US$21.2 bn on the forward cover market (currency markets) was in fact greater than South Africa's gross foreign reserves. Similarly between June and July 1998 the Reserve Bank had an exposure of some R25 bn of forward losses.

The squandering of taxpayers' funds

The lesson to learn here is that the Reserve Bank should not be in the forward market, in essence subsidising South Africa's largest companies. The approach is inefficient, and has already cost the South African taxpayer multiple billions of rands over the past few years alone. It is high time that our companies learn to play in the big leagues and that the cotton wool is removed from their offshore financing deals.

By some accounts the Reserve Bank spent no less than R9 bn during 1996 and R26 bn in May and June 1998 propping up the rand, only to see its efforts ultimately wiped out by seasoned foreign speculators who realise that our level of foreign exchange is too small to adequately defend the currency.

Since 1994 it is estimated that total losses of close to R35 bn have been covered by the taxpayer due to the Reserve Bank's handling of forward cover, in which it in essence subsidises the foreign exchange commitments of the parastatals and the private sector.

If the Reserve Bank withdrew from the forward cover market, this would in effect increase the cost of offshore borrowing and borrowers would turn to domestic credit. It is high time that the Bank got out of meddling in the private sector and let the free market reign. This sort of intervention continues to subsidise the wealthiest companies in the land at the taxpayers' expense. It should not be allowed to continue. South Africa does not have R35 bn to squander in such a fashion.

Exchange controls

By maintaining exchange controls the Reserve Bank will continue to keep an outdated system alive. The taxpayer will have no choice but to sit idly by and pick up a rising price tag of forward foreign exchange losses. This is because exchange controls preclude the creation of a significant free market in forward cover among our commercial banks.

Until enough foreign exchange is generated by significantly increased export volumes and long-term direct foreign investment, our currency will remain at the mercy of foreign speculators who realise its vulnerability. To defend our currency huge levels of foreign exchange not yet seen in South Africa must be generated. A strategy must be implemented, though at present we remain woefully short of any strategy that will convince long-term foreign investment to move here. South Africa, it must be said, is not even on the radar screens of most foreign executives wishing to establish new manufacturing plants outside of their home countries. We are at present a hard sell.

Unfortunately, the longer exchange controls remain the longer foreigners' perceptions will remain negative. Their view, which is well taken, is why should they invest in a country whose own citizens remain so eager to move their savings and investments out of the country, and into other currencies, that exchange controls are needed to prevent a massive outflow?

If the press accounts are true that the Governor of the Reserve Bank, Dr Chris Stals, believes a five-year period is necessary to dismantle exchange controls gradually, then he and the government must be willing to take responsibility for a rand that will remain undervalued, and may well reach 10 to the US dollar by the time exchange controls are truly scrapped.

A weakening rand has numerous other negative results. Take for example the proposed privatisation of South African Airways (SAA). The rand meltdown which began in February 1996 sent South African Airways losses soaring to R300 m for the six months to 31 October 1996. Even worse results were expected for 1998. The prospects of obtaining a premium price for SAA in any privatisation sell-off have become exceedingly poor. The government's procrastination for the last three years concerning SAA's privatisation has no doubt cost the South African taxpayer millions of rands in proceeds lost from any premium price which may have accompanied an earlier sell-off during the ANC's honeymoon period (i.e. its first two years in government).

A narrow focus

Sadly, it seems that the Reserve Bank is out of touch with many of the most critical economic issues facing South Africa. In early 1997 Governor Stals believed the GDP would rise by as much as 3.5% for the year. Needless to say it only grew at some 1.8%. His much reported projection of a 1999 growth rate of 3% will also remain but a pipe dream without a significant change in economic policy on government's part.

Although the Reserve Bank is in agreement that labour market inflexibility is partly to blame for the lack of job creation, the Bank arguably shares the blame for stifling any signs of economic growth by maintaining excessively high real rates of interest (the real prime rate is as much as 16%, after taking inflation into account).

While the current high interest rates cripple the creation and growth of many businesses (and small businesses in particular), the adjustment in the true value of the rand following the forthcoming expected decline in the level of interest rates may also be as sharp and as painful as it was in early 1996. Foreign speculators have bought up large chunks of local South African gilts because of the high rates of return (as high as 10% above international norms, as long as the rand remains stable). When the Reserve Bank is finally pressured to reduce interest rates, this will reduce the attraction of South African gilts, leading to the drying up of such global passive investment and, with it, a weakening in the value of the rand.

The Reserve Bank thus should be less hasty to criticise Cosatu and the labour movement when its own handling of the economy is easily open to criticism. The Bank's repeated announcements that it is focusing on the figures relating to the extension of credit to the private sector (and that a significant fall must first occur before any interest rate cut will proceed) have led many to believe that its view of the economy is far too narrow. The fact that figures for the extension of credit remain high and fail to fall despite South Africa's economy entering a real slowdown, causes some economists to believe that the figures used are outdated.

In July 1998 M3 money supply figures hit 19.4% — a high figure given the dramatic slowdown in the economy following the 30% devaluation of the rand against the pound and dollar. Economists argue that due to the large influx of foreign banks and the lending they are doing, the old staple credit extension figures are somewhat distorted and may no longer be valid — partly due to the fact that many of the loans are not designed to be spent inside South Africa, and so may have little or no impact on inflation inside South Africa.

Is the Reserve Bank losing its grip?

By Dr Stals' own admission the Bank "seems to have lost some of its grip over money supply in the past three years." The Reserve Bank drastically needs to update its financial models and thereby bring its various target measures more in line with reality on the ground. The fact that 50 new foreign banks have opened their doors in Johannesburg has clearly created a new playing field with regard to the extension of credit to South African firms, as well as foreign companies intent on using local borrowings for investment in South Africa.

The recent Budget and Gear proposals allow foreign-owned firms operating in South Africa to borrow up to 50% of their capital in South African currency — dramatically boosting the amount of borrowings they are now permitted to undertake in South Africa. The Reserve Bank and government policies seem out of kilter with each other as government is in effect encouraging foreign firms to increase their borrowings in South Africa, rather than to receive equity (capital) funding from their parents abroad. An incentive for foreign firms to borrow locally is the tax deduction they receive for interest paid on such borrowings — in essence they will pay less tax by using debt; incurring local debt is cheaper for the company than being funded out of after-tax profits generated by an overseas parent.

Developing the South African economy at the expense of a little more inflation may well be what is needed. The question needs to be asked: is it more important to generate thousands of new jobs by developing the economy at 4%–6% or should we retain high

interest rates, thereby slowing down an economy which is already
showing many signs of softening, and stifle any job creation
prospects for 1997, all because we want to hold inflation at 10%
rather than, say, 12% or 13%? Those South Africans without an
income, but who have a good chance of being hired in a strong
growth-oriented economy, would hardly seem to care that the
inflation rate may have gone up a few percentage points,
compared to the prospect of having a job and a regular income.
Sadly our vulnerable rand has not helped our inflation-beating
hawks at the Reserve Bank. By the end of 1998 inflation in South
Africa is expected to be back at around 9%.

Labour and the Reserve Bank

Rather than casting blame either on the rigid labour market (as
the business sector likes to do) or on the Reserve Bank's handling
of interest rates (as the labour movement is keen on doing), we
would be better off reviewing the overall picture. This may help
us realise that a plague on both their houses is in order. They are
in one way or another both accountable for the lack of job
creation and economic growth experienced in South Africa over
the past few years. It should not be up to commercial banks to
lead the Reserve Bank in setting interest rate policy — but the
Reserve Bank's inaction on the interest rate front has often led
our banks to lower their mortgage lending rates well ahead of any
interest rate cut by the Reserve Bank.

Should the Bank finally wake up and provide even a 3% interest
rate cut (in the repo rate) later this year, it will be woefully
insufficient to set South Africa's economy on a significant growth
trajectory. The prime rate needs to come down by as much as
7–8% by the end of 1998 (from a peak of 23%) if South Africa's
economy is to have any chance of exceeding 1.5% economic
growth for 1998. We will be lucky to record even 1% growth in
1998.

How is the economy really doing?

In the first quarter of 1997 GDP registered a negative 0.8%
contraction which shocked many observers. While it might be fine
for the US or Europe to achieve a growth level of around 3%, their
population growth rate remains close to zero in comparison to
South Africa's population growth rate of 2.5%.

Our 1998 GDP growth is expected to be just 0.7% and casts

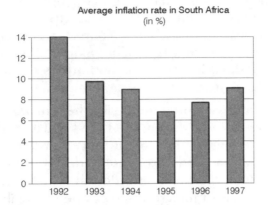

Figure 29 *Average inflation rate in South Africa*

much doubt on the economy's ability to meet Gear's employment targets and economic growth target levels. These are nothing more than a pipe dream. While Gear projected that 250 000 new jobs would be created in 1997, in fact 120 000 were shed from the formal sector. By the end of 1998, South Africa will be close to 1 million jobs behind Gear's employment targets, and our economic growth figures at less than half those projected by Gear. Government itself has recently admitted that Gear's employment figures are unattainable.

Inflation meanwhile nudges double digits once more, reaching 9.7% in mid-1997 (with 9% expected by December 1998). Meanwhile the level of household debt has risen to 67% of disposable annual income, which exceeds the international average of comparable countries by a wide margin. In mid-1998 South Africa experienced its highest real interest rates in two decades, causing even more pain for our citizens. South African property markets are now in the doldrums, as high bond rates hit property sales.

It is clear that South Africa is in a major downturn and requires interest rate cuts to free it from its present strangulation, but the all-important credit extension figure the Reserve Bank appears to have its heart set on fails to fall in any measurable manner.

With business and investor confidence in South Africa dropping to their lowest levels this decade, it is hoped that the Reserve Bank and government won't blow this opportunity to accelerate the relaxation of exchange controls. Prior to the 1996 30% devaluation of the rand, import cover had been at some 8–9 weeks — sufficient levels to have begun the process of meaningful exchange control relaxation. However, that opportunity was blown, and the easing of exchange controls was delayed until 1 July 1997, some 16 months later. The small outflow of funds seen post-July 1997 should inspire our authorities to ease exchange controls in a far more determined fashion in future.

Announcing a phased programme for the remaining removal of exchange control would discourage the speculation that remains inherent in the market due to the uncertainty created by the government's *ad hoc* and inconsistent decision-making in this area. Clearly the opportunity afforded by a stable rand in 1995 and adequate levels of foreign reserves due to sizeable inflows of foreign investment was missed.

The original conditions which made exchange controls necessary (World War II, and the Sharpeville shootings in 1960) disappeared eons ago — it is high time to complete the process finally begun in July 1997. The Governor of the Reserve Bank and the Minister of Finance should at a minimum provide a time-frame and a guideline of required conditions for the complete scrapping of exchange controls, and bring South Africans back into the family of free economic citizens all over the world. Specific targets need to be set so we all know where we stand.

Government's High Debt Levels

The ratio of government debt to GDP rose from just 37% in 1991 to 49.6% by the end of the1993/94 fiscal year, when the ANC took over. However, the level of government debt has since risen to 56% of the GDP. This is just short of the internationally accepted ceiling of 60% of the GDP (acknowledged as a debt trap).

Interest on government debt now comprises almost 21% of the budget or R34.4 bn, the second largest item of our 1996/97 budget after education and it is growing. The total government debt by November 1996 had reached a record R312 bn, 11.4% more than at the beginning of the fiscal year, when the total debt figure was R280 bn. This has meant that government debt levels doubled between 1992 and 1996.

With the dramatic 30% fall of the rand against the pound and dollar in mid-1998, the government's interest bill will grow by some R350 m more than was budgeted for in March 1998. Higher domestic interest rates also upset the budget calculations of an average of 13% capital market yield. It appears that 15–16% yield is to be expected between May and December 1998, pushing up domestic interest payments by government to R25 m more than budgeted for.

Despite the above problems, government continues to borrow from foreign capital markets. Note the outrageous cost of foreign borrowings: due to the depreciation of the rand, the total service costs in rand terms on a 1991–96 German deutschmark loan of R682.5 m averaged 29% per year (including forex capital costs and interest), as opposed to the low coupon rate of 10.5%. It has cost government an additional R536 m to repay the interest on the original loan — this is over and above the original R682.5 m principal which was repaid. As such, the total cost of the loan amounted to R1 176 m, close to double the initial loan.

Government's 1994 loan in US dollars had an initial value of R2.7 bn. At R6.25 to the dollar, R4.7 bn is required to repay the loan — a loss of R2 bn. Total losses in 1998 following the rand crash are estimated at R3.4 bn (including both extra interest and principal). Reserve Bank forward losses will increase State debt by some R10 bn to R15 bn by mid-1999.

Government has too often been sucked into offshore loans by focusing on the low coupon rate and not bearing in mind the drastic toll such foreign loans take on our Treasury as the rand falls. The seemingly low coupon rates now translate into fairly high levels of interest payments, and the principal amounts of the loans have ballooned in rand terms — by as much as 30% to 40% in certain cases.

Sadly, our government appears not to have learned the lesson of 1983–84, when South Africa's foreign debt rose by just 6.6% in dollar terms, but due to the rapid depreciation of the currency, the rand value of this debt shot up by 65.6%, and the proportion of total debt to GDP rose from 32.6% to 45.7%.

Our government deficit is finally moving in the right direction — downwards. But until it is brought under even stricter control it will continue to impact the value of the rand.

Based on our 1997/98 budget **South Africa spends double the amount of money paying off interest on its debt as it spends on either health or welfare**. Another alarming comparison is that by just paying off the annual interest on the debt, government spends ten times the amount of money it spends on housing. These interest payments are choking the rebuilding of South African society, sapping our productivity and our ability to

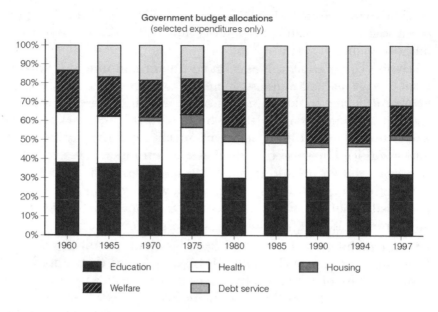

Figure 30 *South African government budget allocations (selected expenditures only)*

compete with the rest of the world, and significantly reducing our standard of living.

Waking Up — how to reduce our huge debt problem

We must realise that in South Africa there are only three ways to pay off our debt: government must spend less, tax more or print more money. Printing more money means that there is a tremendous amount of new money in circulation, which leads to inflation. Since South Africans are already over-taxed, improved collection and tax administration is needed to increase tax revenues, along with a growing economic base, which will add revenue to government coffers. Raising tax rates is not the solution here. The Katz Commission estimated two years ago that every year R21 bn worth of taxes was not being collected. Former revenue chief Piet Liebenberg estimated that as much as 20% of the current tax take is lost (approximately R35 bn).

Growth in government expenditure must be reduced to a level which will over time come close to balancing the budget. With interest rates at exorbitant levels and an unstable rand, South

Africa cannot afford to keep borrowing to finance yearly deficits which only add to our total government debt. If we are serious about reducing government debt we cannot continue to run large yearly budget deficits — it is no different to simultaneously speaking out of both sides of one's mouth.

Being a debtor nation — and a heavily indebted one — means that South Africa has lost much of its control over its own economic policy. Witness the rand freefall and our inability to stem the tide. The rand's fall has severely damaged our economic prospects, setting us back some two years or more.

Current account deficit and the balance of payments

Since 1994 South Africa has been running a current account deficit, which was initially funded by passive foreign investment flows into equities and bonds. However, once the honeymoon terminated in early 1996 and the rand lost 30% of its value against the dollar and pound (between February and October 1996), these portfolio flows reversed themselves, leaving South Africa's balance of payments in an unsustainable weak position. Sadly we did not learn our lesson then, nor again in 1998.

Throughout 1994–96 government was in essence relying on a capital account surplus made up largely of short-term portfolio flows to keep our balance of payments in check. With the reversal

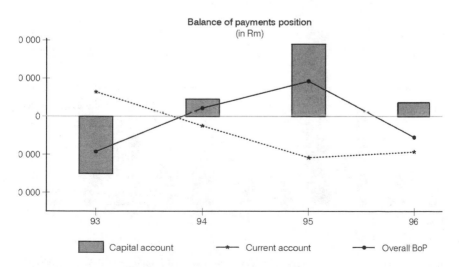

Figure 31   *South African balance of payments (in millions of rands)*

in the rand's fortunes this is no longer possible; nor is it such a prudent policy.

It is imperative that we begin to attract sizeable amounts of long-term direct (fixed) foreign investment in the form of the establishment of new plants and factories in South Africa by foreign firms. Foreign investment is important not for the inflow it generates on the Johannesburg Stock Exchange, but for the number of new long-term jobs it will generate. We need to focus on this form of foreign investment as a leading priority to assist in cutting unemployment. We need to strive to attract foreign investment which will use South Africa as an export base, since this will simultaneously stimulate job creation and export growth, and provide the country with an increased level of foreign exchange reserves.

A country cannot rely upon passive foreign investment, which by its very nature is liquid and tends to be short term.

Manufacturing exports are far too low. The value of gold sales still accounts for one quarter (25%) of physical exports. A further 40% of the country's exports consist of minerals and metals. The prices of these minerals and metals are determined internationally.

The frightening truth is that the real growth in exports that the country has been enjoying over the past few years (56% over the past three years), has mainly reflected improved international

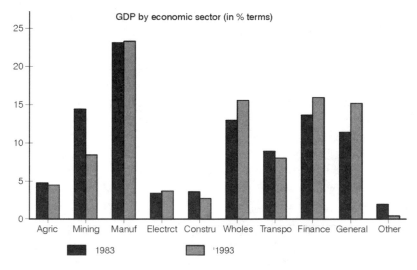

Figure 32   *South African GDP by economic sector (in percentage terms)*

prices. Our true level of manufacturing exports remains abysmally low for a country eager to create at least 400 000 new jobs per year. Our manufacturers have rarely devoted much of their time to generating exports, when they were able to enjoy a captive market inside South Africa protected from real competition by overly generous import duties. Why does a R140 shirt in Edgars cost just R80 in LA? The same question could be asked of numerous South African products.

Manufacturing's share of the country's economic output (measured in GDP) has in fact remained fairly static since the mid-1970s at roughly 25%, reaching 30% in 1983. Today it is at 26% according to most reports. Clearly such a sluggish performance is nothing to get excited about, and a sincere push to develop the manufacturing sector is urgently needed, since it is the sector that can bring the large numbers of labour-intensive jobs to South Africa.

Figure 32 shows the negligible increase in the size of our manufacturing sector over a ten-year period.

South Africa's trade deficit

At the same time, we must turn our trade deficit into a whopping surplus by boosting export growth over the next decade. This will not only help to shore up our country's foreign exchange reserves and generate many new jobs linked to new export markets, but it will also help to pay off our enormous government debt more speedily.

Although government does not have as much control over our trade deficit, it can nevertheless influence its level through tariff policy and entering into favourable trade agreements with various countries. Other influences on our trade deficit include the value of the rand relative to other currencies, as well as the costs of such factors of production as labour and capital, which remain excessively high in South Africa. At present South Africa is paying for its trade deficit through a lower standard of living, rather than through increased productivity and sales.

An unstable rand (sometimes too high and at other times too low) has discouraged investment in South Africa — in plant and equipment, as well as in human capital.

Indeed, the exorbitant interest rates in South Africa have resulted in many companies deciding that the profits generated from possible capital investments are inadequate to meet the high interest rate hurdle. In such an environment little or no significant long-term investment takes place — it is better to bank the money and receive 15–18% interest on it.

Moving offshore

In truth many South African companies have chosen to establish operations outside South Africa. This trend will escalate with the relaxation of exchange controls and the attraction of expanding abroad. A combination of high interest rates, an inadequate supply of skilled workers and a rand that remains unstable will only lead to an increasing number of South African companies selecting other countries in which to establish plants.

Cosatu readily admits that its membership numbers have stagnated since the late 1980s (*NALEDI,* 1994). What better way to increase membership numbers than recruiting new workers to its ranks? Unfortunately, its current tactics have had the opposite effect, and scared off many investors who have the potential to create hundreds or thousands of new jobs in South Africa.

It is therefore a bitter irony that Cosatu, the largest trade union group in South Africa, favours not only raising the cost of labour in South Africa with the help of government legislation (such as a reduced working week and a payroll levy), but has also called for massive government expenditure (for public works programmes and the like), thereby seeking to drive up the budget deficit.

While even China has done away with many socialistic economic notions by offering a broad range of investment incentives, we toil under the burden of Cosatu and the South African Communist Party. More people are becoming unemployed every year. What sort of track record is that to run on?

Solutions

Leading economic studies all point to the fact that trade deficits in particular lead to a loss of jobs in the country running the deficit. It is therefore imperative that South Africa position itself as a very hospitable place for investment: ideally investment in manufacturing, which not only is labour intensive and thus generates a large number of jobs for each investment rand spent, but also investment geared towards capturing export markets, thus turning our trade deficits once and for all into a sustained and growing trade surplus. With these surplus funds we can better protect the rand and ensure its stability, while also ploughing back some of these foreign exchange reserves into paying off our government deficit.

Privatisation — Paying Off our Debt

Paying off government debt through privatisation proceeds remains a sound economic policy — but what are we waiting for? The process needs to be speeded up.

It is critical, however, that state assets which are sold off are not allowed to become private monopolies, with little or no increase in efficiency.

It is therefore vital not to let privatisation become another opportunity for the rich to get richer at the expense of the average South African. It is true that at present only a small pool of investors are wealthy enough to purchase assets from the state as it privatises. It is undesirable to have this small, elite group grab an even greater portion of South Africa's wealth, at the expense of the taxpayers who are the true owners of these state companies.

A ticking time bomb

Our state enterprises harbour vast amounts of over-employment — a ticking timebomb of lay-offs is certain when many state monopolies are finally privatised. Selling off certain state enterprises could also have detrimental effects on services such as Spoornet — private owners may not see fit to continue offering unprofitable train services to particular regions.

The longer the public sector takes to recognise that outsourcing is the way of the future for successful governments, the harsher will be the ultimate lay-offs suffered by the public sector when privatisation gets underway. During the last decade New Zealand successfully outsourced a large proportion of former government services, resulting in slashed government payrolls.

Privatisation in South Africa should have as its central tenet the spreading of shareholder wealth across the length and breadth of the country, to all groups. Individuals who work at the companies being privatised should also be given incentives to purchase equity — they should be assisted in the financing of such purchases.

Privatisation — figures

Total assets based on the historical value of state enterprises amount to about R140 bn. Telkom (the South African telecommunications company) alone has been able to raise R5.5 bn from the sale of a 30% stake. The investment in it by a foreign group represented some two thirds of total foreign direct investment received in 1997.

It is encouraging to note the partial privatisation of Telkom, but SAA, Transnet, Denel, Mossgas, Safcol, Eskom and numerous other partial holdings which government has should also be speedily privatised. If one excludes state land, forests, buildings and entities such as airports and harbours, the market value of state assets is close to R70 bn.

Reasons for privatisation

- Reducing the cost of government debt.
- Encouraging foreign investment.
- Broadening ownership within the economy, and empowering blacks in the process.
- Improving the productivity and efficiency of such vital services as communications and transportation through their management by the private sector.

CHAPTER NINE

Job Creation and the Labour Challenges Ahead

GOVERNMENT MUST MAKE ITS highest priority the creation and stimulation of hundreds of thousands — if not millions — of new jobs. Thousands of new small businesses need to be created by South African entrepreneurs. We must target industries of the future that will be the foundation for new wealth and job creation in South Africa.

Study after study indicates that the majority of jobs in South Africa are now held by employees of small businesses (i.e. enterprises with under 100 workers). The vast majority of new jobs won't come from South Africa's largest companies.

To encourage entrepreneurs and new business development, South Africa's economic fundamentals must change. Interest rates of 20% and more plague our country and put a permanent brake on the stimulation of wealth and new businesses.

Our small businesses are starved for credit and venture capital. Starting a business in South Africa remains one of the toughest challenges for any of our citizens. Banks will not easily lend or free their capital for entrepreneurial ventures. Incentives can, however, be created to encourage greater lending to small businesses.

Interest rates must be reduced if a thriving small business sector — and, indeed, South Africa's consumer purchasing power — is ever to be properly unleashed and the economy permitted to grow by more than a halting 2–3% per annum.

Jobs and GEAR

Gear's aim was to create 126 000 new jobs in 1996, 252 000 in 1997, 320 000 in 1998 and 409 000 in 2000. The reality is that these targets are little more than wishful thinking. We are shedding jobs at an alarming rate of some 100 000 per year.

Although Gear states that the budget deficit should be brought down to a target of 4%, in 1996 government did not meet its own budgeted figure of a deficit of 5.1% of the GDP — it was in reality 5.6%. Gear growth was projected to be 2.9% in 1997, but in reality will amount to no more than 1.8%. In terms of job creation Gear projected a very modest 1.3% increase in the number of new jobs in 1996 — in reality the figure was closer to a 1.3% net loss of jobs. While Gear projected a fall in the real remuneration of workers of 0.55% in 1996, in fact real remuneration was up by 0.5%. Even gross domestic savings have fallen to 15.5% of the GDP (in the first quarter of 1997) from the 16.5% figure achieved in 1996. We are now almost 1 million jobs behind Gear's own job creation targets.

While Gear explicitly states that labour flexibility will be enhanced in South Africa, the Labour Ministry remains out of step with the ideals of Gear by enhancing workers' rights to the hilt, and adding costs through the proposed Basic Conditions of Employment Bill. Labour costs are expected to rise by some 12.5% with this new Act, which intends to boost overtime pay from normal pay plus a third to pay plus a half, while cutting the working week down to 40 hours.

It is evident that the Labour Ministry, in its idealistic eagerness to do away with the remnants of apartheid, has concentrated almost exclusively on the rights of existing workers without stepping back and reviewing the overall picture of how this may affect nationwide job creation. The Ministry could attract more labour to the formal sector through a wide range of apprenticeship and labour-hiring programmes. The Labour Ministry should not just represent those with existing jobs, but also those eager to work, but currently unemployed.

South Africa faces an increasingly daunting challenge — how to create jobs for the annual 429 000 new entrants into the labour market (based on the 1997 figure), in addition to the 35–40% already unemployed (approximately half of whom are younger than 30). With 5–6 million people unemployed and a further 1.4 million likely to be so by 2005, South Africa faces an economic and social crisis that will have far greater influence than the political achievements of the past few years.

Total employment in the formal sector has sadly only increased once since 1989, when it rose in 1995 by 0.7%.

Gear also targeted a reduction of 100 000 jobs in the public sector, but up to 1997 there was a net increase of almost 5% in the number of people employed at central and local government level.

The Gear targets on employment creation certainly appear to be wishful thinking given the current economic constraints: the tax system rewards capital-intensive investment while the inflexible labour system makes it impossible to reduce the workforce even in leaner times, thus discouraging firms from hiring additional workers.

While the Ministry of Labour continues to generate new labour laws and regulations by the month, it appears to have few ideas about how to create new jobs and stimulate the economy. Accordingly, the jobs summit was organised by the Ministry of Trade and Industry.

The Sanctions Legacy

Evidence of the worst effects of sanctions is that between 1985 and 1990 there were only 33 000 new jobs created to satisfy 392 600 new job entrants per year. This represents just one of the reasons for the current high unemployment rate.

Labour Legislation

The private sector seems likely to continue to shed jobs as it has done for the past decade. The slew of recent labour legislation has tipped the balance of industrial relations power dramatically away from employers, and according to many of them has helped to accelerate their move towards increasing automation. Of course, additional labour costs such as payroll levies certainly do not give rise to any optimism that employers will shy away from automation in favour of hiring new workers, which would require the payment of additional company taxes. By reducing the number of employees a factory has in favour of robots and machines, the factory owner will reduce his payroll tax, as well as any further headaches he may encounter from the new labour laws.

Payroll Levy

A proposed 1–1.5% payroll levy will be collected by government, which intends to return only 80% of it to industry to finance industrial training. Notwithstanding the costs of setting up a new government bureau to collect the taxes, surely industry should be the administrator of such a programme? Government has proven its incompetence in collecting taxes over the years.

It has also been said that the levy would use private business monies to finance and train the workforce of state enterprises which may not be privatised for many years to come.

It is clear that South Africa's human resources are under-trained and under-skilled. Companies should be expected to spend funds on improving the skills of their workforce. Since the private sector will be the main payer of such a levy, it is clear that it should have a large say in how the scheme is administered.

Apprenticeships

South African students should be encouraged to enrol in apprenticeship training and technical courses. Companies should be given incentives to sponsor such courses and employ graduates from them. It would be in both the company's best interests and those of the student for companies to be able to offer students the prospect of a secure job, provided they achieve the level of training demanded.

The private sector itself has been found guilty of not investing in the training of its workers. A sharp decline can be seen in the number of newly enrolled apprentices and current apprenticeship contracts. According to a government study, the numbers of persons who obtained artisan status declined by 39% during the period 1988–91. The same report states that among the several state-assisted service training programmes, the number of individuals trained declined from 243 000 to 161 000 over the same period.

While successful international companies have invested more than 5% of their payroll in training and developing their human resources further, South African companies have on average invested no more than 1%.

The new payroll levy will only make the cost of doing business in South Africa even more expensive — making South Africa that much more uncompetitive.

A heart in the right place

Although the Ministry of Labour's heart is in the right place, and South African workers' skills *do* need to be upgraded and expanded, we can learn from other countries such as Mauritius, China and Singapore, which support companies in upgrading the skills level of their employees, often by matching the funds spent by the company.

In Australia, where companies are required to spend 1% of their turnover on training, and this must be confirmed by the company's auditors, no new expensive bureaucratic structures are necessary.

Rather than funding a new bureaucracy to administer a complicated levy which may well eat up half of the proceeds in its own administrative and monitoring costs, let's learn some lessons from abroad.

Taxed labour means less labour

The surest way of getting less of something (i.e. employment) is to tax it. Raising the price of a product invariably leads to reduced consumption. The bigger the price increase in the cost of labour in South Africa, the more adverse will be the effect on the number of new workers hired in South Africa.

Table 4 *Educational levels of Economically Active Population (EAP) in South Africa — 1991 (in % terms of the EAP)*

	Whites	Coloureds	Asians	Blacks	Total
1	26.2	3.9	10.5	2.6	7.8
2	66.4	29.4	57.3	20.9	32.4
3	5.6	50.6	27.5	45.6	37.4
4	1.8	16.1	4.7	30.9	22.4
Total	100.0	100.0	100.0	100.0	100.0

Notes: 1 = high-level manpower — standard 10 plus diploma or degree;
2 = middle-level manpower — standards 8 to 10;
3 = low-level manpower — standards 2 to 7;
4 = low-level manpower — lower than standard 2

Table 5 *Occupational structure of the South African workforce in 1981 and 1990 (%)*

	1981	1990
High-level occupations	11.2	15.0
Middle-level occupations	32.2	35.3
Low-level occupations	56.6	49.7
Total	100.0	100.0

Areas where we can compete

Although South Africa's workforce is largely unskilled, and may not be as cheap as that in the Far East, for higher value-added manufacturing such as in the areas of information technology, we are very price competitive with Singapore, Barbados, Hong Kong and other countries where computer manufacturing, data-base management and other information-related technologies are generating sizeable employment.

South Africa needs to reduce taxes and levies, but we seem to be moving in the opposite direction, while also designing new ways to grow our government bureaucracy.

Copying European labour law and collective bargaining systems, when countries such as Germany have the highest level of unemployment since the days of Hitler, leaves much to be desired.

We should be looking at other developing nations, such as those in South America (Chile, Argentina and Brazil) which have made giant leaps forward over the past few years.

Australia, South Korea and Singapore, to name but a few countries, have encouraged companies to invest in human resource development by introducing national training awards that give recognition to companies which have become leaders in their particular industry.

Why should companies keep ten workers on when one machine can do the same work and no additional tax will need to be paid when purchasing the machine — when in fact a generous tax break (accelerated depreciation) is permitted as a reward? Companies will continue to spend their investment dollars on machinery so long as our tax system rewards that expenditure and discriminates against hiring labour.

Our Minister of Labour would be better served spending his time focusing on how to make labour a more attractive investment relative to capital and machinery. Rather than taxing a firm's labour, he should be designing policies that encourage employers to hire additional workers, perhaps at the expense of capital-intensive investment. A business levy does not address the lack of competitiveness of labour in relation to capital. Imposing an additional tax on labour is shortsighted at this time, especially as it will just increase the advantages that capital investment has over labour as an investment.

While government continues to pursue initiatives that will increase bureaucracy and more than likely reduce employment levels, it might be worth repeating the findings of a recent European Union report which confirmed, much to the horror of left-wingers, that there was a clear statistical link between labour market rigidity and unemployment.

Policies that raise the costs of employing workers contradict the principles set out in Gear, and will continue to undermine its chance of success.

The Labour Ministry continues to focus all its attention exclusively on protecting workers — i.e. those with jobs. Should our Labour Minister not be concentrating on creating labour, not just assisting insiders who already have jobs? His legislation does little or nothing for the unemployed worker who is keen to be rehired. It appears that the Labour Ministry is exclusively focused on protecting workers, to the exclusion of assisting those in the labour market who are unemployed.

A Free Labour Market

South Africa clearly needs a free market for labour, which will in essence mean that unskilled workers will receive low wages as a result of the enormous excess supply at present, while skilled workers will receive high wages corresponding to the relative scarcity of such workers. Given the ability of workers within the managerial and professional ranks to find work internationally, it will be necessary to continue to reward these workers with salaries that are commensurate with international norms.

The most reliable and effective protection that workers have is not solely made up of laws guaranteeing them increased powers and rights against their employer; rather, protection is provided by the existence of many employers. A person who has only one possible employer for the rest of his life has little protection. A worker's real protection is the existence of competition for his services. In a free market, an employer who requires the services of a worker will, in his own self-interest, be willing to pay that worker the full value for his work so as not to lose him to another company.

Given the huge level of unemployment and the few new jobs available in South Africa, competition among employers for low level workers is far from strong. Nonetheless, many of our employers have little alternative but to pay excessively high wages, as they are precluded from hiring alternative labour at the market price, which might be lower than that set by Industrial Councils or demanded by the unions.

When an employer's labour costs rise out of line with his revenue and profit figures, he has little choice but to move his plant to another country, where the price of labour is driven by market forces. This is already happening in South Africa with such firms as Pepkor, which recently established clothing factories in Malawi.

In South Africa at present, those workers on the inside — largely urban, unionised workers who continue to receive wages higher than the free market would bear — have the effect of restricting entry into a wide variety of occupations. When government pays its employees higher wages, those higher wages are at the expense of the taxpayer.

But the reason we should strive for a freer market in labour is simple. When workers receive higher wages from firms which compete with one another for the best workers, and workers compete with one another for the best jobs, these increased wages are at nobody's expense. They only come about through higher productivity, more capital investment and better utilisation of skills. The entire pie grows larger, leaving more for the worker, more for the employer, the investor, the consumer and, believe it or not, more for the tax collector.

It is time that our government and unions understood the benefit of a free labour market. Without it South Africa faces a longer road to recovery and a harder time creating jobs — that is certain.

It is refreshing to see that those same business interests which went along with most of labour's demands in 1995 and 1996 are finally standing up and not acquiescing as readily to new policies emanating from the Labour Ministry.

Union Membership

Total union membership appears to have levelled off at the 3 million mark, representing 37% of South Africa's workers and just half of South Africa's unemployed. However, given the high number of unemployed workers in South Africa, unions represent no more than about 20% of the economically active population. The combined membership of the union federations outside of Cosatu (including Nactu, Fedsal, Sacol and others) totals between 900 000 and 1 million — about 68% of Cosatu's membership.

Historically, the cost of real wages in South Africa rises much faster than, and falls more slowly than, productivity levels. Only once in the past 30 years have the increases in the cost of real wages been outstripped by the gains made in productivity (between 1973 and 1978). The Labour Relations Act of 1996 is seen by most investors as firmly weighted in favour of labour unions; thus it has done little to inspire renewed investor confidence in the country.

As we have seen, tariffs are counter-productive for the South Africa of the future, reducing prospects of foreign investment, and protecting unproductive and unprofitable companies.

The Industrial Council — A Mockery of Free Enterprise

The Industrial Council system, which extends agreements made between employer bodies (read big business in a particular industry) and unions to those smaller participants in a particular industry, has the negative effects of raising the cost of small businesses, and helping big business keep out small businesses. Since Small, Medium, and Macro Enterprises (SMMEs) are universally acknowledged to produce more jobs per unit of output than their counterparts in big business who are able to afford a more capital-intensive approach, any wage hike will affect the small businesses far more: labour often makes up a far greater percentage of their total costs than is the case with big business.

The Industrial Councils' industry-wide wage rates are handed down with a total disregard for the differences in production method and cost structure of different firms. It makes a mockery of the free market.

SMMEs

Many of the new labour regulations and laws are burdensome to small business, which has difficulty complying with all the additional paperwork. Worse still is the bias of these regulations in favour of large businesses and unionised workers. For instance, industry-wide wage agreements are set by the largest companies in negotiation with their unions, forcing small business to pay the same wages and benefits that the big firms are paying, despite lack of size and infrastructure.

The 800 000 SMMEs currently employ about 7 million people in South Africa, approximately half of South Africa's economically active population. By some estimates SMMEs generate 45% of South Africa's GDP. Since small business tends to be fairly labour intensive and create jobs at a lower average capital cost than big business, it is a vital engine for boosting job creation levels.

In terms of the number of new jobs generated worldwide, it is widely agreed that SMMEs are the largest creator of jobs. In the US over the past two decades 60% of new jobs were created by small businesses.

The South African government must do as much as possible to foster the development of small businesses. The government's newly established Ntsika Enterprise Promotion Agency and Khula Enterprise Finance Limited are designed to provide institutional support for SMMEs, but have yet to truly make their impact. Ntsika has had numerous teething problems, not the least of which have been the resignation of its chief executive and the corruption charges at the highest levels of the agency. The National Small Business Council has also recently collapsed after a full year of leadership wrangles and allegations of financial mismanagement. Whether government's SMME support system can withstand the collapse of the Council remains an open question.

Reducing red tape (such as the removal of zoning laws preventing the establishment of a home business), stable fiscal and monetary policy, tax breaks for training allowances and business development expenses, and the removal of burdensome regulations which require a small business to complete as many forms as a large conglomerate, must be achieved soon to provide the best springboard possible to small businesses.

To the extent that SMMEs are far more labour-intensive than big business, they are discriminated against by the tax system, which rewards highly capital-intensive projects through generous tax deductions and incentives.

The Basic Conditions of Employment Bill

The draft of the new labour legislation known as the Basic Conditions of Employment Bill points to an average 20% increase in labour costs in the event that the working week is cut down to 40 hours, as demanded by the unions. Unions are also demanding four months' paid maternity leave, with a total of six months' maternity leave permissible.

The bill also throws the state's projected budget deficit out of line with reality.

Such increased labour costs make the attainment of Gear's employment targets even more of a fantasy than ever before. While tilting the balance of labour policies overwhelmingly in favour of workers and unions (which should not be unexpected, given the ANC's support base), little or nothing is done to encourage increased output and productivity gains. The consequences of a shorter working week, longer leave and holiday entitlements, more overtime pay and time off for family responsibilities will only serve to increase labour costs out of line with productivity gains, thereby driving up the inflation rate and encouraging employers to replace workers with machines which they can speedily write off against tax.

Since business will wish to retain its same margins, it will simply pass on the increased labour costs to the consumer, which will no doubt hamper South African industry's ability to compete on the global markets.

Clearly, additional job creation which would pay a lower wage is better than none at all; however, separating the work force into two tiers does not in itself guarantee that additional jobs will be created. It remains far more important to provide an investor-friendly business environment.

Rewarding job creation

Policies that reward companies for employing additional labour by offering training grants to such operators, as well as employment tax credits based on payroll expenses (such as in Botswana), are arguably far more effective in stimulating job creation than a so-called two-tier labour system, which only provides a myopic view of the labour market, and neglects the larger investment environment necessary to attract new long-term investment and generate additional jobs.

South Africa's investment environment remains weighted towards automation and machines rather than labour intensity. Companies which invest in machines and equipment are continually rewarded through generous tax breaks, including accelerated depreciation allowances and other write-offs. No such tax benefits exist in the case of hiring additional workers.

Labour Costs

Ironically, South Africa is debating all these additional costs and worker protections while the international trend is towards greater worker flexibility — we are clearly in danger of having too much labour regulation and not enough flexibility in our work force. While Cosatu pushes for a 40-hour working week, the rest of the world now averages a 48-hour week. Workers in Singapore and Korea work a 47.5-hour week, while in Hong Kong and Latin America the working week averages 44 hours. It is true that a number of industrialised countries have a 40-hour week, but South Africa's unusually long holidays and many public holidays effectively mean that if the unions get their way, union workers in South Africa would be among the highest paid workers in the world considering the total number of hours worked over a period of 12 months. By comparison, most workers in the US only receive two weeks off a year plus three public holidays, while working a 42-hour week. US workers work more hours during the course of a year than those in any other industrialised country.

Who in Government is Responsible for Job Creation?

Although Gear is designed to catapult the South African economy forward and create as many as a million jobs over a five-year period (1996–2000), no government minister seems to want to take responsibility for meeting the employment targets. More than likely the reason is that Gear's job creation targets are unattainable.

How were Gear's targets for employment generation conceived and how does government intend to meet these targets? Job creation is rarely discussed in a constructive manner in South Africa, and even fewer constructive policies seem to be put in place to achieve any meaningful growth in employment. Our politicians ignore the millions of unemployed voters at their peril — the debate over job creation is central to South Africa's economic health, and the safety and security of all South African citizens. The longer it takes to reduce our unemployment figures, the more likely it will be that our criminal elements will continue to grow and prosper.

High Interest Rates

Through excessively high interest rates the Reserve Bank has reduced prospects for significant economic growth beyond 1–1.5%, and limited any prospects for job creation in 1998, and probably well into 1999. Although the Reserve Bank and government claim success in cutting the budget deficit, stabilising the rand (let's pray for the moment), and attracting inflows of passive foreign investment, the bottom line is that without substantial economic growth South Africa will not be able to even begin reducing unemployment figures. High interest rates have led to a 35% increase in bankruptcies between 1997 and 1998.

Formal Sector

South African gold mines continue to produce the same amount of gold (20 million ounces) as in 1988, but with 34% fewer workers. As the cost of labour relative to capital has been driven up to its highest level ever, it is not surprising that South African companies have attempted wherever possible to become more capital intensive.

South Africa's faltering growth record during the late 1980s and early 1990s has had a serious effect on the average living standards of the population, and on the rates of formal sector employment growth, income distribution and unemployment.

During the period between 1985 and 1991, formal sector employment fell at an average of 0.1% per year, while the available workforce grew by 2.8% per year. What is even more disturbing is that for each South African worker in the formal sector, there now exist 4 dependants (4 to 1). By comparison, the US has a ratio of 1.1 to 1, and Brazil 1.5 to 1.

The Informal Sector

The growth in formal sector employment remains far too low to absorb new entrants into the labour market. Estimates in 1991 suggested that 43% of the workforce found themselves outside the formal sector. This figure masks the disproportionate number of non-whites unable to achieve employment status. The figure also masks the vast number of under-employed workers who have sufficient training and expertise to be engaged in far more productive jobs.

According to 1991 figures, at least 4.4 million people obtain their livelihood from the informal sector. Some 80% earn a subsistence wage at best, according to studies.

The Structural Employment Problem

South Africans recognise the great need for employment-creating economic growth to relieve the country of its economic and social problems. To understand the extent of this need we need to review the relationship between the growth in formal employment as it correlates to a unit of growth in the GDP (also referred to as the employment coefficient). The higher the employment coefficient, the lower the real economic growth rate needed for the alleviation of the country's unemployment and under-employment problems. Between 1961 and 1984 the coefficient was at about 0.5 or above. Between 1985 and 1991 it remained at almost zero, thereby making it that much tougher for the unemployed to benefit greatly from any modest economic growth. Without exceptional economic growth, the roughly 6 million unemployed will continue to suffer, regardless of Gear.

Lack of Skills

High staff turnover continues to cost South African firms dearly — an estimated R2 bn a year. Because of the lack of skills in South Africa, those with good skills are often lured away to other firms by bigger pay packages.

Since all interest groups agree that manufacturing is the sector that South Africa most depends upon to generate jobs, it should concern us that South Africa produces 15 times fewer graduate engineers per million of the population than Japan, eight times fewer than the US, and six times fewer than Australia. Less than 0.5% of black university students are enrolled in engineering courses. Meanwhile, Japan's Ministry of Education remains adamant that Japan does not have an adequate supply of engineers, and is aiming at boosting engineering enrolment figures by 10% per year.

South African vocational education and training institutions produce far fewer graduate engineers and technicians than are being produced in the Pacific Rim. The intake of engineering students at universities in South Africa has declined since 1990. This has occurred at a time when overall university enrolment is up by more than 80% in the past decade alone. An increasingly unhealthy imbalance now exists between the number of students opting for arts and humanities degrees and those choosing science and technology degrees. It is highly debatable whether South Africa can afford the luxury of disproportionately large numbers of students taking 3- and 4-year courses which do not train them to perform work critical for generating economic growth.

At the same time technicians are not picking up the slack. For South Africa to ever achieve sustained growth in excess of 5% per annum, the growing shortage of technically skilled workers must be addressed immediately. It is clear that South Africa is facing an increasing skills shortage in the area of manufacturing which will hamper our economic competitiveness and growth prospects.

While the average ratio of technicians to graduate engineers is approximately 15 to 1 in East Asian countries (Japan, Taiwan and South Korea), in South Africa it is 1 to 2 — a total reversal.

Training — The Huge Lack of Trained Workers

South Africa has 12 technikons, only one of which offers distance tuition. Only one out of 129 technical colleges offers such distance education. Technical colleges specialise in vocational training, while technikons provide tertiary education for middle and high level human resources in technology.

South Africa must train far more technologists, scientists, engineers, technicians and artisans if it is to meet the technological challenge of the 21st century. Currently South Africa has three university students for every technikon student, a ratio which is far too high. We need to strive for the figures found in other developing countries where the same ratio is often reversed, as in Singapore.

According to the National Manpower Commission, approximately 35% of the economically active population in South Africa has a Standard 4 (Grade 6) or lower level of education. As such South Africa has an over-supply of unschooled and semi-schooled workers. The structural imbalance in the labour market is also indicated by the large number of unskilled and semi-skilled workers, which greatly exceeds the number of jobs available, while at the same time there is a shortage of skilled workers.

In 1985 statistics indicated that more than 80% of the workforce had less than a matric, 8% had a diploma or degree, and more than 50%, had less than a Standard 6 schooling. In 1991 almost 60% of the economically active population had an education qualification lower than Standard 7, and 31% of the black population had an educational qualification lower than Standard 2, which is considered almost illiterate. Unfortunately this situation cannot be rectified overnight, and huge demands are now placed on South Africa's training and educational system.

It is clear that vocational training aimed at orientating students towards the needs of the professional world and enabling them to be productive in the workplace is important. The promotion of distance education and training, increasing the number of community colleges and learning centres, and raising the numbers enrolled in apprenticeship training, must be a priority for both private sector and government expenditure.

More co-ordinated training systems nationwide, with agreed-upon accreditation and national qualification structures, need to be implemented immediately.

The development and operation of a national qualification standard to supplement the existing qualification standard for formal education is needed in order to encourage vocational training provided by the private sector and government assistance programmes.

At present, because there are no national standards for a variety of vocational training courses, many employees who receive company-specific training find themselves unable to leave their employers. In order to allow workers to increase their skills, a national structure and a recognised programme should be implemented which allows workers to continually build on previous training.

Education — Skills

While South Africa spends 23% of its national budget on education, the highest among developing nations, 46% of its citizens remain illiterate. Illiteracy rates are detrimental for job creation and the general social and economic upliftment of South Africa's people.

Only 8% of black adults have passed matric; just 43% of the black population is literate, as measured by a Standard 6 level of education or higher. Few South Africans are engaged in higher education (just 7% of school leavers), compared to 42% in

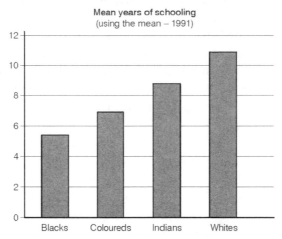

Figure 33 *Mean years of schooling in South Africa (1991)*

Singapore. Estimates are that as many as 2.5 million children do not attend school.

There are numerous districts in KwaZulu-Natal and the Eastern Cape where pupil-to-teacher ratios are higher than 46 to 1. In the former Transkei almost all districts have 48 to 100 pupils per classroom.

South Africa clearly has a very expensive, badly managed and fragmented education system. Apartheid resulted in huge degrees of inequality between the race groups. Blacks living in the former homelands are worst off in terms of poverty, employment levels and high population growth rates.

Education and Severance Packages

Although our Minister of Education fails to take credit for the huge number of experienced teachers who have either been retrenched or accepted severance packages, thus leaving our schools understaffed, in June 1997 he finally acknowledged that there was a problem by putting his department's severance scheme up "for review". This, after losing upwards of 15 000 experienced, long-serving teachers and jeopardising the standard of education in many South African schools. The state paid more than R1 bn in severance packages in the first year of the scheme, double the initial estimate.

As it is, the teaching profession is so underpaid relative to the hours and effort required, that teachers are increasingly forced to take on part-time work and second jobs. For example, a teacher with at least five years' experience, a BA (Honours) degree and a teaching diploma earns just R52 000 per annum (and regional variations may take it lower). Teachers clearly fill one of the key roles in society. They have not received any sizeable pay increases over the past five years that would even merit mention.

We obviously give a low priority to increasing and improving our stock of teachers.

We are not enticing new graduates to teach and train the next generation of South Africans. Education is in huge trouble. The enormous education budget (the largest single item of the budget) continues to be eaten up by the education bureaucrats in the public sector, while only the crumbs are left over for teachers in the classroom. The number of experienced teachers leaving the profession is numbing. Perhaps the teachers' union in South Africa needs to take a leaf out of the book of the powerful teachers' unions in the US.

Teachers in the US are well paid and are known to be ready to strike if their demands are not met. The average teacher's salary in California for an individual with five years' experience is approximately $36 000 per year. Based on equivalent purchasing power rather than the exchange rate, this would amount to well over R100 000, perhaps closer to R150 000.

Although all South Africans agree that our school system needs reforming and that equality must instituted, it is indeed sad that Sibusisu Bengu, the Minister of Education, has remained deaf to the constant calls for modifying his approach. After being rebuffed again and again, 80 Cape Town public schools finally had to resort to taking the Minister to the Supreme Court, with all the time and expense such a move necessitates.

Now that he has lost the case over the method of redeploying teachers, it is hoped that the Minister will finally wake up and smell the coffee. He has already done everything in his power to alienate the majority of teachers in South Africa. In 1997 the matric results were so poor (a 50% failure rate), that there were renewed calls for Bengu to step down.

Expenditure on the part of government alone will not solve South Africa's huge education problems and resultant skills shortage. South Africa needs to spend its limited resources on education wisely. Emphasis must increasingly be placed on technical training. The number of apprentices and artisans in South Africa has declined to disturbing levels, with the number of new indentures declining by 30.4% in 1991/92 (the last year of available figures). Given that training to become an artisan normally takes several years, the fact that the number of artisans who completed training in 1992 was half the number for 1985 portends a negative trend in labour in South Africa. It will have negative knock-on effects in terms of reducing productivity and economic growth.

Education — the sad reality

Despite the enormous education budget, the school book and textbook industry is dying a tragic death in 1998. By May 1998 thousands of schools had not received their new textbooks, as no print orders had been sent to school book printers. Most publishers have had to retrench workers in their school book departments.

Education in South Africa requires a Minister and a task force capable of tough decisions. Teachers' salaries currently comprise 92% of the education budget. Sadly we need to streamline our education system by laying off certain teachers. The big question is which teachers to lay off and how to do it.

Education, despite its huge annual budget (the largest proportion of the national budget), faces the all too familiar triplicate of problems:

- too little money;
- a lack of resources; and
- deteriorating administrative capacity.

Doing something

Although government's proposed teacher-to-pupil ratios of 35:1 in primary schools and 40:1 in secondary schools are very high, they are able to succeed. Currently though, a large number of teachers in South Africa lack adequate training and skills. As such we need to monitor teachers' performances and sack those who underperform. Performance appraisals need to be put in place for teachers. Teachers, especially those with less than a matric, need to have their qualifications upgraded through continuing education courses. An accreditation system for continued education courses for teachers should be put in place.

Needy schools need to be identified and prioritised — and various categories developed — in order to establish a focus as to which school areas require the most help. The Eastern Cape is a case in point. The province needs 15 000 more classrooms immediately, and less than a quarter of its existing classrooms have electricity. Nearly 70% of principals are underqualified. The province spends an extra R3 bn a year on pupils who go to school for 41/2 years longer than the national average to obtain their matrics. Clearly the Eastern Cape inherited two of the most impoverished bantustans, but spending 94% of its budget on teachers' salaries allows little room for improving infrastructure in the province.

Solutions exist. Staff could be reduced, paid less, work more part time, in order to free funds to improve the classroom infrastructure. Richer schools in South Africa will need to make do with less. The shifting of certain teachers from advantaged schools to disadvantaged schools (even on a temporary basis) would help.

The constitution does not give the Ministry of Education control of how much the provinces spend on education. Although the total budget is R36 bn, the Minister has control over just R5.5 bn. Given that education is free and compulsory for the first ten years, the number of new pupils is rising dramatically. Since government is unable to spend much more on education, the private sector should consider assisting. A development fund of just 1% of JSE-listed companies' capital (market capitalisation) could raise R14 bn for the purpose of improving school infrastructure. These funds would have to be kept separate from other state funds.

By prioritising the major structural weaknesses in our school system we would be better able to identify solutions. Just throwing good money after a bad system is no good. A radical overhaul of our education system is required. Local business communities should begin to work closely with provincial governments in this regard. It is in their best interests — the pupils of today are their workers of tomorrow.

An education tax credit could also be offered to the private sector, in order to provide incentives to companies to fund education infrastructure and teacher training.

By raising funds from the private sector in either of these two ways, one may also overcome the problem of having to retrench numerous teachers.

To ensure equality in public education, the bulk of the funds should be earmarked to go to disadvantaged schools and less to the elite.

Although retrenching teachers is unpopular it may allow for the replacement of certain teachers with new recruits, at a lower cost. Averting the threatened June 1998 strike by the South African Democratic Teachers Union over the retrenchment of thousands of teachers, seems only to have served to postpone the crisis.

Why Does Little Old South Africa Need to Maintain the Highest Standards in the World?

Maintaining the highest standards in the world for many of our professional qualifications appears to be out of tune with the realities of South Africa. For example, South Africa desperately requires thousands of new black accountants, but we can't fill the posts due to some of the highest educational standards in the world. Whereas in the United States accountancy graduates rarely fail their board examination, in South Africa failure rates of 40–50% have not been uncommon among those who have managed to survive four gruelling years of accountancy studies in the first place to even have the pleasure of writing the final board exam.

The system deters even the smartest students, who have been known to fail. How then can one expect to encourage black students who have not had the benefit of a good basic education to enter such a course of study? What is the purpose of maintaining the highest standards in the world when a country such as the US does just fine with a far lower standard of accounting tests and examinations? On-the-job training in the US remains the vital ingredient in making their accounting system among the best in the world. The South African accountancy profession is now offering two lower level qualifications in order to keep its protectionist approach alive. It is high time that this profession and others is held more accountable to global norms.

Creating an Entrepreneurial Energy in South Africa

In South Africa the overwhelming majority of young graduates and workers never consider starting a small business — they prefer to go into the corporate sector where a guaranteed monthly pay cheque and less risk exists.

In South Africa the impression is given that the only people who operate their own businesses are rebels or those who have failed to find work in the formal sector. This is not true — many people feel far more satisfied running their own exciting venture than being just another small fish in a huge pond. Many individuals are more motivated to work in their own businesses, and experience direct satisfaction and rewards from building them up. In Taiwan, the Czech Republic and Hungary, for instance, the growth in small businesses has resulted in low unemployment, a dynamic economic growth rate and the transformation of those countries into successful free markets built upon the enterprise of small businesses.

Lack of Venture Capital

South Africa lacks the venture capital to boost the size of many small businesses. A passion for small business must be fostered and *quickly* in South Africa. The sooner we focus on how to facilitate a highly motivated and energetic entrepreneurial class with global aspirations, the better.

Government must promote the notion of people starting their own small businesses, at the same time as this sector is deregulated and freed from red tape. Certain labour laws, including those of the Industrial Councils, should not apply to this sector. The current lack of delivery of the R874 m set aside for the support of small businesses is therefore disturbing. It is clear that although the small business sector represents 40% of the private sector's share of the economy and offers one of the main hopes for job creation, government gives it little attention. These views are echoed by Nafcoc, the largest organisation representing black-owned businesses in South Africa. According to Steve Skhosana, executive director of Nafcoc's 4 000-member National Industrial Chamber, by July 1997 no more than ten of his members had received any financial assistance from Khula Enterprise Finance Ltd with a budget of R260 m, which was established by government to finance the growth of small businesses.

The lack of a formalised venture capital market or private equity market hampers the creation of small businesses and a new generation of entrepreneurs. In turn this has led to few upstart companies being listed on the Johannesburg Stock Exchange (JSE). The JSE, which is almost exclusively comprised of long-established businesses, has over the past few years seen a spate of new listings. But when one investigates the nature of these listings they are most often comprised of established companies which have been recently privatised, unbundled or restructured, or have received a new listing in an alternative JSE sector.

The sad truth is that more companies have been listed on the US Nasdaq (a nationwide electronic exchange) in just the past ten years than have ever been listed in the history of the United Kingdom. Why South Africa continues to mirror the European capital markets such as the London Stock Exchange is a mystery. It is high time we developed a capital market to service and reward high-growth companies, whether they be Internet companies or young, successful companies, if they have defined a profitable niche catering to the townships and are headed for a prosperous future. At present South Africans cannot easily access and invest in any new upstart companies, so they have their equity (shareholdings) primarily in long-established firms with little potential to expand at the high growth rates of many young companies. The large South African conglomerates dragged the JSE down in 1997 and 1998. The JSE All Share Index fell by 8% between July 1997 and July 1998 while the S+P 500 US Index was up 70% in rands, as was the UK FTSE Index. The giant Microsoft was not even listed on a stock exchange 15 years ago. Today it is one of the largest companies in the world.

It is unlikely that Anglo American will double its turnover level from in-house growth in the near future, whereas a profitable young company could well achieve such growth within a year. We should all be able to increase our wealth by being able to invest in a diversified range of younger or more dynamic companies.

At present our smaller companies have little prospect of reaching a national investment audience and are too often acquired and swallowed up by the old guard of established South African companies — all due to the fact that these smaller companies are starved of the equity capital they need to expand.

Bad Policies Drive Businesses Underground into the Informal Sector

The Labour Relations Act, in its zeal to protect all workers, requires that all businesses register in order to pay minimum wages. Of course spaza shops, street hawkers and the like cannot comply, and thus remain in the so-called underground economy.

A number of the labour laws introduced by the Ministry of Labour have the effect of driving businesses underground, where they remain because they do not have the means (either financially or administratively) to comply with all government's requirements.

Entrepreneurs create jobs and remain one of the most vital elements in driving our economy forward. More than anything else, entrepreneurs detest bureaucracy — but that is exactly what the Ministry of Labour has given them, by continually seeking ways to expands its turf. Small business is hamstrung still further by new red tape.

Southern African Consumers Suffer

The absence of competitive conditions and natural market forces in our labour market means that the South African consumer suffers. As productivity rarely keeps up with wage increases, employers just pass on their costs to the consumer. This fuels inflation, and at the end of the day we all lose. In most cases the South African consumer is captive to a few large companies providing any given product.

The workers who may have thought they were receiving higher wages find that they do not have any more buying power, while others who did not receive wage increases can now only buy less.

It is interesting to note that a recent survey conducted by the South African Institute of Race Relations found that some 53% of ANC supporters say that unions are at least partially to blame for the high unemployment rate in South Africa. This is surprising and also refreshing, considering Cosatu's prominence in the ANC political alliance.

South Africa's Conglomerates

South Africa's productivity is bound to improve as companies strive to keep up with their competitors. The oligopolistic nature of an economy dominated by a handful of conglomerates with interlocking directorships and cross-shareholdings has led to highly concentrated power in the hands of a few.

Effective competition in South Africa has suffered due to such varying characteristics as:
- the role of the mining houses in South Africa's economy;
- the small size of the domestic economy;
- the policy of keeping foreign firms at bay;

- exchange controls and import tariffs;
- disinvestment and sanctions;
- the unstable labour market;
- high import tariffs protecting domestic industries; and
- the large number of laws and regulations discouraging the development of an entrepreneurial class.

CHAPTER TEN

The Need for a New Tax System

SOUTH AFRICA'S TAX SYSTEM needs to be drastically reformed to match those of our trading partners, and at the same time South Africa needs to become far more aggressive in attracting long-term foreign investment.

Special interest groups should no longer be subsidised by the South African taxpayer. It is scandalous that we allowed our largest conglomerates to receive billions of rands in subsidies through the now discredited GEIS export incentive. By some accounts over 80% of the subsidy payments from government under this programme went into the coffers of the ten largest companies in South Africa.

GEIS cost the South African taxpayer more than R2 bn in the 1993/94 fiscal year; often we subsidised such behemoths as Anglo American and Barlow Rand in their export ventures. Motor vehicle manufacturers are one of the sectors not benefiting from GEIS. However, they were more than compensated by the special rebates they received on their imported inputs and other materials. Thankfully, GEIS was eliminated at the end of 1997.

Tax incentives in South Africa should be aimed at attracting viable investment projects that might otherwise be designated for location in a different country. However, providing huge tax rebates to projects that on their own merits remain marginally viable is cause for concern.

Tax treaties

With the Secondary Tax on Companies (STC) still in place at 12.5%, our first target in tax reform must be to rid ourselves of it. It acts as a form of penalty for foreign investors in particular, since our tax treaties do little to help them avoid this penalty tax, while their home countries' tax rates are most often no more than 35% (as is the case in the US, for instance).

The STC tax in effect penalises companies wishing to distribute dividends. Shareholders may not receive the best value for their money, since the system encourages companies to reinvest even if there remain few suitable investments.

As far as possible we should strive to incorporate tax-sparing provisions as part of our treaties, as these would allow foreign companies wishing to take advantage of our tax holidays the benefit of not then having to pay tax back home instead of in South Africa.

At least a tax-sparing provision means that the home country — say France, the UK, the US or Germany — recognises the South African tax holiday granted to any of its companies, and will not seek to top up their taxes, i.e. to charge them the missing tax upon repatriation of profits from South Africa.

Ill-conceived tax holidays

Our tax holidays are in many cases ill-conceived in relation to the needs of foreign investors. In view of the unemployment problem in South Africa, it is clear that additional tax incentives which promote the use of capital over labour are not required, and will in fact have detrimental results. (Section 37(e) of the Income Tax Act goes even further as it leads directly to the subsidisation of projects, with the help of the Industrial Development Corporation (IDC); projects which might not be viable without using the taxpayer-owned funds of the IDC in conjunction with enormous capital investment write-offs which reduce tax rates to a fraction.) Government seems happy to provide tax write-offs for select capital-intensive projects (Columbus, Saldanha), but remains opposed to a larger-scale tax incentive programme that would foster labour-intensive investment such as the export processing zones and related options mentioned in Chapter 7.

Our inheritance

One of the problems of the Margo and Katz Commissions has been their failure to recognise the power of tax- and investment-related incentives.

The Margo Commission recognised that the tax incentives which were on offer in South Africa during the mid-1980s favoured particular industries. In fact, the unfairness of the system was such that if your industry was powerful enough to have a voice on the national political stage you could qualify as one of a selected group of beneficiaries. The Margo Commission did its investigation under siege economy conditions and cannot be blamed for not being overly concerned with the foreign investor's viewpoint. At the time, being concerned with attracting foreign investment was a somewhat useless activity given South Africa's isolation.

Although the removal of the tax incentive programme made the tax system far more neutral and less biased, a country desperately requiring investment and job creation cannot always strive for taxation policies that appear in textbooks. It should not emulate the practices of more industrialised nations which have enough internal capacity and a sufficiently large industrial and manufacturing base to be less concerned with attracting foreign investors to their shores.

Need for practical solutions

No matter how laudable such textbook versions of taxation are, South Africa should follow the proven success of nations in the past two decades which have thrown out notions of avoiding tax incentives because they affect the principle of neutrality. In the real world of global investment, trade and tax incentives have proven to be the engine of many a success story over the past 20 years. The principle of neutrality was etched in stone by Oxford dons and World Bank theorists at the time of Bretton Woods in 1948. However, based on empirical evidence over the past two decades, the notion of not using tax incentives is outdated, especially when a country such as South Africa is so dependent on attracting long-term foreign investment.

It is interesting to note that despite the recommendations of the Margo Commission, the many tax incentives which were almost exclusively for the benefit of local operators were hardly off the statute books when the new Section 37(e) of the Income Tax Act was introduced in 1991.

Arguments against tax incentives

To their credit, opponents of tax- or investment-based incentives do not just rely on the neutrality concept. They argue that such incentives distort the tax system unnecessarily, are open to potential abuse and discriminate against particular groups. Ironically, those arguing most vehemently against the creation of tax and trade incentives such as Export Processing Zones (EPZs), are precisely the same companies which were for years the greatest beneficiaries of numerous tax incentives which discriminated against other sectors of the South African economy and against foreign investors.

Targeted incentives that are linked to an economic plan — such

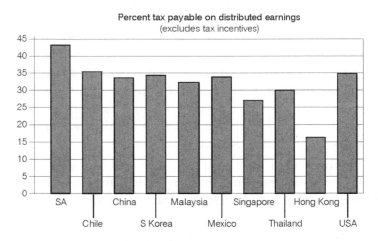

Figure 34 *Percentage tax payable on distributed earnings, world comparison (excludes tax incentives)*

as boosting South African exports and creating large numbers of jobs, by permitting foreign investors to set up manufacturing plants primarily for export purposes in specially designated low-tax EPZs — continue to be opposed by the entrenched South African conglomerates, which, after years of being subsidised for their own exports (under GEIS and the export marketing assistance scheme), now complain because a new type of programme may become more inclusive. Ironic, is it not?

Unlike certain wealthy countries which have few tax or investment incentives, South Africa cannot operate a tax system that does not provide considerable advantages to investors, if it seriously hopes to attract long-term capital to its shores. As previously discussed, South Africa certainly cannot compete with other countries based on its cost of labour or its productivity.

Tax competitiveness

South Africa currently ranks poorly in comparison studies with other countries' investment-friendly tax systems. In fact, South Africa's high effective 43% corporate tax rate (taking into account STC at 12.5% plus the 35% corporate tax rate) makes it rank as an unfriendly tax climate for foreign investors.

The recently released findings of the Katz Commission propose a tax system which will not discriminate against domestic investment in favour of foreign investment. Specifically the commission states that general incentives aimed purely at encouraging foreign investment should not be introduced. In effect, this rules out some of the attractive fiscal and investment policies for which there is empirical evidence of success in a number of other countries, including Singapore and Australia.

The Commission did recognise the need to remove tax disincentives for foreign companies which wished to use South Africa as a base for regional holdings, finance and service companies.

The Commission specifically states that no further tax incentives should be implemented to stimulate savings and investment, while any existing preferences should be abolished. This is unfortunate in the light of South Africa's high tax system.

If South Africa ignores the international rules of the game, it will remain at a competitive disadvantage in attracting foreign investment.

Furthermore, because of South Africa's high tax rate for foreign investors, we currently discourage such investment. High labour costs and exchange controls certainly do not help. Only belatedly did Gear begin to address the notion of implementing tax incentives and becoming more competitive in emulating the benefits numerous other countries offer. However, as mentioned above, our incentives do not take into account the tax rules of foreign countries, and therefore in many cases are not as attractive as they may appear on paper from a South African perspective. In fact few takers have been found for the tax holidays implemented by Gear due to their impractical provisions, and short-term nature.

The lack of South African tax incentives specifically targeted at foreign and domestic investment is somewhat disturbing in the light of the proven success they have had in a diverse number of countries, including Brazil, Uruguay, Chile, Singapore, Malaysia, Mexico, China, Mauritius, Ireland and Taiwan. Incentives such as low tax rates for export-oriented investment could play an important role in developing South Africa's export earnings potential by encouraging greater numbers of investors to manufacture and assemble their products in South Africa for export, or use South Africa as a regional administrative base.

At present the investment incentives in South Africa are very weak and unattractive. This is not what one would expect from a developing country supposedly desperate for long-term investment.

Indirect taxes

Most experts agree that indirect taxes such as Value-Added Tax (VAT) are far more efficient than direct taxes such as personal income tax. This is because a flat rate VAT cannot be avoided, and therefore does not affect people's preferences. However, VAT is regressive, since poorer people spend a larger proportion of their income on what they consume.

South Africa must increasingly move away from excessive reliance on direct taxes (personal income taxes alone comprised 40% of the total tax revenue in 1996, while corporate tax made up just 14%) in favour of the indirect taxes which at present only comprise VAT (26% of total tax revenue) and excise duties (12.5%).

Although VAT may appear to be ineffective as a means of redistribution, if the revenue raised by the tax were to be used to improve the plight of the poor, it would in essence be redistributed.

The reason why VAT and other consumption taxes have become increasingly popular internationally is that it has become accepted that the main role of taxes is to finance expenditure, and that government expenditure should be largely responsible for redistributing wealth across the economy from the wealthy to the poor.

Changing our tax system

Since the personal income tax burden is largely shouldered by a small group of wealthy individuals, many believe that the maximum level of taxes is already being extracted from this group, and that any further attempts to depend on personal income tax as a percentage of total taxes collected should turn to lowering personal tax rates while broadening the tax base. The low threshold of the maximum marginal tax rate remains uniquely low — a 45% marginal tax rate of R100 000 — as compared to the far lower tax rates on personal income found in other successful nations. This R100 000 threshold needs to be increased in line with international norms to at least R150 000, making it a more efficient personal income tax system.

The highest marginal rates of income tax should not be

designed to capture more than the top 5% of income earners.
Moving the threshold up to R150 000 is in fact insufficient, but is
at least a start — South Africa cannot afford to reduce the tax
burden any further at the present time.

Foreign investors who wish to relocate management or
supervisors to a new operation in South Africa face a tax cost
which is often steep. An employee who is relocated to South Africa
from the US, for instance, will incur at least 8% more tax on his
salary and bonuses. This drives up the cost to his employer, who
must fork out a higher salary in order to make his compensation
commensurate with the after-tax earnings the employee would
have received for working elsewhere in the world.

However, the wealthy have additional resources and are able to
avoid taxes — spending considerable resources to do so. They are
the most mobile, and if progressive rates remain excessively high,
are able to make use of emigration and capital flight.

A growing economy is the best approach to raise additional tax
revenues in South Africa other than by spreading the tax base and
having better tax administration and collection.

Wealth taxes

Capital or wealth taxes on South African estates, such as the Katz
Commission's proposed capital transfer tax (CTT), which will tax
trusts, will no doubt lead to wealthy South Africans attempting to
hive as much of their funds as possible into offshore tax havens
where secrecy and confidentiality are ensured. The Katz
Commission itself concedes that South Africa does not have the
capacity to police assets on a worldwide basis, and thus according
to the Commission, capital taxes should only be imposed on a
South African source.

The Commission has urged that donations tax and estate duty
ultimately be merged into a future CTT which taxes trust assets at
intervals of 25 to 30 years. In addition, the Commission has
invited Inland Revenue to design anti-avoidance measures to deal
with trust structures, while the distribution of capital from a trust
will also be subject to the CTT rate.

To many this appears like overkill: from a present position
where hardly any tax is paid on family assets, to one where there
would be three tiers of tax — periodical levies, tax on the interest-
free loans often used by trust structures, and taxes on capital
distributions made from trusts.

Regional headquarters

In one of its boldest moves the Katz Commission recommends that a particular incentive be introduced to facilitate the establishment by non-resident investors of wholly owned regional base companies in South Africa that provide managerial and financial support services to related companies outside South Africa. Although this is encouraging, whether South Africa will follow the bold moves of Ireland, Australia and Singapore, which all offer significantly low tax rates (ranging from 3% to 10%) to regional headquarters of companies, remains to be seen. We do not need to reinvent the tax wheel. We do, however, need to be less arrogant and learn from other more successful nations which have used tax policies to attract long-term foreign investment.

Transfer pricing

The Commission recommends that a facility be established to provide multinational corporations with the possibility of obtaining advance pricing agreements, along with measures to counter transfer pricing abuse. A facility to provide foreign investors with advance tax rulings has also been recommended, and should be implemented along the lines of arrangements in the Netherlands. This provides companies with security, something severely lacking in South Africa's tax system.

Conclusion

Since many MPs and elected leaders have no training in the private sector, many economic issues are delegated to bureaucrats who are often thrust into positions without the necessary qualifications or experience. It is high time that more chartered accountants, business people, bankers, doctors, teachers, sociologists and individuals experienced in the private sector played a role in national politics and government.

They would not do it for the money, but for love of their country. The onus is also on our political parties to co-opt the best brains and minds for their leadership ranks. Otherwise these lopsided tax loopholes, pork-barrel spending projects and other quietly kept secrets will continue to favour those wealthy special interest groups who can sweet-talk our leaders and distort the facts.

CHAPTER ELEVEN

Conclusion

I DID NOT SET OUT TO write an academic work, but rather a book accessible to the layman concerned about South Africa's future.

Almost 70% of the South African public surveyed by the Human Sciences Research Council in February 1998 expect the economy to worsen or to stay the same. The roughly 30% minority who believed that the economy would improve, has no doubt shrunk since July 1998 — given the rand's 30% decline against leading currencies. If, after reading this book, you comment that it was interesting, but do nothing more, then I have not succeeded in what I set out to do.

South Africa requires concerned citizens who are knowledgeable about our country's problems and will follow through on their concerns.

Of course we all believe that we are patriotic citizens. I have covered a lot of ground in this book, some of which may have confused you along the way. I have explained the nature of the horrible economic mess we have inherited from decades of ruinous government policies, and I have attempted to address the many difficulties which will arise if we do not do something about this inheritance. I have shown that current inaction will inevitably lead to a reduced standard of living for all South Africans. After looking at the dangers South Africans face both economically and politically, I have proposed a number of viable solutions necessary to prevent many of today's inappropriate policies robbing our children and grandchildren of their rightful inheritance.

Take action

In order to make a difference it is vital that you become more active. If there were ideas and suggestions which you agreed with in this book contact the leader of your favourite political party or write to the Office of the President, at Private Bag X83, Pretoria 0001.

Tell politicians about the suggestions which make the most sense to you, and ask them to act on these suggestions.

If you feel strongly enough, write a letter to the editor of your local newspaper — these have more influence than you might think, and are widely read.

It is incumbent upon all South Africans to learn more about ways to improve our country. By remaining passive and not exerting any pressure on those in public office to provide substantive answers to many of the tough issues raised in this book, we have not fulfilled our duty as true patriots. The Appendix (see page 259) lists issues which every candidate for political office and his/her party should be able to answer, prior to the next election.

This is no time for South Africa to be following Europe's lead in the labour field. Europe has created few new jobs since 1960, while its unemployment rate has tripled. The US, by contrast, has an unemployment rate of just 5% (close to one third of France's and Germany's) and since 1960 has doubled the number of jobs available. Unlike Europe, where lifetime employment for one company remains the norm, and where labour laws entrench this system, workers in the US frequently change jobs — on average seven times in their careers.

The only way to meet the aspirations of our nation of some 42 million people is to grow the South African economy by at least four to five times its present size — from roughly R600 bn to between R2.5 trillion and R3 trillion. To do this requires sustained economic growth of 5–6% per annum over the next 25 years.

When will the out-of-control crime wave recede? Only when the government feels enough pressure to believe that it may lose an election. This will put it under sufficient pressure to adopt bold strategies for job creation, and to ensure that crime is controlled and citizens are protected. If a government cannot even protect its citizens, what use is it?

Sadly, there is no such pressure being brought to bear on our government at present. This allows it to release 9 000 prisoners, six months before their release date, thus sending a message to the world that we reward crime. To really crack down on crime we need a referendum on capital punishment and numerous Meyer Kahns running divisions of the police force.

South Africa's political imperative

The 6 million unemployed South Africans and their dependants are now also voters, and they cannot be neglected by any freely elected government. The imbalance between the aspirations of the employed and the unemployed will ultimately cause trade unions to have less power, and the highly concentrated industrial oligopolies who now employ them to have less influence. Arguably, it may be in the best interests of labour and employers to band together to preserve the status quo so that market forces have little effect, and South African consumers have no choice but to buy their higher-priced goods — effectively a hidden tax on every consumer. But, by allowing manufacturing costs to rise out of line with improvements in productivity, inflation follows, and the consumer pays again.

I understand that many of the views expressed here will not be politically correct — but this does not make them any less factually correct. Remaining silent is far worse, and in fact unpatriotic. South Africa can no longer afford a bunch of *ja-broere* who remain *poep* scared to challenge their leaders.

Is it not high time that South Africa begins to move a little quicker in the right direction by taking decisive action to combat crime, and grow the economy at a sustained 6% level, thereby fostering job creation?

Surely the ANC, with no viable opposition on the horizon, is in the perfect position to make bolder moves on many fronts? It should begin to energetically strive towards the creation of a new South Africa that will be admired by the rest of the world.

Most recently, the sudden depreciation in our currency has had many negative repercussions, not the least of which are the perceptions abroad that South Africa is not a stable economy in which to invest for the long term, and that even if a foreigner could make a R100 profit by manufacturing widget X, it may not be worth all the effort when at the end of the day it will translate into less than 19 dollars or 10 pounds.

Perhaps even worse, though, is the rise in inflation in tandem with the 30% devaluation in our currency both in 1996 and in 1998. Inflation almost doubled from a low of 5.5% in mid-1996 to 9.9% in April 1997. The same scenario is set to occur by mid 1999 as inflation is set to almost double between May 1998 and May 1999.

A combination of high interest rates, an unstable rand and a workforce that is not well trained continues to persuade South African manufacturers to build plants in other countries where all three factors are superior.

As South Africa becomes a debtor nation we increasingly lose control over our own economic policies.

We need to bring more professionalism to our economic, education, health and crime policies if we are to seriously attack the root causes of many of our problems, and even *begin* to gain the upper hand in this fight. We need to adopt more efficient and productive private sector managerial systems in government. We need our Cabinet members to have strong business and private sector backgrounds as is occurring all over the world — particularly in the US, UK, Canada and Latin America.

Emigration continues in droves, facilitated by the rampant crime and school and health systems whose internationally competitive standards continue to drop. Ethical standards in the public sector have reached such a low point that the gravy train has not only gathered steam, but is breaking all speed records. The levels of corruption and inefficiency that exist and are being exposed almost daily continue to hamper any chance South Africa has of achieving sustainable economic growth.

We have a large number of weapons in our economic armoury to grow our economy at the required 5–6%. Bold leadership is required — tough choices need to be made and implemented. These steps include an economy free of huge red tape, attractive investment incentives and job creation policies.

Historians are likely to look back on those in leadership positions today and judge them on their responses to our critical needs as we approach a new millennium.

Less political posturing and more determination to resolve South Africa's problems in a non-partisan manner would go some way towards raising the public's esteem for our politicians. After all, what are our elected leaders in office to do? First and foremost it should be to improve the living standards of all South Africans.

South Africa remains Africa's leading economic power and at the same time its sleeping giant. Sadly, if we continue on our present course, we will soon squander any hope of being the engine which drives an African economic renaissance.

Fortunately, with the right policies and an accountable and responsive government, we can still overcome our many problems and pass on a more prosperous South Africa to future generations. But the opportunity to do so is rapidly slipping away. The signs of peril exist.

An enormous national debt, exorbitant interest rates, an out-of-control crime wave, trade deficits, an education system in disorder, high taxes and high unemployment – all are on the verge of ruining the prospects of a prosperous future for all South Africans. It is high time that South African citizens no longer sit around and watch in disbelief as their quality of life diminishes.

We have the ability to solve these problems and to lift ourselves up by our own bootstraps. The big question is: Do we have the will?

It is time for action — today.

Appendix

A checklist for all South African Political Candidates

This Appendix serves as a summary of many of the most important issues affecting our country's future. Our political candidates need to know that we care about these issues and that we will vote according to candidates' positions on them. Once they are elected we should continue to hold them accountable for their answers to these questions.

What are your political candidates' plans to:
- encourage job creation and dramatically reduce unemployment?
- eliminate the huge government debt?
- reduce crime substantially?
- build sufficient housing for our citizens?
- attract foreign investment?
- increase exports and generate foreign exchange?
- improve our educational system?
- reduce the government's size?
- get rid of unnecessary regulations?
- assist those industries which will create new wealth in South Africa?
- address political corruption in South Africa?
- reform the tax system?
- pass laws to prevent special interest groups giving large sums of money to political candidates?
- get rid of unnecessary perks for elected officials?
- pass laws to stop Parliament exempting itself from the laws it imposes on the rest of the country?

Bibliography

Abedian, Iraj and Standish, Barry. *Economic Growth in South Africa*. Oxford: Oxford University Press, 1992.

Ginsberg, A.S. *International Tax Planning: Offshore Finance Centres and the EU*. Boston and The Netherlands: Kluwer Law and Taxation Publishers, 1994.

Ginsberg, A. S. *Tax Havens*. Englewood Cliffs, NJ: Prentice-Hall, 1991.

Ginsberg, A. S. *International Tax Havens*. 2nd ed, Durban: Butterworths, 1997.

Maasdorp, Gavin. *Can South and Southern Africa Become Globally Competitive Economies?*, London: Macmillan Press, 1996.

National Labour and Economic Development Institute. *Unions in Transition: Cosatu at the Dawn of Democracy*. Johannesburg: Naledi, 1994.

Nattrass, Nicoli. *Intermediate Macroeconomic Theory*. 2nd ed, Cape Town: University of Cape Town, 1996.

Porter, Michael E. *The Competitive Advantage of Nations*. New York: The Free Press, 1990.

South African Foundation. *Growth for All*. Johannesburg, 1996.

South African Government. *Growth Employment and Redistribution: A Macroeconomic Strategy*. Pretoria, 1996.

South African Institute of Race Relations. Various publications. Johannesburg.

Sunter, Clem. *The High Road: Where Are We Now?* Cape Town: Tafelberg Human & Rousseau, 1996.